BEN GOLDSTEIN

The BIG Picture

B1+ INTERMEDIATE Student's Book

Richmond

CONTENTS UNITS 1–6

	GRAMMAR	VOCABULARY	READING & LISTENING	PRONUNCIATION
1 COMMUNICATION *page 4*	• Tense review • Question forms • State & dynamic verbs	• Communication • Senses	(R) Describing photographs • Behind the curtain (L) Four interviews	• *-es* & *-ed* verb endings • Intonation: stress

page 12 **FUNCTIONAL LANGUAGE:** BREAKING THE ICE *page 13* **SPEAKING TASK:** OUTLINING A PROMOTIONAL CAMPAIGN
page 152 **WRITING BANK:** A PROMOTIONAL POSTER

	GRAMMAR	VOCABULARY	READING & LISTENING	PRONUNCIATION
2 A GOOD READ *page 14*	• Past simple & past continuous • Past perfect & past simple • *Used to* & *would*	• Reading • Books & genres	(R) Extracts from two novels • Descriptions of three plays • Mobile novels (L) Discussing four novels • Talking about manga	• *Used to / use to* • Intonation: stress

page 22 **FUNCTIONAL LANGUAGE:** AGREEING AND DISAGREEING *page 23* **WRITING TASK:** THE STORY BEHIND THE PHOTO

	GRAMMAR	VOCABULARY	READING & LISTENING	PRONUNCIATION
3 ART EVERYWHERE *page 24*	• Gradable & absolute adjectives • *As ... as*, comparatives & superlatives • Adjectives & adverbs	• Art • Gradable & absolute adjectives • People-watching	(R) A portrait is worth a thousand words • A newspaper article (L) Describing artwork	• Word stress for emphasis • Intonation: stress

page 32 **FUNCTIONAL LANGUAGE:** ADDING EMPHASIS *page 33* **SPEAKING TASK:** A CLASS SURVEY
page 153 **WRITING BANK:** SUMMARISING THE FINDINGS OF A REPORT

page 34 **REVIEW A**, UNITS 1–3 *page 37* **BRING IT TOGETHER** 1, 2 & 3

	GRAMMAR	VOCABULARY	READING & LISTENING	PRONUNCIATION
4 MAN AND NATURE *page 38*	• Present perfect simple • Present perfect continuous	• Landscapes & natural disasters • Natural world collocations • The environment	(R) Three traditional villages • Plastic: A toxic love story (L) A report on plastic bags	• Word stress in expressions • Intonation: responding to news

page 46 **FUNCTIONAL LANGUAGE:** CHECKING INFORMATION *page 47* **WRITING TASK:** DESCRIBING A PLACE TO STAY

	GRAMMAR	VOCABULARY	READING & LISTENING	PRONUNCIATION
5 BRIDGES, BORDERS AND BARRIERS *page 48*	• Future forms (1): plans, intentions, hopes & fears • Future forms (2): predictions	• Connections & prevention • Future plans & intentions • Describing trends	(R) The dangers of social networking • The Oresund Bridge • The endless city (L) Social networks • A news report	• Reduction in auxiliary verbs • Intonation: sounding friendly/ unfriendly

page 56 **FUNCTIONAL LANGUAGE:** AT PASSPORT CONTROL *page 57* **SPEAKING TASK:** A CLASS DEBATE
page 154 **WRITING BANK:** AN OPINION

	GRAMMAR	VOCABULARY	READING & LISTENING	PRONUNCIATION
6 GLOBAL AND LOCAL *page 58*	• Sentences with *if*: real situations • Modal verbs: making deductions • Future time clauses	• Celebrations & festivals • Recommendations • Qualities	(R) Carnival of cultures • An article about travel disruption (L) A festival • A podcast about superheroes	• Modal verb stress in making deductions • Intonation: being emphatic

page 66 **FUNCTIONAL LANGUAGE:** CLARIFYING *page 67* **WRITING TASK:** DEBATING AN ISSUE IN A BLOG POST

page 68 **REVIEW B**, UNITS 4–6 *page 71* **BRING IT TOGETHER** 4, 5 & 6

CONTENTS

	GRAMMAR	VOCABULARY	READING & LISTENING	PRONUNCIATION
7 IS THIS YOURS? *page 72*	• Quantifiers • Using *one* & *ones* • Articles	• Possessions • Organisation • Toys & games	R Say Yes to Mess • The history of three objects L A podcast about toy museum • Childhood games	• *One / ones* • Intonation: stress

page 80 **FUNCTIONAL LANGUAGE:** USING VAGUE LANGUAGE *page 81* **SPEAKING TASK:** DESCRIBING AN IMPORTANT OBJECT
page 155 **WRITING BANK:** SAYING THANK YOU

	GRAMMAR	VOCABULARY	READING & LISTENING	PRONUNCIATION
8 TELLING A DIFFERENT STORY *page 82*	• Reported speech • Reporting requests & instructions	• Storytelling • Travel activities • The media	R Not the whole story • Citizen journalism L Unseen tours • A conversation	• Word stress – three- & four-syllable words • Intonation: stress

page 90 **FUNCTIONAL LANGUAGE:** PHONE MESSAGES *page 91* **WRITING TASK:** TAKING NOTES

	GRAMMAR	VOCABULARY	READING & LISTENING	PRONUNCIATION
9 RULES AND REGULATIONS *page 92*	• Permission, prohibition & obligation (1): present • Permission, prohibition & obligation (2): past • Talking about ability (past & present)	• Permission & prohibition • Internet • Verbs with *law*	R Two anecdotes L Discussing internet restrictions • A news story	• *Are / aren't* in permissions and prohibitions • Intonation: using *please*

page 100 **FUNCTIONAL LANGUAGE:** MAKING POLITE REQUESTS *page 101* **SPEAKING TASK:** COMPLAINING
page 156 **WRITING BANK:** FILING A COMPLAINT

page 102 **REVIEW C**, UNITS 7–9 *page 105* **BRING IT TOGETHER** 7, 8 & 9

	GRAMMAR	VOCABULARY	READING & LISTENING	PRONUNCIATION
10 INSIGHTS AND INNOVATIONS *page 106*	• Passives • *Who, which, that*	• Ideas & solutions • Phrasal verbs (1) • Footwear • Metaphorical language	R A blog post about bikes • My epiphany moment L A conversation • Audio messages	• Sentence stress • Intonation: saying *thanks*

page 114 **FUNCTIONAL LANGUAGE:** GETTING THINGS DONE *page 115* **WRITING TASK:** DESCRIBING A PROCESS

	GRAMMAR	VOCABULARY	READING & LISTENING	PRONUNCIATION
11 A SENSE OF IDENTITY *page 116*	• Imaginary situations: present or future • *If only / I wish*	• Identity • Gaming • Personality adjectives	R A book review • Positive visualisation L Discussing video games • Discussing imagined futures	• *I'd, it'd, wouldn't* • Intonation: stress

page 124 **FUNCTIONAL LANGUAGE:** GIVING ADVICE *page 125* **SPEAKING TASK:** MAKING A GOOD IMPRESSION
page 157 **WRITING BANK:** AN ONLINE PROFILE

	GRAMMAR	VOCABULARY	READING & LISTENING	PRONUNCIATION
12 MEMORIES *page 126*	• Imaginary situations: past • Review	• Remembering • Phrasal verbs (2) • Review	R Thanks, Grandad! • What's new? L Describing photographs	• Contractions with *had / would have* • Intonation

page 134 **FUNCTIONAL LANGUAGE:** APOLOGISING *page 135* **WRITING TASK:** CHILDHOOD MEMORIES

page 136 **REVIEW D**, UNITS 10–12 *page 139* **BRING IT TOGETHER** 10, 11 & 12

page 140 **GRAMMAR REFERENCE** *page 152* **WRITING BANK** *page 158* **COMMUNICATION BANK**
page 162 **SELECTED TRANSCRIPTS** *page 168* **IRREGULAR VERBS**

1 Communication

a

b

d

e

1 **a** Work in pairs. Look at the photos. Answer the questions.

1 What do the photos show?
2 What is the connection between the photos and the unit title?
3 Which photo is the most striking? Why?

b Work in pairs. Complete **A** in the KEY VOCABULARY PANEL. Can you think of any other types of communication? Add them to the list.

2 1.1 Listen to six people talking about the photos. Match speakers 1–6 to photos a–f. Do you agree with their descriptions?

3 **a** Complete the extracts from transcript 1.1 with the verbs in the box. Match the extracts to the photos.

communicate say speak tell

1 They're not just .... with words...
2 This gesture .... a thousand words.
3 ... she's using a placard to .... her message.
4 ... each dance .... a story.
5 ... it's amazing how a hand gesture can .... so much!
6 ... or perhaps they're .... with someone else.

b Read transcript 1.1 on page 162 and check your answers.

4 Work in pairs. Complete **B** in the KEY VOCABULARY PANEL.

c

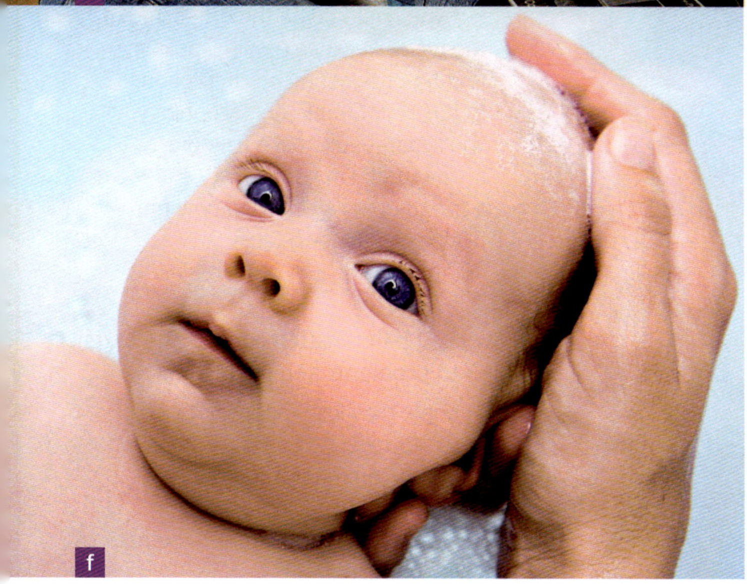

f

5 **a** Complete the questions with the correct form of *say*, *tell* and *speak*.

1 How many languages can you ....?
2 Who is the one person you .... to most often?
3 Who was the first person you .... to today?
4 What was the first thing you .... this morning?
5 Are you good at .... jokes?
6 Do you know anyone who's good at .... stories?
7 Are you generally good at .... people what you think? Why?/Why not?
8 Have you ever .... to a crowd of people? How did you feel?

b Work in pairs. Choose three questions. Ask and answer.

Key vocabulary

Communication

A Types of communication

- Match the expressions in the box to the photos. You can match more than one expression to each photo.

body language	facial expressions
hand gestures	instant messaging
placards & signs	sign language
social networks	the written word

B *Say, tell, speak*

- Complete the word maps with *say*, *tell* or *speak*.

1

your mind
complete rubbish

two languages
English very well

very quietly
loudly
quite quickly

in public
a room full of people

TO | my friend
my mother on the phone

2

hello
goodbye
yes
no

something interesting/ important | TO ME

a lot about something

what you think
how you feel

3

the truth
a lie
a story
a joke

ME
HIM
THEM | what you want
what to do
what you're thinking

SOMEBODY ABOUT | yourself
your holidays
your family

Notice *say & tell*

We use *say* + *to* + personal pronoun, e.g.
What did he say to you?
We use *tell* + personal pronoun, e.g.
Tell me what the problem is.

1.1 COMMUNICATION BREAKDOWN

- PRACTISE TENSES
- TALK ABOUT COMMUNICATING

SPEAKING & VOCABULARY: communication

1 **a** Match the communication expressions in A to the categories in B. Use a dictionary to help you.

A

chat to friends and family on Facebook | discuss politics | give talks/lectures/presentations/speeches | have arguments | speak on Skype | talk in public | talk to children/the elderly/pets/strangers | text, tweet or email friends | use my body to express myself

B

I do it a lot. | I never do it. | I can do it in English. | I rarely do it. | I enjoy doing it. | I hate doing it. | I'm good at it. | I'm bad at it.

b How do you communicate in your everyday life?

2 Work in pairs. Compare your answers. What differences did you find?

READING

1 **a** Look at the images. What kinds of communication do they show?

a

b

c

b Read texts 1–3 and match them to images a–c.

2 Match texts 1–3 to one or more of the types of communication in SPEAKING & VOCABULARY 1a.

1 I have a lot of trouble talking to people. I find it easier being with animals ... you can communicate in different ways with them. I've had lots of dogs. Playing with the ball or stroking the dog's back, these actions communicate simple things, everything is more simple and straightforward. Human communication is too complex.

2 When I first started dancing, I went to dance class every day. I was very tense, I don't think I realised what I could do with my body. At first I got really frustrated. But now I think I can say so much more with my body and I have real problems with speaking!

3 I often find myself in this situation. You're in the same room as someone, but you could be on the other side of the world because they're speaking, texting or tweeting on their phones. In the end, I think this technology will separate us, make us more introverted. I'm going to try and meet a friend every week from now on, just to chat face-to-face!

3 Work in pairs. Match each of the texts 1–3 to problems a–c described.

a People may lose the art of talking face-to-face.

b Human communication can be complicated and confusing.

c Some people can't express themselves with words.

4 Read the texts in 2 again. Which of the people prefer another form of communication to speaking? Which form and why?

5 Work in small groups. Discuss the questions.

- Do you know anybody who communicates with their body? What are different ways you can do that (e.g. dance, mime)?
- Do you sometimes prefer the company of animals to humans? Why/Why not?
- Is face-to-face communication always preferable? Why/Why not?

GRAMMAR

1 **a** Work in pairs. Match extracts 1–6 to images a–c without looking back at the texts in READING 2.

1 I have a lot of trouble talking to people.
2 When I first started dancing,...
3 ... this technology will separate us,...
4 I've had lots of dogs.
5 ... they're speaking, texting or tweeting on their phones...
6 I'm going to try and meet a friend every week...

b Look at the sentences in 1a again. Underline the verbs. Which are talking about a) the present? b) the past? c) the future?

2 Complete 1–6 in the GRAMMAR PANEL with the sentences in 1a.

3 **a** Choose the correct form of the verb. In one sentence both are possible.

1 I*'ve never been* / *never went* to a photo exhibition.
2 I*'m speaking* / *speak* to my mother on the other line.
3 Children who grow up with animals *communicate* / *are communicating* better.
4 I don't think computers *will change* / *are going to change* the way we communicate in the future.
5 I*'ve done* / *did* a lot of dancing when I was younger.
6 I*'m going to study* / *'ll study* art at university next year.

b Match sentences 1–6 to the uses in the GRAMMAR PANEL.

TENSE REVIEW

A Present simple or present continuous?

a We use the present simple to refer to habits and routines.
(1) ....

b We use the present simple to refer to repeated actions or situations.
I go to dance class every day.

c We use the present simple to describe things which are generally true.
Human communication is too complex.

d We use the present continuous to talk about things that are happening now or around now.
(2) ....

B Past simple or present perfect?

e We use the past simple to talk about completed actions in the past.
(3) ....

f We use the past simple to talk about habitual actions in the past.
I went to dance class every day.

g We use the present perfect to talk about experiences you have had in your life up to the present. You do not say when it happened.
(4) ....

C Future: *will* or *going to*?

h We use both *will* and *going to* to make predictions.
(5) ...., *this technology is going to change us.*

i We use *going to* to talk about intentions and plans.
(6) ....

See page 140 for grammar reference and more practice.

PRONUNCIATION: *-es* & *-ed* verb endings

1 **a** Work in pairs. Write the third person present simple and the past simple forms of the verbs.

	Present	Past
start	*starts*	*started*
watch		
text		
dance		

b Read the verbs out loud. Underline the verb forms that have two syllables.

2 **a** 1.2 Listen and check. Answer the questions.

1 When do we add *-es*, and not *-s*, to a verb in the present simple?
2 When do we pronounce the *-ed* ending as an extra syllable?

b Check your answers on page 158.

3 **a** 1.3 Listen and write the ten verbs you hear.

b Read transcript 1.3 on page 162 out loud. Pay attention to the *-ed* endings.

SPEAKING

1 Work in pairs. Think about three or four different situations where people have difficulty communicating, e.g. when they don't speak each other's language or when the internet connection is weak. What can you do to repair the communication in each situation? Add some of your own ideas to the list.

Use sign language, use simpler language, ask someone to help...

2 **a** Think about the situations below. What do you think would be the best way to repair the communication?

- You make a joke in an online chat room, but your friend thinks you're being serious and takes offence.
- A friend asks you for advice, but you're distracted, watching your favourite programme on TV and you answer without really listening. Your friend looks hurt.

b Share your ideas with the class. Who has the best solutions?

1.2 SIGN OF THE TIMES

- PRACTISE QUESTION FORMS
- TALK ABOUT SIGNS AND THEIR PURPOSE

a

b

SPEAKING & VOCABULARY: communicating

1 Work in pairs. Look at the photos. Answer the questions.

- Where do you think the people are?
- What is the purpose of each sign?
- Which are protests? Which are giving information?
- Which is the most effective? Why?

2 a Match sentences 1–6 to one (or more) of photos a–d.

1 This person is **making a** very serious **point**.
2 This person isn't trying to **change** anybody's **mind**.
3 This person doesn't really have a particular message to **put across**.
4 This person isn't trying to persuade anyone, they're simply **speaking their mind**.
5 This person is **standing up for** animal rights.
6 This sign certainly makes you stop and **pay attention**.

b Match the words and expressions in **bold** in 2a to definitions a–f.

a express a personal opinion ....
b support and fight for something ....
c transmit information successfully ....
d influence someone's opinion ....
e express a particular argument ....
f look at or listen to something very carefully ....

3 a Complete the questions with the expressions in 2a.

1 Which sign do you think makes people .... the most ....? Why?
2 What rights is the man in the mask ....ing .... for?
3 Do you think any of these signs can actually .... people's ....? If yes, which?
4 Which sign do you think is ....ing the most important ....?
5 Do you think making a sign is the best way to .... a message ....? Why/Why not? What other ways are there?
6 Do you ever .... your .... in public like this? Why/Why not?

b 1.4 Listen and check.

4 Work in pairs. Ask and answer the questions in 3a.

c

LISTENING

1 a 1.5 Listen to interviews with the four people in the photos. Match interviews 1–4 with photos a–d.

b Listen again. Match statements 1–4 to photos a–d. More than one answer may be correct.

1 The person wanted to be funny and serious at the same time.
2 The person made the sign with a friend.
3 The person talks about how the problem is affecting their mood.
4 The person wants to be the first.

2 Work in groups. Discuss the questions.

- Do you ever see people carrying signs?
- What types of signs are they?
- In what way are they similar to the signs in the photos?

d

GRAMMAR

1 a Match questions 1–8 to answers a–h.

1 How long will you stay here for?
2 What made you want to dress like a polar bear?
3 How long did it take to make the sign?
4 How long have you been here?
5 Who gave you the idea?
6 Do you think the sign will work?
7 Did he say anything to you?
8 Who is the sign for?

a It's a powerful symbol...
b Nobody. I just love this footballer.
c Well, about an hour, I think.
d Well, for nobody really... it was just a joke.
e ... as long as necessary...
f I hope so, but I just don't know...
g No, unfortunately not.
h Twenty-four hours, I slept here overnight.

b 1.5 Listen again and check.

2 a Look at the questions in 1a again. Underline all the question words, circle all the subject pronouns and highlight all the auxiliary verbs.

b Which questions don't have a) question words? b) subject pronouns? c) auxiliary verbs?

3 Check your answers in the GRAMMAR PANEL. Complete 1–4.

4 a Correct the mistakes.

1 When the last protest was held in your town?
2 What it was about?
3 When played your local football team their last game?
4 Who did win?
5 You have ever queued to buy something?
6 What you wanted to buy?

b Work in pairs. Ask and answer the questions in 4a.

QUESTION FORMS

Yes/No **questions** do not need a question word. The auxiliary verb always comes (1) *before / after* the subject except with questions with the verb *to be*.
Did you make the sign?

Wh- **questions** begin with a question word such as *how, which, what, who, why, where* and *when*. Some *wh-* question words can also combine with other words. Add more examples.
How much/many/old/(2) ....?
What sort/kind/type...?

In **Object questions** the question word is the object of the verb.
What did you make? We made a sign.
The auxiliary always comes (3) *before / after* the subject. We use *do* and *did* to form questions in the present and past simple.

Subject questions start with *who, what, which* or *how much/many*. The question word is the subject of the verb.
Who made the sign? We made the sign.
There is no subject pronoun and we (4) *need / don't need* to use *do/did* in the present and past simple.
Who made the sign? NOT Who ~~they did make~~ the sign?

See page 140 for grammar reference and more practice.

NOTICE QUESTIONS ENDING WITH PREPOSITIONS

We usually put prepositions at the end of a question.
What is he talking about? Who do you live with?

SPEAKING

1 Work in pairs. Have you ever made a sign? What was it for? Tell your partner about it.

2 Write your own sign. Think about
- its purpose and its message. Is it funny or serious?
- where you would like to show it.
- who you would like to show it to.

3 Show the sign to your partner. Ask and answer questions about your signs.

1.3 WHEN COLOURS SPEAK

■ PRACTISE STATE AND DYNAMIC VERBS
■ TALK ABOUT THE SENSES

SPEAKING

1 Work in groups. Discuss the questions.

- Do you have a mobile phone? Is it a smartphone? What do you use it for?
- What other technology do you use to communicate with other people?
- What else can you use it for?

READING

1 a You are going to read a post from a blog called *Behind the Curtain*. Look at the headline and the description of the blogger. What do you think the post is going to be about?

b Read the blog post and check your answer.

2 a Work in pairs. What is the connection between the images and the story?

b Read the post again and answer the questions.

1 How has his new phone changed the writer's life?
2 What can he do now that he couldn't do before?
3 What two features of the iPhone does the writer talk about and how exactly do they work?
4 In what way do they change the way the writer communicates with his mother?
5 What else can he do with them?
6 Which application is the writer most impressed by? Why?

3 a Find words/phrases in the blog post that mean

1 switch something on
2 told you that something has happened
3 moved something across a surface
4 unclear images
5 walked around with no particular purpose or direction
6 makes something better or stronger

b Think of an adjective to describe the blog post. Tell the class why you chose it.

Behind the Curtain

My First Week with the iPhone

Posted by Austin Seraphin

Austin Seraphin, the man 'behind the curtain', has been blind from birth. In his blog he discusses a range of topics, including advances in computer technology that affect and help blind people.

Last Wednesday, my life changed forever. I got an iPhone. I consider it the greatest thing to happen to blind people for a very long time, possibly ever. It changed my life in 24 hours.

I went to the store with my mom. We asked the salesman about VoiceOver, a program that reads the text on the screen as you touch it. He knew about it and how to activate it, but he didn't know how to use it. 'Can he get text messages on this?' my mom asked. 'Well, yes, but it doesn't read the message,' the salesman said. Mom's hopes sunk, but mine didn't. 'Well, let's see, try it,' I suggested. She pulled out her phone and sent me a text message. Within seconds, my phone alerted me, and said her name. I simply swiped my finger and it read her message: Hi Austin. She almost cried.

The other night I downloaded an app that identifies colors. It uses the phone's camera and speaks the names of colors. Some of them have very surreal names, such as Atomic Orange, Cosmic, Hippie Green, Opium and Black-White. I have never experienced this before in my life. I can see some light and color, but just in blurs, and objects don't really have a color, just light sources.

The next day, I went outside. I looked at the sky. I heard colors such as 'Horizon', 'Outer Space' and many shades of blue and gray. I used color cues to find my pumpkin plants, by looking for the green among the brown and stone. I spent ten minutes looking at my pumpkin plants, with their leaves of green and lemon-ginger. I then roamed my yard and saw a blue flower. I then found the brown shed and returned to the gray house. My mind felt blown. I watched the sun set, listening to the colors change as the sky darkened. The next night, I had a conversation with mom about how the sky looked bluer tonight. Since I can see some light and color, I think hearing the color names helps my perception and enhances my visual experience. Amazing!

Archives
Links
Recent Posts
Blogstats
Blogchats
Blogrolls

VOCABULARY: senses

1 **a** Look at the extracts from the text in READING 1b. Underline the verbs and answer the questions.

1 I looked at the sky.
2 The sky looked bluer tonight.
3 I can see some light and color.

In which sentence is the verb
a describing an ability?
b describing a conscious action (something you decide to do)?
c introducing a description?

b Match the verbs in the box to the categories. Use a dictionary to help you. Some verbs can fit in more than one category.

~~feel~~ ~~hear~~ ~~listen~~ look see smell sound taste touch watch

Ability	Conscious action	Description
feel	*feel*	*feel*
hear	*listen*	

2 Complete the sentences with the verbs from 1b. More than one verb may be possible.

1 Don't .... that! It's hot!
2 Can you .... that sound? What is it?
3 Mm. That .... nice. What are you cooking?
4 Is that Ana singing? She .... really good!

3 **a** Choose the correct verb to complete the questions.

1 How well can you *look* / *see* ? Do you need to wear glasses? Do either of your parents wear glasses?
2 Do you prefer to *hear* / *listen* to music quietly or at full volume? Why?
3 Does it get very cold in your hometown in winter? Do you *feel* / *touch* the cold?
4 Do you like food that *feels* / *tastes* hot and spicy, or do you prefer more subtle flavours? Why?

b Work in pairs. Ask and answer the questions in 3a. Which sense do you think is most important for you? Why?

GRAMMAR

1 **a** Which of the sentences are true for you at the moment?

1 I'm looking out of the window.
2 I can see something strange out of the corner of my eye!
3 I can hear the sound of children playing in the distance.
4 I'm thinking about this exercise.

b Work in pairs. Compare your answers. Answer the questions.

a Which sentences describe a conscious action that is in progress at the moment?
b Which describe perceptions (things you can sense using your five senses)?

2 Complete 1–4 in the GRAMMAR PANEL with the sentences in 1a.

3 Choose the correct verb to complete the sentences.

1 I've got a bad cold and *I can't smell* / *I'm not smelling* anything.
2 *I see* / *I'm seeing* the boss about my holiday dates tomorrow.
3 What are you doing? *I taste* / *I'm tasting* the soup to see if it's got enough salt in it.
4 *I can feel* / *I'm feeling* the sun on my skin. It's so hot! I think *I burn* / *I'm burning*!

4 **a** Write three sentences describing what you are doing right now and three sentences describing what you can perceive through your senses.

b Work in pairs. Compare your sentences. How many of them are the same?

STATE & DYNAMIC VERBS

A State verbs

State verbs describe an emotion, a thought or a sense. They are not usually used in a continuous form.

I don't see very well without glasses NOT ~~*I'm not seeing*~~ *very well without glasses.*

We often use the verbs of the senses (*see*, *hear*, *smell*, *taste*, *feel*) with *can* or *could*.

I can see some light and colour.

(1) ....

(2) ....

B Dynamic verbs

Dynamic (or action) verbs describe actions we decide to perform. We use dynamic verbs with continuous verb forms to talk about an action that is in progress.

I'm listening to a really interesting podcast.

(3) ....

(4) ....

Some verbs can be both state verbs and dynamic verbs, e.g. *see*.

I can't see without glasses. (*see* = sense)

I'm seeing Jane on Friday. (*see* = meet)

See page 140 for grammar reference and more practice.

1.4 FUNCTIONAL LANGUAGE: BREAKING THE ICE

TUNE IN

1 Work in pairs. Look at the images. Discuss the questions.

- Do you ever use these topics to start a conversation?
- What other topics do you use?
- What kinds of questions would you ask about them?

2 Work in pairs. Match verbs 1–6 to nouns a–f. More than one option may be possible.

1 hear	a wet
2 watch	b better
3 get	c the match
4 have	d the news
5 feel	e people
6 know	f plans

3 **a** The expressions in 2 can all be used to start a conversation. Think of the conversation opener for each expression.

hear the news → *Have you heard the news about Jenny?*

b 1.6 Listen and compare.

4 1.7 Listen and match conversations 1–5 to situations a–e.

a strangers on a train
b work colleagues at the coffee machine
c work colleagues in the lift
d a couple at home
e strangers at a party

NOTICE *HOW'S THINGS / HOW'S IT GOING?*

These are common conversation starters. They are more informal than *How are you?*

How's things? is grammatically incorrect (it should be *How are things?*), but many people say it this way.

5 Listen again. Which conversations change topic and which follow the topic in the opening line? What does this tell you about conversation starters?

FOCUS ON LANGUAGE

6 **a** Look at the statements and questions. Which would you use with a) strangers? b) friends/family? c) both?

1 Do you know something? Your face is really familiar.
2 Excuse me, can I give you a hand with that?
3 How are you feeling today?
4 So, how do you know Sergio then?
5 What's the problem? You look terrible.
6 What did you say your name was again?
7 Hi, what are you up to?
8 Did you sleep OK?
9 Hi, what brings you here at this time?
10 You don't know me, but...

b Work in pairs. Which do you think might be useful for breaking the ice?

Stress

1.8 Listen to the statements and questions in 6a. Underline the main stress.

Do you know something?

Listen again and repeat with the correct stress.

OVER TO YOU

7 **a** Work in pairs. Choose one of the situations. Student A starts a conversation with Student B. You are strangers. How long can you can keep the conversation going?

1 standing at a bus stop
2 sheltering from torrential rain
3 standing in a long queue for tickets
4 waiting to check in at an airport

b Act out your situation to the class. Can other students guess where you are?

8 Work in groups. How easy do you find it to break the ice if you are interested in talking to somebody? What other typical ways can you think of?

TUNE IN

1 Read the online article. Match statements a–d to paragraphs 1–4.

a It can help create goodwill and a positive image for your product.
b It may be expensive and time-consuming.
c A personal touch can help a lot.
d It can help get people interested in what you offer.

HOW TO RUN A SUCCESSFUL CAMPAIGN

Communication has always been the most important process in the success of any business. Here are four ways to get your message across.

1 Advertising

Choose from radio or TV, print flyers, online sites, billboards and other digital resources. All these media can help you transmit your message to a lot of people. But costs are high and it can take time and effort. If that is the case, consider social networking sites.

2 Promotion

Consider product displays, product samples or different promotional offers like discounts or free trials. The main objective is to create interest with your strategy so that people recognise your brand.

3 Public Relations

What about sponsoring events and having product launches to introduce your business to your clients? You can have press conferences or stands at trade shows. This will all help the image that you want to present.

4 Direct Selling

Sometimes you need to go straight to your clients. Organise one-on-one meetings, so you can talk to your clients on a personal level. But don't forget, before anything else, make sure you know who to go to – always consider who your target market is!

2 Underline the different marketing strategies in the article.

PREPARE FOR TASK

3 Work in pairs. Discuss the pros and cons of

- email
- wikis
- Twitter
- online banners
- merchandising
- cold-calling
- word of mouth

It seems to me that cold-calling doesn't work for anything – people just hang up when they hear someone selling on the phone.

4 Work in pairs. Which of the marketing strategies in the article and in 3 could work for these products?

- events
- mobile phone service
- last-minute travel deals
- free invitation to concert
- football team

Print flyers and email can work well for events...

5 How would you design a promotional campaign for your English textbook? Brainstorm some initial thoughts about it.

TASK

6 a Work in small groups. Outline a promotional campaign for *The Big Picture*. Include

- the customers you are targeting
- the promotions you are going to adopt
- the form of communication you are going to use for your campaign

target: teachers
promotions: launches at events
communication: spread the word on Twitter, Facebook, YouTube

b Look at the strategies on page 158. Choose the one you think is the most effective for your campaign. Explain why and give more details where possible. Can you think of any other strategies?

I think a big event is important, it should give a good impression to the customers, so luxury hotels would be ideal.

REPORT BACK

7 Present your campaign to the rest of the class. Whose campaign is the most attractive, commercial, original? Which is the 'hardest sell'? Why?

➔ Go to Review A, Unit 1, p. 34 ➔ Go to Writing bank 1, p. 152

2 A GOOD READ

a

b

d

e

1 **a** Work in pairs. Look at the images. Answer the questions.

1 Where are the people?
2 What do you think the people are reading? How do you know?
3 Are they reading carefully or casually? Why?

b Work in pairs. Complete A in the KEY VOCABULARY PANEL.

2 **a** 2.1 Listen to a photographer talking about the images. In what order does she talk about them?

b Listen again. What does she like about each image?

3 **a** Match the extracts from transcript 2.1 to images a–f.

1 This is a good place to **check out** the football news. ....
2 He **scrolls down** the text on the screen. ....
3 You hear people **reading out** a script, but you never see them. ....
4 You **glance at** a few lines of a novel and then close your eyes... ....
5 They're **looking through** their notes for the last time. ....
6 This guy seems to be **looking up** some important information. ....

b Complete B in the KEY VOCABULARY PANEL.

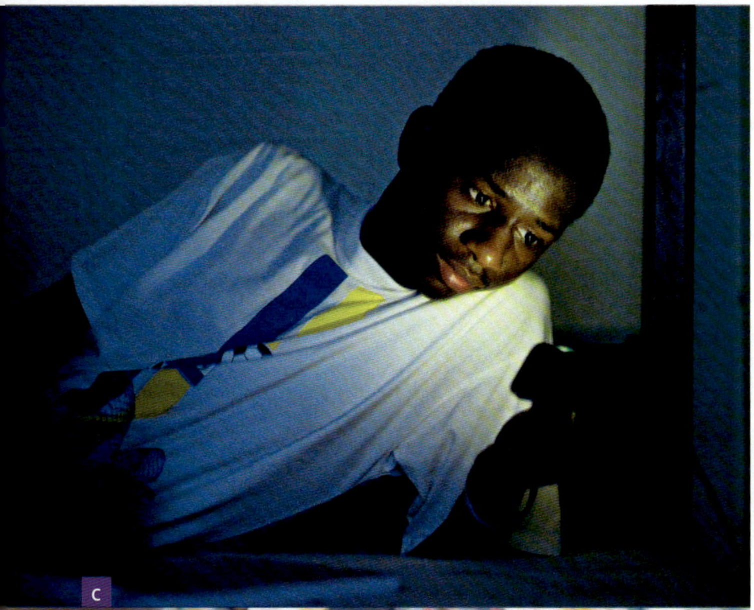

c

f

KEY VOCABULARY

Reading

A Types of reading material

- Match at least one word or phrase to images a–f.

blog dictionary email encyclopedia
instruction manual letter magazine
newspaper notes novel reference book
script (for a speech or film or play)
short story travel guide text message

- Put the words from the box in the correct category.

Reading for pleasure

....

Looking for information

....

Reading as part of your job or studies

....

- Answer the questions.

1 What kind of reading do you do most?
2 What do you think is the most relaxing: reading a book, listening to music or watching a video or TV programme? Why?

B Reading verbs

- Complete the definitions using the verbs in 3a.

flick/.................. **through** *a newspaper, notes, a novel*
to look at something quickly and superficially, sometimes just turning the pages

.... **at** *pages/the lines of a book*
to look at something for a very short time

.... **out** *a speech, a statement*
to speak the words aloud as you read

.... **out** *a piece of news, a news story, a text message*
to look at something to see what information it can give you

.... **up** *information, a word in a dictionary*
to use a reference book or website to find specific information

.... **down** *a screen, a text message*
to use a cursor, your finger or mouse to move the text down on a screen

4 **a** Use words in B to complete the sentences. One does not apply. More than one answer may be correct.

1 I sometimes .... the covers of magazines in shops, but I never buy them.
2 I always .... my notes just before an exam.
3 When I want to .... a word, I always go to an online dictionary.
4 I always .... the weather report on my computer first thing every morning.
5 I've never had to .... a speech .... to an audience. It'd terrify me!

b Are the statements true for you? Share your answers with the class.

5 Work in pairs. Discuss the questions.

- Where do you prefer to read?
- What do you like reading there?

- Practise past simple & past continuous
- Talk about books

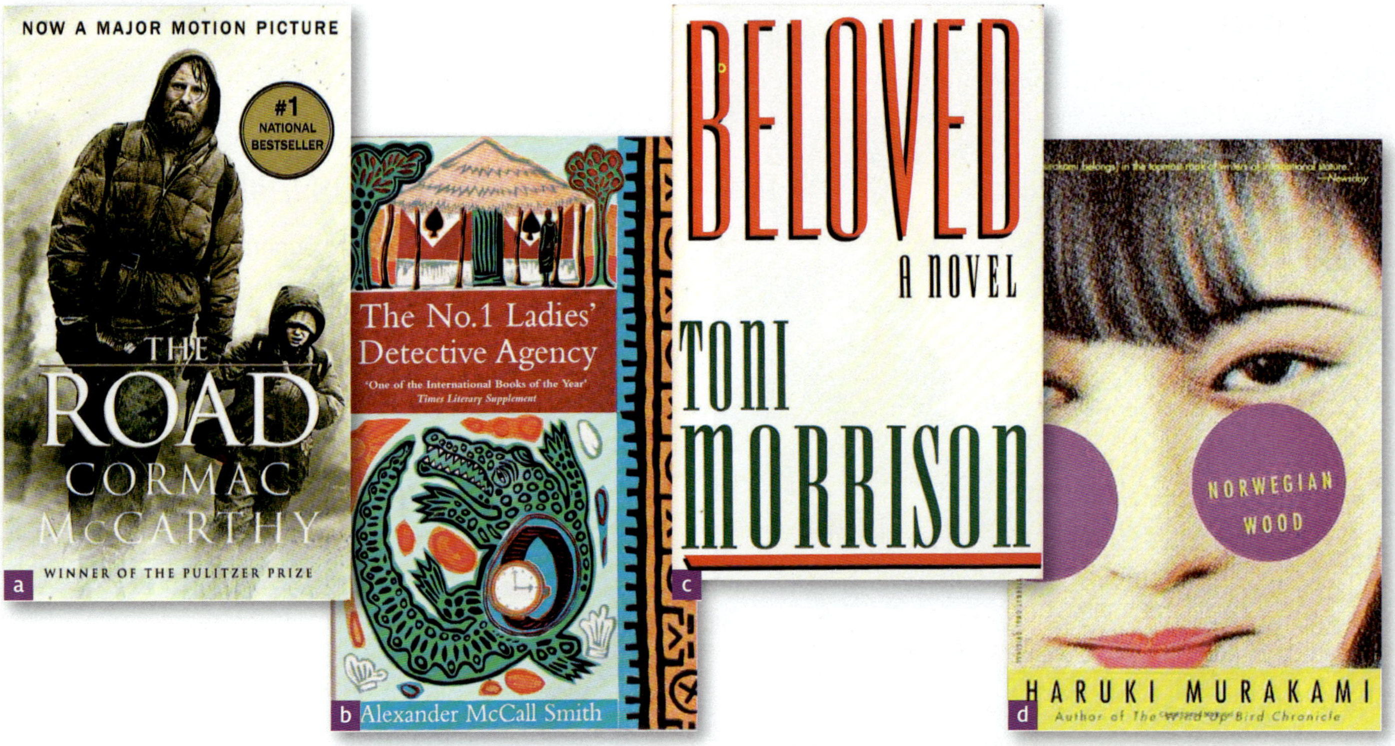

Speaking & Vocabulary: books & genres (1)

1 a Work in pairs. Add the words in the box to the two groups. Use a dictionary to help you.

1 Different kinds of books ....*anthology*....
2 Different types or genres of fiction (novels or films) ....*action-adventure*....

> action-adventure anthology autobiography biography comedy crime/detective fiction historical horror humorous love story manual non-fiction novel picture book recipe book romantic science-fiction storybook textbook tragedy war

b Answer the questions.

- When was the last time you bought a book?
- What kind of book was it?
- Was it for you or for someone else?
- Why did you choose that particular book?

2 a Tick the statements that are true for you.

When you choose a book what do you do?

.... I look at the cover – the image and the design tell me a lot about the book.
.... I read the blurb on the back and maybe the information about the author.
.... I flick through the book and maybe read the opening page or a short extract.
.... I only buy a book if someone has recommended it or if I've read a good review.

b Compare your answers with a partner.

Listening

1 a Look at the covers of four novels. Answer the questions.

1 Do you know any of the novels?
2 Look at the titles and the images. What kinds of books do you think they are? Choose from the genres in Speaking & Vocabulary 1a.
3 If you were in a bookshop, which one might you pick up?

b Discuss your answers in small groups. Did you all agree?

2 2.2 Listen to someone talking about the four novels. Check your answers to 1a.

3 a Listen again. Match the novels to the facts. More than one answer is possible for one of the sentences.

1 It seems very real and this makes it powerful.
2 It's the story of a parent and a child.
3 The novel is like a flashback.
4 The novel is a vision of the future.
5 It gives a real flavour of the place where it is set.

b Work in pairs. Answer the question.

What do the books have in common?
a They are not easy to classify.
b They are/were all best sellers.
c They are all controversial novels.

4 Work in pairs. Discuss the questions.

- Have you read any of these books?
- Would you like to? Why/Why not?
- Would you prefer to see the film?

Reading

1 **a** Read two extracts from one of the novels on page 16. Which novel do you think they come from?

b Work in pairs. Compare your answers and explain why.

2 **a** Read the extracts again. Answer the questions.

1 How many characters are there in each extract? Who are they? Which is the main character?
2 Where is the action taking place? What is the main action?
3 What do you think happened after the scene?

b Work in pairs. Would you like to read the novel? Why?/Why not?

a

Note Makoti was travelling on a bus down from Francistown. He was sitting in the front, his trumpet case on the seat beside him. She could not help but notice him, nor fail to notice the high cheek-bones and the arched eyebrows. It was a proud face, the face of a man used to being looked at and appreciated. Who was this man? A musician, with that case beside him; a clever person from the University perhaps?

The bus stopped in Gaborone. She stayed in her seat, and saw him get up. She felt her heart jump; he had looked at her; no, he had not, he was looking out of the window.

Suddenly, without thinking, she got to her feet and took her bag down from the rack. She would get off the bus.

b

There were very few people in the Botswana Book Centre. Three or four men were looking through magazines, and one or two people were reading books. The assistants were leaning over the counters, gossiping idly, and even the flies seemed lethargic.

Mma Ramotswe noticed that the two girls were at the far end of the shop. They were standing there, talking to one another, and one of them was laughing. Mma Ramotswe returned to her perusal of her book.

She looked up sharply. Her book had so absorbed her that she had not been paying attention to the girls and now – where were they? – gone. They were gone.

Grammar

1 **a** Look at the verbs in **bold** from the extracts. Which describe

a a single action?
b an action that was in progress at the time?

*Note Makoti **was travelling** on a bus down from Francistown. He **was sitting** in the front. The bus **stopped** in Gaborone. She stayed in her seat and **saw** him get up.*
*They **were standing** there, talking to one another, and one of them **was laughing**. Mma Ramotswe **returned** to her perusal of her book.*

b Complete the GRAMMAR PANEL.

2 Complete the sentences with the correct form of the verbs.

1 Mma Ramotswe .... (*stand*) at the counter of the shop when Mma Makutsi .... (*run*) through the door.
2 I .... (*stop*) on my way back from my cattle post. It .... (*be*) a hot day and I .... (*rest*) under a tree.
3 She .... (*sit*) on the bed when the neighbour .... (*come*) in and .... (*say*) that she would get somebody to take her to her father.
4 As she .... (*walk*) down the front steps of the hotel, she .... (*see*) Dr Komoti in the mall.
5 She .... (*turn*) around sharply. A woman .... (*stand*) in the doorway, wiping her hands on a cloth.

Past simple & past continuous

We often use the (1) .... to talk about single events, especially when we are telling a story.
She paid her bill and left.

We often use the (2) .... to explain the background to the story and describe a situation or action that was in progress at the time.
She was waiting under a tree.

See page 141 for grammar reference and more practice.

Speaking

1 **a** Think of a book or the film of a book you have read or seen recently. Would you recommend it to your classmates? Why/ Why not?

b Work in groups. Tell your group about your book or film.
It's set in...
It tells the story of...
It's all about...

2 **a** Work in groups. Decide which book or film you would like to recommend to the class.

b Present your choice to the class. Take a vote to see which book or film most people would like to see or read.

■ PRACTISE PAST PERFECT & PAST SIMPLE
■ TALK ABOUT FILMS

LISTENING

1 Work in pairs. What do you know about manga? Look at the images to help you. Do you know anyone who is a fan?

2 2.3 Listen to a manga fan, Tanya Kowitz, talk about manga's growth in the world. Answer the questions.

1 In what order does she mention the images?
2 What other uses of manga are not illustrated?

3 **a** Listen again. Change the sentences so that they are true.

1 Manga represents nearly half of what Japanese people read.
2 Tanya lives in Tokyo now.
3 Hiroshima has a special bookshop devoted to manga.
4 The plot of the manga *Hamlet* is similar to the original version.
5 *1 World Manga* are comics which look at local Japanese issues.
6 Large manga faces are used on TV commercials.
7 Tanya's final point is that manga is a purely Japanese phenomenon.

b 2.4 Listen and check your answers.

VOCABULARY: books & genres (2)

1 Match the words from LISTENING 2 to the categories.

adaptation best seller character comic book graphic novel plot series setting theme version

1 Type of reading material ....
2 Elements of a story ....
3 Different representations of a story ....

2 **a** Complete the sentences with words from the box in 1. In some cases, two answers may be possible.

1 I loved the original, but the film .... was terrible.
2 I like Lisa Simpson, she's my favourite .... in the programme.
3 The book was great, but I had trouble understanding the .... It was really complicated.
4 *Tintin* was the first .... that I read as a kid.
5 I mostly read fiction, though not ...., I'm not so interested in them.

b 2.5 Listen and check.

3 Work in pairs. Change or add any words in the sentences in 2a to make them true for you. Continue the sentences to tell your partner why.

1 I loved the original 'Batman' comic but the film version was terrible. It's much better in my imagination.

Reading & Speaking

1 Work in pairs. Look at the images on page 18 again. Which one shows a famous work of literature? Do you know anything about the original story?

a

b

2 **a** Look at the film posters of two other plays by the same writer. Do you know what they are? Choose from the list.

Romeo & Juliet *The Tempest* *The Merchant of Venice*
A Midsummer Night's Dream *Macbeth* *Twelfth Night*

b Read the descriptions of *Hamlet* and the two plays in the posters. Match them to the images on this page and page 18.

1 Two young people met and fell in love. But their two families **had been** at war for years, so they had to keep their love a secret. When the boy discovered that he **had killed** his lover's cousin in a fight, the two lovers planned their escape.

2 A rich businessman borrowed some money from a moneylender. The businessman **had promised** to give the moneylender a pound of his flesh if he couldn't repay the money. He **had thought** it was a joke, but the moneylender was deadly serious.

3 His father **had** only **been** dead for a few weeks when the Prince met his ghost. He listened amazed as his father's ghost told him what **had happened** and who **had killed** him. The Prince had no other choice. He had to seek revenge for his father's death.

3 Work in pairs. Have you seen either of the films in 1? Would you like to? Which stories from your country have been made into a film or comics?

Grammar

1 **a** Look at the verbs in **bold** in Reading & Speaking 2b. Which are describing

a an event which happened before the main action in the story?

b a situation that had been in progress for some time before the story started?

b Complete 1–3 in the Grammar panel with sentences from the texts in Reading & Speaking 2b.

2 **a** Choose the correct form of the verbs to complete the story.

Luke (1)*was / had been* a simple farm boy. He (2)*lived / had lived* with his uncle and aunt. His mother died when he was born and he (3)*never met / had never met* his father. Not, that is, until one day, when he was repairing an old robot that he (4)*bought / had bought* from some travellers and he accidentally (5)*unlocked / had unlocked* a message that would change the course of his life.

b Work in pairs. Compare your answers. Do you know what film it comes from?

3 Work in pairs. Write the story (50 words) of a famous film or piece of literature. Read it to the class. Can they guess what it is?

Past perfect & past simple

A Past perfect

We use the **past perfect** to

- talk about an event that happened **before** a point in time in the past

(1) ....

- describe a situation that was in progress up to a point in time in the past.

(2) ....

We form the past perfect with *had* + past participle.

B Past perfect & past simple

We use the **past simple** to describe the main events in the story. We use the past perfect to explain that one event happened **before** another.

(3) ....

See page 141 for grammar reference and more practice.

cliffhanger **1** a melodramatic TV series in which each episode ends in suspense, **2** a situation full of suspense at the end of a chapter in a book, a scene in a film or an episode in a radio or TV series, **3** a dramatic situation where the outcome is uncertain up to the very end

a

b

c

SPEAKING

1 **a** Work in pairs. Look at the images. What is the connection between the images and the dictionary definition?

b 2.6 Listen and check.

2 Work in groups. Think of five popular TV series in your country. Compare your list with your group and answer the questions.

- Why are they so popular? Why do people get addicted to them?
- Have you ever been hooked on a TV series? Why/Why not?

READING

1 **a** Read the article and make a note of

1 the two forms of literature which are being compared.
2 the main similarities between the two forms.
3 the main differences.

b Work in pairs. Check your answers and discuss the questions.

- Do you know if any mobile phone novels have been published in your language?
- Have you ever read a mobile novel? Would you like to? Why/Why not?

Mobile novels: a new way of reading?

You look at your mobile phone to check the time and see the latest chapter of your favourite novel flash onto your mobile phone. There's nothing new in reading a novel on the train to work, nor in reading texts on your mobile, but the growth of mobile novels is new. So what are they exactly?

The first mobile novel was written in Japan in 2003 by a young writer calling himself Yoshi. He posted his novel in instalments on a website that his readers then accessed on their mobiles. It became an instant success. His fans found out about it by word of mouth and soon he had more than 20 million hits. His first novel, *Deep Love*, was such a success that it re-appeared as a paperback book, a manga story, a TV series and a film.

So, what's so new about mobile novels? It's just a novel read on a screen, isn't it? Well no, there's more to it than that. As Yoshi writes and publishes his novel bit by bit, his readers visit his website and tell him how they feel about the plot and the characters. Yoshi listens to his readers' opinions and if he notices that fewer people are downloading his story, he changes the plot.

Interactive novels, written in instalments and changing in response to their readers' comments – people are saying this is a revolution, but is it really that new? Back in the nineteenth century, in Victorian England, the novels of Charles Dickens were written in just the same way, each instalment ending with a cliffhanger to keep the readers' attention.

Grammar

1 **a** Look at the sentences. Complete them with Yoshi (Y) or Dickens (D).

1 .... writes and publishes his novel bit by bit.
2 .... used to write his novels one instalment at a time.
3 .... listens to his readers' opinions.
4 .... changes the plot.
5 .... would listen to the reactions of his readers.
6 .... would drop a storyline if it wasn't successful.

b Read the article in Reading 1a again and check your answers. How did you know which was which?

2 **a** Underline the verbs in the extracts in 1a that speak about Dickens. What two forms are used? Find more examples of both forms in the article.

b Complete 1–2 in the Grammar panel with examples from the article.

3 **a** Work in pairs. Look at the Grammar panel again. In which sentences can you replace *used to* with *would*?

1 I used to love reading comic books when I was younger, but now I find them really boring.
2 My dad used to read stories to us every night before we went to sleep.
3 My favourite bedtime stories used to be stories about pirates and robbers and superheroes.
4 I used to do a lot of reading in bed, but now I just fall asleep!

b Are any of the sentences true for you? Share your ideas with your partner.

Dickens used to write his novels one instalment at a time. The instalments would appear in magazines, once a month, over a period of a year or more. Readers used to wait anxiously for the next instalment to come out. They'd discuss the plot and characters all month until it came out. Children would press their noses up against the glass of the bookshop window to look at the illustrations. And Dickens would listen to the reactions of his readers. If a character was particularly popular, then he or she would make another appearance in the plot; if a story line wasn't successful, then he would drop it and start another.

Dickens' novels were interactive, much-loved, popular best sellers, just like these new twenty-first century novels which are appearing on mobiles, slowly but surely, all around the world.

Used to & would

We can use both *used to* and *would* to talk about things that happened regularly in the past or past habits.

Examples
(1) ....
(2) ....

We can use *used to* to talk about feelings, states and actions.

They used to read them over and over. (action)
People used to be anxious to read the next instalment. (feeling)

We can only use *would* with actions, not with feelings.
Feelings: *They used to love the stories.* NOT *They ~~would love~~ the stories.*
Actions: *They would wait anxiously for the next instalment.*
They used to wait anxiously for the next instalment.

Note: In questions and negative forms there's no *d* at the end of *use*.
Did you use to read a lot as a child?
No, I didn't use to like reading very much.

See page 141 for grammar reference and more practice.

Pronunciation: *used to / use to*

1 **a** 2.7 Listen to this short exchange. How do we pronounce the underlined words? Does it change at all?

A Did you use to watch a lot of TV when you were a kid?
B No, we didn't use to have a TV, but we used to go to the cinema a lot.

b Work in pairs. Listen and repeat. Ask and answer other questions beginning *Did you use to...?*

Speaking

1 **a** Work in pairs. Discuss the questions.

- What are the ingredients of a successful children's book or TV programme?
- In what ways are they different from books and programmes that appeal to adults?
- Can you think of any books, films or TV programmes that are equally popular with kids and adults? Why do you think that is?

b Share your answers with the class. Which book or programme was the most talked about?

TUNE IN

1 Work in pairs. Look at the image. What does it say about reading today?

2 a 2.8 Listen to journalist Louise Fryer talking about how we read today. Tick the sentence which best summarises her opinion.

We read badly because

.... 1 there is too much to read.
.... 2 we read anxiously.
.... 3 we can't concentrate.

b What examples of reading online does she mention?

emails, weather forecast...

3 a 2.9 Listen to six people giving their personal opinion about the topic. How many of them agree with Louise and how many disagree?

b Work in pairs. What do you think? Do you agree or disagree? Why?

FOCUS ON LANGUAGE

4 Work in pairs. Match the two parts of the phrases from 3a.

1 I don't agree	a that way,
2 I really see	b about that.
3 I agree	c at all.
4 I don't see it	d Louise's point, but...
5 I couldn't	e to some extent,
6 I'm afraid she's wrong	f agree more, but

5 Which phrases mean *agree* and which *disagree*? Which express this strongly and which in a more polite way?

	Agree	Disagree
Politely		*I don't see it that way*
Strongly		

> **Stress**
>
> 2.10 Listen to the phrases in 4.
> Underline the main stress.
> *I don't agree at all.*
> Listen again and repeat with the correct stress.

6 Listen again. Which words are used before the expressions?

You know, I don't agree at all...

OVER TO YOU

7 a Look at the opinions. What is your reaction to them? Do you a) strongly agree? b) agree to a point? c) disagree on the whole? d) strongly disagree?

1 Professional sports people are paid too much.
2 Our schools don't prepare children for the modern world.
3 The internet is the best invention of the last 100 years.
4 Printed books will soon be a thing of the past.

b Work in pairs. Compare your answers. Explain why you agree or disagree. If you and your partner disagree on any of the points, then try to persuade your partner to change his or her mind.

8 Report back to the class on your discussion. Which statement provoked the most disagreement in the class?

TUNE IN

1 Look at the photo. What can you see? Who do you think took it? Was it planned or accidental?

2 Read a short article from the *Lonely Earth* website called *The story behind the photo* and check your answers to 1.

> I took the photo at Leeds bus station where I was waiting to start my journey, though I can't remember where I was going now. I saw the couple from the entrance of the bus station. Eventually they kissed… they were obviously saying goodbye. I took just one shot and that was it, I didn't think of it again. I had forgotten all about the photo, then one day I was looking at some old files and found it. I printed it in colour to start with, but that seemed to lose a bit of the romance, so I converted it to black and white. I stuck it on the wall of my flat and people started telling me what a good shot it was. However, they always asked me the same question: had I set the whole thing up? My answer is 'No, I never do that'.

3 Work in pairs. Read the article again and answer the questions.

1 What did he think of the photo after he took it?
2 Why did he change it to black and white?
3 What was people's reaction to it?

PREPARE FOR TASK

4 a Work in pairs. Look at the photo and complete the text with the correct form of the verbs in the past simple, past continuous or past perfect.

b 2.11 Listen and check.

5 What similarities can you find between the two descriptions?

I (1) .... (*take*) this photo in Patagonia in Argentina. The two narrow peaks that you can see are called Fitzroy and Cerro Torre. We (2) .... (*spent*) a few weeks trekking around that area and this (3) .... (*be*) the end of the last day of our trip. We (4) .... (*drive*) back on that desolate highway, and the light (5) .... (*die*) when I (6) .... (*catch*) a glimpse of the mountain range in the rear view mirror and (7) .... (*think*) 'I just need to take one last photo of that horizon'. It (8) .... (*turn*) out to be the best photo I (9) .... (*take*) on that whole trip.

TASK

6 Think of a photo that you have taken on holiday and that has a good story behind it. Make notes about

1 *the main* actions/events in the story.
2 the *background* events/actions.
3 the events that took place at a *previous time*.
4 what happened *after* you took the photo.

7 Write your own story behind the photo. Use your notes from 6.

REPORT BACK

8 a Read out your story to the class.

b Listen to the stories and decide

a if there are any similarities between the photos and/or the stories that students chose.
b the most interesting story behind the photo.

➔ Go to Review A, Unit 2, p. 35

3 Art everywhere

a

b

c

d

1 Work in small groups. Look at the images. What do they show? What do they have in common? What is the link with the unit title?

2 a Complete A in the Key vocabulary panel. Discuss the questions.

- Are there any sculptures or other works of art on display in the open air in your town or area? Where are they?
- Are they permanent fixtures or part of a temporary exhibition?
- Are there any art galleries or museums in your town? What kind of art is on display there?
- Do you often visit art galleries and museums? Why/Why not?

b 3.1 Listen to five conversations. Answer the questions.

1 Which image of art are they discussing in each conversation?
2 Which image <u>don't</u> they discuss?
3 Do they like them? Why/Why not?

f

e

3 a Complete **B** in the KEY VOCABULARY PANEL.

b Complete the extracts with adjectives from **B**.

1 It's .... how he uses these derelict old buildings and turns them into a work of art.
2 Yes, but the images are pretty .... sometimes. I mean, all those rats!
3 We were really .... when we came across this last installation.
4 It was so .... All these people taking photos on their phones!
5 The kids look really ...., don't they? But actually they're just imitating the statue's pose.
6 I tell you, this one was so lifelike that the first time you saw it, it was ....

4 a 3.2 Listen and check. Which other adjectives could you add to the sentences in **3b**?

b Do you agree with the speakers' opinions? Why/Why not?

KEY VOCABULARY

Art

A Works of art

- Match the words in the box to images a–f.

drawing exhibition graffiti installation
mural painting photo sculpture
street art statue work of art

B -*ed* and -*ing* adjectives

- ***-ed*** and ***-ing*** adjectives are formed from verbs that describe emotional reactions.

interest interested interesting

- Adjectives that end in ***-ed*** describe emotional reactions and responses. They usually follow a linking verb such as *be*, *seem*, *look*.

I was interested in the photos.

- Adjectives that end in ***-ing*** describe the thing, place or person that provokes the emotion.

The photos were interesting.

- Match the pairs of adjectives 1–8 with the emotions a–h they are associated with. The first has been done for you.

Adjectives	Emotions
1 annoyed/annoying	a sympathy or empathy
2 disturbed /disturbing	b anger
3 bored/boring	c extreme fear
4 surprised/surprising	d impatience or lack of interest
5 amazed/amazing	e reaction to something unusual
6 shocked/shocking	f surprise (something bad)
7 moved/moving	g surprise (something good)
8 terrified/terrifying	h unhappiness and worry

- Can you think of any more adjectives that have both an *-ed* and an *-ing* ending?

NOTICE ADJECTIVES

We can combine a noun and an *-ing* verb to create adjectives.

thought-provoking
breath-taking
mind-blowing

Use each adjective to describe one of the works of art.

- PRACTISE ADJECTIVES
- TALK ABOUT GRAFFITI

a

b

portrait *noun [countable]* a painting, drawing or photograph of a person, especially their face. Portraits can take many forms, e.g. ***a painting, a photo or a caricature.***

SPEAKING & READING

1 Work in pairs. Look at images a and b and the dictionary definition. Discuss the questions.

- Is there anywhere in your town where people draw or paint on the street? What kind of things do they usually paint or draw?
- Have you ever had a portrait taken or made of you? If yes, what kind of portrait was it? Did you like it? Do you still have a copy?

2 **a** Look at paragraph 1 of the article and the two portraits c and d and answer the questions.

1 What two things do the portraits have in common?
2 What do you think the rest of the article is about?

b Read the rest of the article. Match the artists to their portraits. What messages are the two artists trying to express?

3 **a** Read the article again and match the facts to Liu (L), Zhang (Z) or both (B).

1 He doesn't live in the country of his birth. ......Z......
2 The title of his work is easy to understand. ....
3 His work is connected with how he sees himself. ....
4 His art is a performance that the public can watch. ....
5 His work has a very personal significance. ....
6 His body becomes part of the artwork. ....

b In what ways are the two artists similar? In what ways are they different? Which portrait do you prefer (if any)? Why?

A portrait is worth a thousand words

1 The tradition of painting portraits is an old one. And artists have always been interested in self-portraits, but there are two Chinese artists who are doing something very different with this old tradition. Instead of painting pictures of themselves, they pose and their assistants paint *on* them. If you're confused, then read on...

2 Zhang Huan asked three calligraphers to paint very small Chinese characters all over his face. First a few words, then more and more. The tiny characters slowly filled his whole face until you can't read anything anymore. His whole face is covered in black ink. Art critic Alina Balanescu says, 'I find this work extremely **interesting**. It's called *Family Tree*. Most of the text comes from Chinese folklore. The title isn't very easy to understand, but I think Zhang, who now lives in the US, is showing the influence of his [Chinese] roots, he's trying not to forget his family tree. He's doing it in a very **special** way of course, and the result is totally **fascinating**'. The artist has a more negative view: 'At the end, I cannot tell who I am. My identity has disappeared'.

d

c

3 Compare this with the work of Liu Bolin in *Hiding in the City* – a series of photographs taken in urban locations. It's a very **good** title, because it's almost impossible to see Liu in his photos. People walking by when the photos are being prepared often have no idea Liu is there until he begins to move. Preparing for these photographs requires a lot of patience. Liu has to stand still for hours while an assistant paints him from head to toe, until he disappears into the background like a human chameleon. It's great fun and makes for an absolutely **fantastic** collection of images. But there is another more serious side to his art. Liu makes himself invisible to highlight the difficulties that many artists have in his country. This is a silent protest which is completely **unique** to him.

GRAMMAR & VOCABULARY: gradable & absolute adjectives

1 a Work in pairs. Look at the pairs of adjectives and answer the questions.

interesting/fascinating good/fantastic special/unique

1 Find the adjectives in **bold** in the article. What is each adjective describing?
2 Which adjective is stronger in each pair?
3 What word comes directly before each adjective?

b Complete 1–8 in the GRAMMAR PANEL with words from 1a. Are these rules similar in your language?

2 a Look at the adjectives in the box. Make seven more word pairs with similar meanings. Use a dictionary to help you. Which adjectives would you not normally use to describe a work of art?

bad beautiful big delicious difficult exhausted huge impossible small stunning tasty terrible tiny tired

b Decide which adjectives you can use with

a very *beautiful*, ..., ..., ..., ...
b absolutely *stunning*, ..., ..., ..., ...

3 a Work in pairs. Look at pages 24 and 25. Write a sentence about three of the pieces of art you can see, with the adjectives and modifiers in 1 and 2.

b Work with another pair. Read out your sentences. Can your partners guess which piece of art you're describing?

PRONUNCIATION: word stress for emphasis

1 a 3.3 Listen and notice the stress on the words in **bold**.

1 A Mm, this isn't very nice.
B Not very nice? It's **to**tally dis**gus**ting!

b Listen and repeat.

2 a Complete the sentences using absolute adjectives.

1 A This is quite interesting.
B Interesting? It's absolutely ....!

2 A I'm quite tired after that walk.
B Tired? I'm completely ....!

3 A Hey, this is quite good, you know.
B Good? It's really ....!

b 3.4 Listen and compare your answers. Were they the same?

3 a Listen again and mark the stress. Practise reading the exchanges in 2a in pairs.

b Write two similar exchanges. Read them out in pairs.

GRADABLE & ABSOLUTE ADJECTIVES

A Gradable & absolute adjectives

Some adjectives are **gradable** – we can make them stronger or weaker: *it's quite nice* (weak), *it's very nice* (strong).

Examples: *good*, (1) .... (2) ....

Other adjectives are **absolute** – the quality either exists or it doesn't. They cannot be made stronger or weaker.

Examples: *fascinating*, (3) .... and (4) ....

B Modifying gradable & absolute adjectives

To make **gradable** adjectives stronger use *very* or (5) ....: *very small Chinese characters*

To make gradable adjectives weaker use *quite* or *fairly*: *It's quite difficult.*

To emphasise **absolute** adjectives use (6) ...., *absolutely* or *completely*:

I find this work absolutely fascinating.

We cannot use *absolutely*, *completely* and (7) .... with gradable adjectives. We cannot use (8) ...., *very* and *fairly* with absolute adjectives.

We can use *really* to add information about both gradable and absolute adjectives.

It's really nice. It's really stunning.

See page 142 for grammar reference and more practice.

SPEAKING

1 a Work in pairs. Look at the different examples of graffiti on page 158 and discuss the questions.

- Who do you think painted them?
- Why do you think they painted them?
- Which do you think has a personal meaning? Which has a political message? Why?
- Which could be viewed as art and which as an act of vandalism? Why?

b Tell another pair about one of the pieces of graffiti. Can they guess which one it is?

I think this was probably drawn by a very angry person.

2 Work in pairs and discuss the questions.

- Is there a lot of graffiti in your neighbourhood? If yes, where is it? What kind of graffiti is it?
- Is graffiti illegal in your country? Do you think it should be?

Listening

1 **a** 3.5 Look at the image. What can you see? Where do you think it is? Listen and find out.

b Listen again and answer the questions.

1 What is a plinth?
2 Why is this plinth empty?
3 What is the competition established in 2010?
4 Who decides the winner?
5 How long will the first two statues stand on the plinth?

2 **a** Look at the final six short-listed entries a–f and match them to the descriptions.

1 A colourful statue of aristocrat and businessman, Sir George White.
2 A giant bright blue cockerel.
3 A huge slice of Battenburg cake (a popular cake in the UK, possibly named after a German prince who married into the Royal family) made of bricks.
4 A mountain landscape in the shape of Britain.
5 A brass statue of a boy on a rocking horse.
6 A cash machine below an enormous organ.

a

b

c

d

e

f

b What exactly do they represent do you think?

3 **a** 3.6 Listen to Estefanía, Luke, Camelia and Miguel talking about the contestants and answer the questions.

1 Which is each person's favourite?
2 Which of the six artworks don't they talk about?
3 Which one do they think will win?

b Listen again. Which artwork, according the speakers

1 is easy to relate to?
2 is just a crazy idea?
3 has a historical significance?
4 is similar to another statue nearby?

4 **a** Listen a third time and match the phrases to the four artworks they speak about.

1 'It's definitely the funniest and by far the most colourful.'
2 'It's much more elegant than the bird.'
3 'I think it's the most intelligent one, actually.'
4 'I think it's a little more appropriate, that's all.'
5 'I think it's as funny as the cake.'
6 'It's not as strange as the others.'

b Work in small groups. Discuss the questions.

- Do you agree with the speakers? Why/Why not?
- Which piece of art do you think would look best on the plinth? Why?

Grammar

1 Look at the descriptions in **Listening 4a**. Which

1 describe a difference between two things?
2 describe a similarity between two things?
3 say that one thing is better than all the others?

2 a Look at the descriptions again. Underline the adjectives. Which are

a comparatives (used with *more* or *-er*)?
b superlatives (used with *most* or *-est*)?
c used with *as ... as*?

b Complete gaps 1–2 in A in the **Grammar panel** with sentences from **Listening 4a**.

3 a Look at the sentences in **Listening 4a** again. Which of the words in the box are used with

a comparative
b superlative
c *as ... as*

a little by far much

by far the most colourful...

b Complete 3–5 in B in the **Grammar panel**.

4 Look at the three versions of the Mona Lisa and complete the sentences with the correct form of the words in brackets.

1 I really like the third one – the Banksy. It's .... in my opinion. (*by far/good*).
2 Really? No, I prefer the cartoon. I think it's .... than the Banksy. (*much/original*).
3 I find it really difficult to choose between them. I think the Banksy is .... the cartoon. (*as ... as/original*).
4 I agree, they're both great, but I still prefer the Kucherenko. It's more colourful, I don't know, and just .... the other two I suppose. (*a little/fun*).

Notice *fun*

We can use *fun* as both a noun and an adjective.
This is great fun. (noun)
It was a fun day out. (adjective)
We say *more fun/most fun*.
Playing tennis is much more fun than watching it!

1 Kucherenko
2
3 Banksy

5 a Look at the three versions of the Mona Lisa again. Which do you prefer? Write three sentences using the structures in the **Grammar panel** to explain your answer.

b Compare your answers with a partner. Do you agree?

As ... as, comparatives & superlatives

A *As ... as*

We use *as* + adjective + *as* to show the **similarity** between two things. (1) ....

We use *not as* + adj + *as* to show the **difference**.
(2) ....

B Modifying comparatives & superlatives

- **Comparative adjectives**

We use *a lot*, *much*, *far* to show a big difference.
(3) ....

We use *a little*, *a bit*, *slightly* to show a small difference.
(4) ....

- **Superlative adjectives**

We use *By far* to emphasise a superlative adjective.
(5) ....

See page 142 for grammar reference and more practice.

Speaking

1 Work in small groups. Think of a sculpture, a fountain or a monument in your town and answer the questions.

- Where is it?
- What does it look like? Do you like it? Why/Why not?

2 a Work in groups. Your local town council wants to place a new sculpture in one of the main squares in your town. Your group is going to put forward a proposal. Think about the questions.

- Where do you think it should be?
- What should the sculpture represent?
- What kind of sculpture do you think would look best?

b Present your ideas to the class. Vote on the most original idea and the most traditional idea.

Eric Molinksy is a freelance radio reporter with an interesting hobby. He likes sketching people secretly on New York City's subway using his iPhone. Read this interview with him.

1 ______________________?

'I love the technology side of it, it feels right for my work. I use an iPhone app called Sketchbook. I use my finger to do the drawings, I think they come out really well, better than if I was using a normal sketchbook and pencil. And of course people don't know you're drawing them. It works beautifully.'

2 ______________________?

'Because I don't want them to pose. If somebody realises I'm drawing them and gets annoyed then I delete the drawing. I don't want to annoy people. But most people are friendly or they don't notice.'

3 ______________________?

'There isn't very much time. People are coming in and out and it can get crowded, so I have to draw them really fast. The initial black and white drawing only takes about 30 seconds. Often I finish the details at home. And I add layers of colour.'

4 ______________________?

'It's not easy, every day it's like a hunt – a hunt for a great-looking face. Like, you think, wow that guy's got a great beard! Real people are always more interesting than what I would have come up with in my own head.'

5 ______________________?

'I post my drawings to a blog. I have more than 300 sketches on the site, so people can easily go and check if they're there! The faces look so different, they're the faces of New York: babies and the elderly; burkas and sundresses; skaters and executives.'

6 ______________________?

'I'm happiest when I feel like I've captured somebody to the point where you look at the drawing and you think the person is just going to start talking to you.'

Reading

1 Work in pairs. Look at the sketches and answer the questions.

- Where do you think the people are?
- What are they doing and thinking?
- In what way are these sketches different from photos? Do they give us more, or less, information about the people?

2 a Read the newspaper article about the sketches and answer the questions.

1 Who drew them?
2 Where were they drawn?
3 What's unusual about them?

b Read the article again and match a–f to gaps 1–6 in the article.

a What do you look for in a face?
b What does technology add to your work?
c What are the problems of working on the subway?
d What do you do with the sketches afterwards?
e What's the best part of your work?
f Why don't you warn people that you are going to draw them?

3 a Complete the summary of the interview.

Eric Molinsky loves sketching (1) .... who are travelling on the (2) .... He uses his (3) .... so that no-one will notice what he's doing because he doesn't want people to (4) .... and look unnatural. He uploads the sketches to his (5) .... He has more than (6) .... faces on his site. These faces represent for him the many faces of (7) ....

b Work in pairs. Discuss the questions.

- What do you think of Eric Molinsky's hobby?
- Would you be happy for him to sketch you on the subway? Why/Why not?

Grammar

1 a Work in pairs. Look at the extracts from the interview. What do the words in **bold** refer to?

1 ... **it** feels right for my work. *working with an iPhone*
2 ... **they** come out really well.
3 **It** works beautifully.
4 But most people are friendly or **they** don't notice.
5 People are coming in and out and **it** can get crowded.
6 I have to draw **them** really fast.
7 It's not easy, every day **it**'s like a hunt – a hunt for a great-looking face.
8 ... people can easily go and check if **they**'re there!

b Read A in the Grammar panel. Look at the sentences in 1a again and find all the examples of a) adjectives and b) adverbs of manner.

2 a Look at your answers to 1b and answer the questions.

1 Which two adverbs can also be used as adjectives?
2 Which adjective can also be used as an adverb?
3 Which word ending in *-ly* is not an adverb?
4 What is the adverb form of *good*?

b Complete 1–5 in B in the GRAMMAR PANEL.

3 Choose the correct option to complete this short description of the Sketchbook app.

File Edit View Tools Message Help
Reply Reply All Forward Print Delete Previous Next Addresses

I've just downloaded Sketchbook onto my iPad. It's (1)*great / greatly*! It downloaded so (2)*quick / quickly* and it's so (3)*easy / easily* to use. To start with I drew very (4)*careful / carefully*. It was the first time I'd drawn with my fingers. But then I started to feel more (5)*confident / confidently* and I found that I could draw really (6)*good / well*, and really (7)*fast / fastly*. Much better than I had ever done with a pencil or brush before. There's an (8)*enormous / enormously* range of colours and effects to choose from. And the final results look really (9)*professional / professionally*. Try it out for yourself! I'm sure you'll be (10)*impressed / impressedly*.

4 a Do you have an interesting app on your phone or computer? Write three or four sentences explaining the app. Use as many adjectives and adverbs as you can.

b Compare your answers with a partner. Have you ever tried your partner's app?

ADJECTIVES & ADVERBS

A Adjectives & adverbs of manner

Adjectives add information about people, things or places. They can come

- **before** a noun: *He has a great beard.*
- **after** a linking verb *(be, get, look, feel)*: *It sounds strange, but it's true.*

Adverbs of manner add information about how we do something. They usually come after the verb they are describing. *It works beautifully.*

NOTE: We do not use adverbs after linking verbs: *It sounds beautiful.* NOT *It sounds ~~beautifully~~.*

B -ly adverbs

Many adverbs of manner are formed by adding *-ly* to an adjective:
beautiful → (1) ...., *easy* → *easily*, *gentle* → *gently*

NOTE: Not all words which end in *-ly* are adverbs. Some are adjectives: (2) ...., *lovely*, etc.

Some adjectives and adverbs are the same.
(3) ...., (4) ...., *late*, *early*.
I had a late night. (adjective) *I worked late that night.* (adverb)

NOTE: The adverb form of *good* is (5) ....

See page 142 for grammar reference and more practice.

SPEAKING & VOCABULARY: people-watching

1 a 3.7 Listen to Toni talking about the café in the photo. What does she like about it? What does she like doing there?

b Listen again and match the two parts of the sentences.

1 I love sitting here with a coffee and **watching**
2 ... a huge variety of people walk along this street, all **going**
3 It's so much more interesting than just **staring**
4 Sometimes I watch the people at the next table and **tune**
5 I know I shouldn't really **listen**
6 ... but on the whole they're simply **passing**

a ... **about their business**.
b ... **in on** other people's **conversations**...
c ... **in to** their conversations.
d ... **the time of day**...
e ... **the world go by**.
f ... **into space**.

2 a Work in pairs. Look at at the phrases in **bold** in 1b. Can you guess what they mean?

b Check your answers on page 158. Do you have any similar phrases in your language?

3 Work in small groups. Discuss the questions.

- Do you enjoy people-watching? Why/Why not?
- Where are the best places to watch the world go by in your town?
- Think of the last time you were in one of those places. Who else was there? What were they doing? Did you see anyone particularly interesting?

TUNE IN

1 **a** Work in pairs. Look at the building in the photo. Do you like the design? Why/Why not?

b Read a short text on page 161 and find out more about the building.

2 **a** 3.8 Listen to Frank, Jane, Adrian and Sally talking about the building. How many people are in favour of the project and how many are against the project?

b Listen again. Who says the following? Complete the chart.

	Frank	Jane	Adrian	Sally
The building...				
1 is embarrassing.			✓	
2 ruined a beautiful place.				
3 is modern like its contents.				
4 is an artwork in itself.				
5 is a topic of conversation.				
6 is a technological wonder.				
7 is not functional.				

3 Work in pairs. Compare your answers and answer the questions.

- What do you think about the building?
- Do you know of any other controversial modern public buildings? Do you like or dislike them?

FOCUS ON LANGUAGE

4 Look at how we make sentences more emphatic by changing the word order. Do you add emphasis in a similar way in your language?

The design is the problem. → The problem is the design.
The colour is the most important thing. → The most important thing is the colour.
I really hate the colour. → What I hate is the colour.

5 **a** Work in pairs. Match 1–6 to a–e to make phrases.

1 What I like is that it	a about it
2 That's the best thing	b is that people are talking about it
3 The most important thing	c is the position
4 The problem is that	d matches what's inside
5 What I hate about it	e the architect is famous

b 3.8 Listen and check.

Stress

3.9 Listen again to the statements in 5a. Underline the main stress.
What I like is that it matches what's inside.
Listen again and repeat with the correct stress.

6 **a** Make the sentences more emphatic. Begin with the word in brackets.

1 I don't like much pop music. All the tracks sound the same. (What I don't like about pop music is...)
2 I love travelling by plane, but I hate the jet-lag. (The only problem with travelling...)
3 It's a good idea to go shopping with somebody else so you get a second opinion. (The best thing about going shopping...)

b Change the sentences so that they are true for you.

OVER TO YOU

7 Work in pairs. Look at the list. Write a sentence giving your opinion on five of the topics.

- Sundays
- the English language
- art galleries
- summer holidays
- politicians
- mobile phones
- fast food
- professional footballers
- pets
- beaches

The worst thing about Sundays is that they only last 24 hours.

8 **a** Show your sentences to another pair. Find the topics where there was most disagreement.

b Try to convince the others to change their mind. Be emphatic! Report back to the class.

TUNE IN

1 Work in pairs. Look at the photo. Discuss the questions.

- Where are the people? What do you think they're talking about?
- When was the last time you were asked to answer a survey? What was it about?
- Did you stop and answer the questions or did you walk on? Why?

2 a 3.10 Listen to the woman talking to a few people on the street and answer the questions.

1 How many people does the woman approach?
2 How many of them agree to complete the survey?
3 What do they get if they complete the survey?

b Listen again and write in the answers that you hear.

1 Age ☐under 18 ☐18–25 ☐26–30 ☐over 30

2 Gender ☐M ☐F

3 Do you have a digital camera?
Tick the ones you have
☐a digital camera
☐a digital video camera
☐a smartphone
☐other (give details) ....

4 Do you ever print your photos on photographic paper?
☐No, never. Please explain why not.
....
☐Yes, on special occasions.
☐Yes, always.

PREPARE FOR TASK

3 a Work in pairs. Write the other questions in the survey using the prompts.

5 when / usually / take photos?
6 what kind / photos / usually take?
7 what / usually do with / photos?
8 ever alter / photos in any way?

b Which questions in 3a do options a–d relate to?

a photos of my friends and family
b landscapes
c holiday snaps
d action photos, sports events, etc.

4 Write options for the other questions in 3a.

5 3.11 Listen again to the woman asking people if they would be happy to complete her survey. Complete her questions.

1 Excuse me, do ....?
2 Excuse me, I wonder ....
3 Good morning, do ....?
4 OK, thank you. Just ....

TASK

6 Work in pairs. Interview three or four different classmates using the survey questions and options you have practised.

7 a Read the short report from the survey in 2a. Are the results similar to the results in your surveys?

We were surprised to see that **most of the people we questioned** did not actually own digital cameras, but preferred to use the cameras on their phones. **Two or three people** occasionally printed out their photos on photographic paper, but **the majority** prefer to upload them onto a photo sharing website.

b Compare your results and prepare to present them to the class. Use the phrases in bold to help you prepare your report.

REPORT BACK

8 Present your results to the class.

9 Compare the results from all the pairs and write a short paragraph about the information you have collected. Use the text in 7a to help you.

➜ Go to Review A, Unit 3, p. 36 ➜ Go to Writing bank 2, p. 153

VOCABULARY

Say, tell, speak

1 a Complete the sentences with *say*, *tell* or *speak*.

1 I find it difficult to .... goodbye.
2 I usually .... quietly.
3 I don't know how to .... jokes.
4 I can .... more than two languages.
5 I can't .... in public.
6 I can .... a good story.
7 It's hard for me to .... what I feel sometimes.

b Work in pairs. Compare your answers. Which of the sentences are true for you, your partner or both?

Communicating

2 a R1 Listen to Gisela talking about different forms of communication in her life. Match forms of communication a–g with people 1–6.

a lectures/presentations
b chat
c Skype
d arguments
e tweeting
f discussions
g email

1 work/business colleagues
2 friends
3 acquaintances
4 family
5 strangers
6 boyfriend

b Work in pairs. Do you share her opinion? What would you change?

Tweeting can be with work colleagues as well as with friends...

Senses

3 Work in pairs. Answer the questions.

1 How many senses do we have?
2 How many verbs can you think of that are linked to our senses?
3 Write five sentences using some of the words in 2a to describe where you are and what you can sense now.

GRAMMAR

Tense review

1 Complete the sentences about Gisela's life in the correct tense with the best verb from the box.

be able give have speak use

1 I .... to my boss about a work problem last week
2 I .... a talk next week to some new recruits.
3 I .... the phone for personal calls at work, it's not allowed.
4 I .... to speak to my mum for ages, it's terrible...
5 ... and I don't think I .... time this week either.

Question forms

2 Make questions using the verb in brackets.

1 What .... *(you/do)* last night?
2 .... ever .... *(you/travel)* to the UK?
3 Who .... *(you/meet)* this evening?
4 What .... *(you/prefer)* to do after class?
5 What .... *(you/happen)* in class yesterday?

3 Work in pairs. Ask and answer the questions.

State & dynamic verbs

4 Work in pairs. Which of the sentences are incorrect? Why are they incorrect?

1 I'm seeing the dentist tomorrow.
2 I'm seeing what you're trying to say.
3 I'm not seeing anything without my glasses.
4 I'm having lots of friends.

FUNCTIONAL LANGUAGE

Breaking the ice

1 a Write the words in the correct order.

1 a you give I Can hand that? with
2 me know I'm don't but you Carl Hello,
3 it going? how's Hi
4 do How know you then? John

b Complete the mini conversations with expressions from 1a.

1 A ....
B I met him at a party like this one!

2 A Hi! ....
B Hello, I'm Mary.

2 R2 Listen and check. Then practise breaking the ice with your classmates.

LOOKING BACK

- Think of three different forms of communication that you take part in everyday.
- Think of three phrases you think might be useful in a conversation with a new friend or acquaintance.
- Think of five useful phrases you have learnt in this unit. Why are they useful?

VOCABULARY

Types of reading material

1 Work in pairs. What type/types of text might you read in each situation?

1 You need to know the meaning of a word or expression.
2 You need information on how a piece of equipment works.
3 You want something to read on the beach.

Reading verbs

2 **a** Match the verbs to the prepositions and complete the sentences. In some cases there are two possible answers.

verbs: flick scroll glance look
prepositions: up down at through

1 .... with your cursor and click on 'open' to download the files.
2 I .... it but I haven't read it in detail yet, so I'll wait before I sign if that's ok.
3 If you don't know, ... it .... using this tool.

b What text type do sentences 1–3 refer to?

Books & genres

3 **a** Work in pairs. Think of a film, book or series for each genre in the box.

adventure comedy detective historical
horror romantic science-fiction war

b Do you prefer one genre? If yes, which one and why?

GRAMMAR

Past perfect & past simple

1 **a** Complete the gaps in Fabian's story with the best form of the verb in brackets.

I love romantic stories and one of the best I know is how my parents (1) .... *(meet)*. Apparently, they were sitting next to each other on a plane to Sydney. As soon as they (2) .... *(start)* talking, my mum knew that she (3) .... *(meet)* somebody very special. They (4) .... *(have)* lots of things in common. Both of them were going to visit family in Australia and that was exciting because neither of them (5) .... *(be)* there before – it was their first time. They (6) .... *(both, get)* divorced recently and both were thinking about starting a new life in a new land. In the end, they (7) .... *(decide)* that they (8) .... *(can)* do that together. Isn't that incredible, just from one conversation on a plane?

b R3 Listen and check.

2 Do you know how your parents or your grandparents met? Tell your partner about it.

My mum met my dad at a party, they were dancing together and...

Used to & would

3 **a** Cross out *would* in the sentences where you cannot use it.

When I was younger...
1 I *used to / would* have long hair.
2 I *used to / would* spend a lot of time playing.
3 I *used to / would* be quite naughty.
4 I didn't *use to / wouldn't* like studying much.
5 I *used to / would* go to bed and get up earlier.

b Make the sentences true for you. Compare with your partner. Report back to the class.

Both of us used to have long hair...

FUNCTIONAL LANGUAGE

Agreeing and disagreeing

1 Complete the mini conversations with expressions agreeing or disagreeing. Use the expressions in 4 on page 22.

1 A I think reading aloud is a great way to learn a language.
B ✗✗ ....

2 A Some people can tell entertaining stories and jokes, and others just can't.
B ✓ ....

3 A I love reading a good book.
B ✓✓ ....

b R4 Listen and check.

2 Work in pairs. Look at the conversations in 1a and give your opinions. Do you agree or disagree with the statements?

LOOKING BACK

- Which phrases or expressions from this unit do you consider the most useful? Why?
- What do you think you will read in the coming weeks? What will you enjoy the most? Why?
- Which task do you remember most clearly from the unit? Why?

VOCABULARY

-ed and -ing adjectives

1 a Choose the correct option to complete the sentences.

1 It's *amazing / amazed* how many things today can be called 'art'. I think a lot of it is rubbish!
2 He was really *moving / moved* by a work of art.
3 A lot of modern art is very *shocking / shocked*. I don't like that because I think they only want to provoke.
4 I feel really *annoying / annoyed* when I read about artworks being worth so much money!

b Do you agree/disagree with 1–4? Why? Discuss in pairs.

Gradable & absolute adjectives

2 a Find the pairs of a) gradable and b) absolute adjectives which have a similar meaning.

a	b
interesting	delicious
tasty	huge
difficult	tiny
tired	fascinating
small	stunning
beautiful	terrible
bad	exhausted
big	impossible

b Make sentences with any adjectives of your choice. Share them with your partner.

GRAMMAR

Modifying gradable & absolute adjectives

1 a Correct the incorrect modifiers.

1 A That painting is *extremely stunning*, don't you think?
B No, it doesn't do anything for me. I think it's *totally difficult* to understand what the artist is trying to say.

2 A I'm *very exhausted*, galleries really tire you out!
B Yeah, I'm *absolutely tired* as well. Let's have a rest.

b Change your sentences in VOCABULARY 2b to include modifiers.

As … as, comparatives & superlatives

2 a Look at the artworks. Choose the best option to complete the sentences.

1 A is *much / a bit* cheaper than C.
2 C is *by far / much* the most expensive.
3 B is *not as / as* expensive as D.
4 A is *slightly / far* cheaper than B.

b Work in pairs. Make the sentences true for you and your partner. Use *a lot, much, far, a little, a bit, slightly* where possible.

1 My partner is *(tall / short)* than me.
2 My English is *(good / bad)* than last year.
3 My partner lives *(near to / far from)* the school than me.
4 I find these exercises *(difficult / easy)* than before.

My partner's hair is far shorter than mine…

Adjectives & adverbs

3 a Choose the correct option to complete the questions.

1 Do you look *good / well* in black?
2 Do you talk *fast / fastly* in English?
3 Do you feel *confident / confidently* speaking English?
4 Do you drive *careful / carefully*?
5 Can you do this exercise *easy / easily*?

b Work in pairs. Ask and answer questions 1–5.

FUNCTIONAL LANGUAGE

Adding emphasis

1 Write the words in **bold** in the correct order.

A **about like that is What I it** it's free..
B Yes, **thing the best that's** about the show for me. The exhibition is really good value.
A **is only that problem The** I don't like any of the art!

2 R5 Listen and check. Then use the same prompts (or negative versions) to talk about another topic of your choice.

LOOKING BACK

- Think of ten useful phrases that you've learnt in this unit.
- Think of five different ways that you can talk about things emphatically.
- Think of five things that you have been interested in or amazed by recently.

LISTENING

1 Work in small groups. Look at the people practising their language skills. What do you think they are doing? Think of at least five more ways of improving your language skills outside class.

2 a R6 Listen to three people talking about the things they do outside class to practise and improve their language skills. Answer the questions.

1 Do they mention any of the ideas on your list in 1?
2 What languages are Xavier and Sue talking about?
3 Are they talking about the past or the present?

b Work in pairs. Compare your answers.

3 a Work in pairs. Choose the correct options.

1 **Xavier**

I'm really lucky. (1)*I have / I'm having* a few English-speaking friends. They're exchange students studying at my university. They (2)*don't speak / aren't speaking* much French – one's Dutch, another's Brazilian – (3)*we meet / we're meeting* up once a week and do a language exchange, a little bit of French, a little bit of Portuguese, not much Dutch! But the main language we use together is English – it's really helping me. I feel so (4)*much / many* more confident ... it's definitely the (5)*better / best* way to learn.

2 **Sue**

When I (6)*was studying / had studied* Spanish at school I (7)*used to listen / was listening* to the radio in Spanish all the time – absolutely anything, the news, the weather, sport, I didn't care. And every now and then they (8)*would show / were showing* a film in Spanish on the TV – I (9)*used to like / would like* watching them with the subtitles in English over and over again until I (10)*understood / was understanding* every single word they said.

3 **Kat**

Music has to be one of the (11)*more / most important* things for me. It is (12)*absolutely / very* incredible how easy it is to remember words when you associate them with music. (13)*I spend / I'm spending* hours and hours watching videos of my favourite bands and reading their lyrics online. What did people (14)*used / use* to do before YouTube? It is a (15)*totally / very* amazing language-learning tool. And it's not just music, of course, there are chat rooms and so much more. (16)*I don't think / I'm not thinking* you need a language-learning classroom anymore. You can learn it all online!

b Listen again and check.

SPEAKING

4 a Work in groups. Look back at your list in 1 and discuss the questions.

- Which are possible where you live and study or work?
- Which do you already do? How often? Which do you find most useful? Why?
- Which would you like to be able to do? Why? Why can't you at the moment?

b Report back to the class. Make a class list of the ways you are going to practise your English outside class over the next month. In one month's time, look back and see if you kept to your plans.

QUICK CHECK

Complete the checklist below.

Can you...	Yes, I can.	Yes, more or less.	I need to look again.
1 explain what you can see, hear and feel?	☐	☐	☐
2 start a conversation with someone you don't know?	☐	☐	☐
3 talk about past habits and routines?	☐	☐	☐
4 summarise the plot of a book or film?	☐	☐	☐
5 express agreement or disagreement?	☐	☐	☐
6 express your opinion about a work of art?	☐	☐	☐
7 compare the qualities of two or more things?	☐	☐	☐
8 add emphasis to help you get your message across?	☐	☐	☐

Compare your answers with a partner.

- What else do you know now after studying units 1–3?
- Do you need to look again at any of the sections?
- Do you need any extra help from your teacher?

4 MAN AND NATURE

1 Work in small groups. Look at the photo. Answer the questions.

- What does the photo show?
- Where do you think the photo was taken?
- What does it show about the relationship between man and nature?

2 **a** Complete A in the KEY VOCABULARY PANEL.

b Which of the words in A can be used to describe the landscape in the photo? Which can be used to describe landscapes in your country?

There are lots of resorts and golf courses on the coast in my country, but not inland.

3 **a** Look at the photo on page 159. What does it show? What do you think it has in common with the photo in 1?

3 **b** 4.1 Listen to an environmentalist talking about the photos and check your answers to 1.

4 **a** Listen again and answer the questions.

1 Why has man changed the landscape in both cases?
2 What are the consequences of these changes?

b Compare your answers with a partner.

5 Complete the extracts from transcript 4.1 with words from A in the KEY VOCABULARY PANEL.

1 The best way to see man's destruction of the Amazon rain .... is from the air.
2 Farmers and .... owners have cut down an enormous number of trees.
3 This golf course is part of the Bab Alms Resort built in the middle of the .... in Dubai.
4 ... the specially planted .... provide some shade for the golfers.

6 Work in small groups. Discuss the questions.

- Which situation do you think is the worst example of man's destruction of nature? Why?
- Think about where you live. Are any changes to the landscapes recent? Do you think they are positive or negative?

7 Work in pairs. Complete B in the KEY VOCABULARY PANEL.

8 Work in pairs. Have any of the disasters in B been in the news recently?

There have been floods as a result of heavy rain...

KEY VOCABULARY

Landscapes & natural disasters

A Man-made & natural landscapes

- Put the words in the box in the correct column. Use a dictionary to help you.

crops desert dune farm fields
forest grass hills mountains
palm trees path plain plantation
ranch resort sand

Man-made	Natural
crops	*desert*

B Natural disasters & extreme weather

- Tick the disasters 1–7 you heard in transcript 4.1.

1 forest fire
2 earthquake
3 drought
4 hurricane
5 famine
6 flood
7 tsunami

- Match disasters 1–7 to definitions a–g. Use a dictionary to help you.

a when there is too much rain and water covers land that is usually dry
b when movement in the earth under the sea causes very large waves
c when there isn't enough rain and water levels are dangerously low
d when the earth moves
e when there is not enough food
f when there is an uncontrolled area of fire in a forest
g when there are very strong winds

- Which of these disasters could be provoked by man?

NOTICE PHRASAL VERBS WITH *DOWN*

Plantation owners have cut down an enormous number of trees...

We use other verbs with *down* to mean *destroy* or *break*.

A fire burns down a forest.

The wind blows down a tree.

a

b

c

d

- Practise present perfect simple
- Talk about disasters

Speaking

1 Work in groups. Look at signs a–d and discuss the questions.

- What dangers are they warning of?
- Which of these dangers are natural and which could be man-made?
- What countries are particularly prone to these problems?
- What can we do to avoid them?

Listening & Vocabulary: natural world collocations

1 **a** What is the connection between the words in the box and signs a–d? Use a dictionary to help you.

Cigarettes are connected to sign d because they can cause fires…

cigarette	deep water	flatlands	flooding
forest	heat	shelter	shore	waves

b 4.2 Listen to a radio programme about dangers. Check your answers to 1a and match the four reports to signs a–d.

2 Listen again. Are the sentences true or false?

1 The Outback, Australia
   a) Local people are very aware of the danger.
   b) There have been no forest fires yet this year.

2 Coastal areas, Thailand
   a) There was an enormous tsunami in 2009.
   b) Preparations have been made for future tsunamis.

3 Norfolk, UK
   a) Roads often get flooded in this area.
   b) Motorists are very careful and don't go out in their cars if there's a flood warning.

4 Recife, Brazil
   a) There have been two fatal attacks this year.
   b) Children and tourists are most at risk.

3 **a** Match 1–8 to a–h to form expressions from transcript 4.2.

1 wind	a water
2 higher	b current
3 deep	c level
4 torrential	d ground
5 water	e rain
6 strong	f direction
7 flash	g attack
8 fatal	h flood

b Look at the expressions in 3a again. Which reports do they come from? Read transcript 4.2 on page 162 and check your answers.

Grammar

1 **a** Look at the pairs of sentences. Which reports do they come from? Which report is not included?

1 a We've **already** had three major fires this year, and it's only February!
  b People have lost their homes, their businesses, but luckily no one's lost their life – **yet**!
2 a We haven't seen anything like it...
  b We've built new evacuation sites...
3 a Have you ever seen a shark attack?
  b No, I haven't. I've seen sharks in the waters, and they come up really close to the shore. But we've always been able to warn people in time. I've never actually seen one attack a person.

b Look at the sentences again. Underline the verbs in the present perfect. Match the pairs of sentences in 1a to times a–c and answer the questions.

a since December 2004
b during the last two months
c during the speaker's life

1 Are these periods of time
  a) finished? b) continuing up to the present?
2 Are the actions
  a) finished? b) continuing in the present?

2 Complete 1–4 in the Grammar panel.

3 **a** Look at the words in **bold** in sentence 1 in 1a again. Answer the questions.

Which is
a) emphasising that an action has happened before now?
b) emphasising that an action has not happened before now?

Which is being used in
a) an affirmative sentence?
b) a negative sentence?

b Complete 5–8 in the Grammar panel with *already* or *yet*.

4 **a** Complete the sentences with *already*, *always*, *ever*, *never* and *yet*. More than one answer is possible.

1 I've .... seen snow.
2 I've .... wanted to visit Australia.
3 Have you .... seen a shark?
4 I've .... been to Brazil three times this year.
5 We haven't been to Thailand .... – that's the next place on our trip.
6 Have you finished the exercise ....?
7 Yes, I've .... finished it and checked it!

b Write four sentences about yourself using *ever*, *never*, *already*, *yet* and the present perfect. Compare your answers with a partner.

Present perfect simple

We can use the present perfect simple to talk about a completed action or series of actions that happened during a period of time which (1)*has finished / continues up to the present*.

There have been three shark attacks in the last month.
(= the past month up to and including today)

We often use the adverbs *always*, *ever* and *never* with the present perfect simple.

Have you (2) .... *seen a shark attack? I've* (3) .... *seen a shark attack.* (= in my whole life up to today)

We've (4) .... *been able to warn people in time.* (= in my experience up to today)

Already & *yet*

We use the present perfect with *already* or *yet* to emphasise that an action has/hasn't happened before now. We usually use (5) .... in affirmative sentences and (6) .... in negative sentences. We use (7) .... between the auxiliary (*has/have*) and the main verb.

We use (8) .... at the end of the sentence.

There have already been three attacks this year.
Luckily we haven't had any attacks on this beach yet.

We can use *already* and *yet* in questions. There's a difference in the meaning.

Questions with *yet*: *Have you finished yet?* (= I expect you have, I'm just checking.)

Questions with *already*: *Have you already finished?/Have you finished already?* (= I'm surprised, you did that very quickly!)

See page 143 for grammar reference and more practice.

Speaking & Writing

1 Discuss the questions in small groups.

- Has your area ever been affected by a natural or man-made disaster or by extreme weather?
- Where was it? Do you know how it was started?

Yes, last winter in my hometown... there was an enormous storm and a tornado swept through the town... it did a lot of damage to the beach.

2 **a** Choose one of your stories from 1. Write a short news story as if the event has happened recently.

Good evening, this is the 9 o'clock news. We have news coming in of...

b Read your story out loud to the class, as if you were a radio or TV news presenter.

Blending in

- Practise present perfect continuous
- Talk about different types of houses

a

b

c

Reading

1 **a** Look at the images. What can you see? Match images a–c to one of the words or expressions in each group.

1 materials: mud rock slate wood
2 locations: in caves in a desert on stilts on a terraced hillside

b Work in pairs. Discuss the questions.

- Where do you think the villages are?
- Which settlement do you think is the oldest? Why?
- What do you think would be the advantages and disadvantages of living in each of the three places?

2 **a** Read texts 1–3 about traditional villages around the world and match them to images a–c.

b Read the texts again. Match villages 1–3 to statements a–d.

a The villagers are looking for new ways to earn a living. ....
b The houses need constant maintenance. ....
c The houses are warm in winter. ....
d We don't know exactly how old they are. ....

3 Find words/phrases in the texts which mean

1 to emerge
2 a place where people live permanently
3 to destroy little by little
4 to replace
5 the side of a hill or mountain
6 a curved area of coast
7 money which you earn

4 Work in small groups. Discuss the questions.

- What are traditional homes like in your country? Do you know why they were built that way?
- Are there any unusual settlements in your country? Do people still live there? If yes, how do they make a living?
- Which of the three settlements in the images would you most like to visit? Why?

1 Ait Benhaddou

People have been building their homes out of the red earth of Northern Morocco for thousands of years. Ait Benhaddou is one of the best preserved of these adobe villages which seem to grow out of the desert that surrounds them. No-one knows exactly how long people have been living in this particular settlement, but it must be at least 1,500 years old. There are still families living there today, and the houses and walls of the village need constant care as the wind and the rain eats away into these incredible, almost living structures.

2 Kullu Valley

Kullu Valley, or the Valley of the Gods, in the foothills of the Himalayas is in one of the most fertile agricultural regions in the whole of India. The people of Kullu Valley have been growing crops on its terraced hillsides for at least 3,000 years. In recent years, apple trees and other fruits have been taking over from more traditional crops, making Kullu Valley the 'fruit basket' of the Himalayas. In the image we can see traditional Kullu houses, built of local wood and stone, with heavy slate roofs that insulate the homes against the cold temperatures of winter when snow covers the slopes of the nearby mountains. They are built just above the irrigated rice fields that provide the backbone of the Kullu people's daily diet.

3 Ko Panyi

Ko Panyi is a fishing village in the bay of Phang Nga in southern Thailand. The village was founded in the eighteenth century by two Indonesian fishing families, and the descendants of these two families have been fishing in the bay ever since. What makes the village unusual is that it's a floating village, built on stilts. This is because, at the time, non-Thai nationals were not allowed to own land, so the fishermen built their homes on water. Recently the villagers have been supplementing their income from fishing by inviting tourists to visit the village. There are no hotels, but plenty of restaurants specialising in local seafood.

Grammar

1 **a** Match the two parts of the sentences. Check your answers in the texts in Reading 2a.

1 Families have been living in this Moroccan settlement
2 The village has been making money from tourism
3 The villagers have been fishing in the bay
4 The villagers have been growing crops

a since the eighteenth century.
b since the 1990s.
c for thousands of years.
d for generations and generations.

b Look at the underlined verbs in 1a again. Tick the correct options to complete the explanation. Complete 1–4 in the Grammar panel.

The verbs are talking about
a an action that was completed in the past.
b an action that started in the past.
c an action that continues in the present.

2 **a** Read A in the Grammar panel. Choose the correct form to complete the sentences. Sometimes both forms are correct.

1 I've *been knowing* / *known* my English teacher for a year.
2 I've *been living* / *lived* in this town all my life.
3 I've always *been wanting* / *wanted* to visit Morocco.

b Work in pairs. Change the sentences so they are true for you. Compare your answers.

3 **a** Look at the second half of the sentences in 1a and complete B in the Grammar panel.

b Complete the time expressions with *for* or *since*.

1 .... I was a child
2 .... last year
3 .... ten years
4 .... a long time
5 2010

4 **a** Write sentences about yourself or your hometown using the time expressions in 3b.

b Compare your sentences with a partner.

5 **a** Complete the sentences with the present perfect continuous form of the verbs in brackets.

1 How long .... (*you/study*) English?
2 How long .... (*you/live*) in your present home? Do you know when it was built?
3 How long .... (*people/live*) in your home town? Do you know when it was first founded? And who founded it?

b Work in pairs. Ask and answer the questions in 5a with time expressions with *for* or *since*.

Present perfect continuous

We use the present perfect continuous to talk about actions that started (1) .... and continue (2) ....

The people of Kullu Valley have been growing crops for 3,000 years.

The village has been supplementing its income through tourism.

We form the present perfect continuous with (3) ..../ *has* + (4) .... + verb + *-ing*.

A Present perfect continuous or simple?

We don't use the present perfect continuous with state verbs (verbs that describe feelings and thought processes).

I've always liked... NOT *I've always ~~been liking~~*

I've known my boss for ten years. NOT *~~I've been knowing~~ my boss for ten years.*

Note: We can often use both the present perfect continuous and the present perfect simple with very little difference when we are talking about an action that has continued over a long period of time up to the present.

I've lived here all my life.

I've been living here all my life.

B Time expressions with *for* & *since*

We can use time expressions with ***for*** or ***since*** to talk about a period of time which started in the past and continues in the present:

We use (5)*for / since* + the point in time when the action started.

We use (6)*for / since* + the period of time.

See page 143 for grammar reference and more practice.

Speaking

1 Look at the houses in the photos. They both use a mixture of traditional and modern materials and ideas. Which would you prefer to live in? Why?

2 **a** Work in pairs. Student A, turn to page 159. Student B, turn to page 161.

b Tell each other about the homes. Would you still prefer to live in the same one?

- PRACTISE WORDS RELATED TO THE ENVIRONMENT
- TALK ABOUT PLASTIC

READING

1 **a** Work in pairs. Look at the images on the cover of this book. Can you identify all the objects? Which do you think is the most useful? Which do you use most?

b Look around you. Name all the plastic objects you can see. How many of them do you use on a daily basis? How many of them do you think are essential? How many could you live without?

a

b

NOTICE *PLASTIC*

We can use the word *plastic* to refer to credit cards.

How did you pay for it? With cash or plastic?

Can you do the same in your language?

Plastic: A Toxic Love Story by Susan Freinkel

Plastic built the modern world.

Try to imagine the world without pacemakers, polyester, computers, cellphones, sneakers or chewing gum. (Plastic in gum? Yep!). It would be like going back in time.

Plastic has been part of our day-to-day life for over a hundred years, but after a century of living with plastic, we're starting to realise it's not so healthy. We use fossil fuels to make plastic. The process releases harmful chemicals into the environment. We litter our landscapes with plastic waste and it is slowly destroying marine life. And yet each year we use and consume more and more. We've produced as much plastic in the past decade as we did in the entire twentieth century. We can't live with it, we can't live without it. We've reached a crisis point.

In her book, Freinkel takes us through the history and science of plastic. She explores the role of plastic in the global economy and assesses the real impact of plastic in our lives. She tells her story through eight familiar plastic objects: the comb, dental floss, Frisbee, I.V. bag or drip, disposable lighter, plastic bag, plastic water bottle and credit card. Each object shows us a different aspect of our synthetic world, and together they help us take a new look at a substance that has become such an important part of our age.

And what is Freinkel's conclusion? We cannot continue like this. And we don't have to. In *Plastic*, Freinkel offers a solution, a new and creative way of living with the material we love to hate, but can't seem to live without.

2 **a** Look at the title of the book. What do you think the book is about?

b Read a description of the book. Check your answers in 2a.

3 **a** Work in pairs. Read the description again and choose the best summary of the main message of the book.

1 We need to stop using plastic altogether.
2 We need to rethink how we use plastic.
3 There's nothing wrong with the way we use plastic.

b Answer the questions.

1 According to the writer, what damage does plastic do?
2 Why does the writer say we have reached a 'crisis point'?
3 What do the eight objects represent?

4 Would you like to read this book? Why/Why not?

LISTENING

1 **a** Think about the last time you used a plastic bag. Answer the questions.

- Where did you get it from?
- If you got it from a shop, did you buy it or was it free?
- What did you use it for?
- After using it, what did you do with it?

b Work in pairs. Discuss your answers with a partner. Were they similar? Report back to the class.

c

d

2 a Work in pairs. Look at the plastic bags in the images. Where are they in each one? Put them in the order of a typical lifecycle of a plastic bag.

b 4.3 Listen to a report about plastic bags. Check your answers in 2a. Answer the questions.

1 What are governments trying to do?
2 Which particular environmental problem does the report describe?

3 a Listen again. What does the reporter say about

- where plastic bags come from?
- how we dispose of plastic bags?
- what happens to plastic waste in the sea?

b Work in pairs. Compare your notes and write a short summary of the report. Use no more than 50 words.

4 Do you know of any campaigns to reduce the use of plastic? Do you think they have any effect? Why/Why not?

VOCABULARY & PRONUNCIATION: the environment

1 a Work in pairs. Match 1–7 to a–g to make expressions from the texts in READING 2b and LISTENING 2b.

1 fossil	a bins
2 harmful	b chemicals
3 litter	c container
4 marine	d dump
5 production	e fuels
6 recycling	f life
7 rubbish	g line

b Which of expressions 1–7 refer to

a) the natural world?
b) waste disposal?
c) industry?

2 a Look again at the expressions in VOCABULARY 1a. Mark the syllable which carries the main stress.

fossil fuels

b 4.4 Listen and check.

3 Work in pairs. Write three sentences about the topic of the lesson using as many expressions from 1a as you can.

4 a Change partners. Dictate your sentences to a partner. Make sure you use the correct stress pattern on the expressions in 1a.

b Compare your sentences. How many of the expressions did you use? Report back to the class.

SPEAKING

1 a Work in pairs. Write down all the plastic objects you have used so far today.

A *I woke up and went to the bathroom, the toothbrush was plastic!*
B *Yeah, and my alarm clock is plastic…*

b Look at your list and discuss the questions.

- Which of the objects on your list could you substitute with an object that is not made of plastic?
- Can you think of ways you could reduce the amount of plastic in your life?
- Imagine that you have to live without plastic. What changes or sacrifices would you have to make?

2 Report back to the class on your discussion. Who would find it easiest to have a plastic-free life?

Tune in

1 Work in pairs. Look at the images. Which do you think is the most dangerous to get lost in: rough seas, a desert or a snowstorm? Why? What would you need to do to survive?

2 4.5 Listen to the story of three teenage boys and answer the questions.

1 Where were they lost?
2 How long were they lost for?
3 What did they do to survive?

3 **a** What did the people say about the following things?

- rainwater
- seawater
- a seagull
- raw fish
- a tuna boat
- a memorial service

b Listen again and check.

Focus on language

4 **a** Listen again and write the questions.

1
A Have you heard the story about the three boys who were rescued after 50 days at sea?
B No... ....?

2
A Yeah, apparently they survived by drinking rainwater and they even managed to catch a seagull...
B ....? How did they do that?

3
A Yes. It landed on the boat and they ate it raw.
B ....?

4
A They ate raw fish too it seems... but raw fish is supposed to be more salty and makes you thirsty.
B ....? Ah, yes, I suppose so, from the seawater.

5
A ... at the end they'd even started drinking seawater.
B ....? That's supposed to be really bad for you, isn't it?

6
A Their families thought they were dead – they'd already held a memorial service for the boys...
B ....?

b We often use echo questions to check information. Here are three common types. Complete the examples with questions from 4a.

1 Repeat the object of the action
A *They ate a seagull.* B ....?
2 Use a subject pronoun and an auxiliary verb
A *Raw fish is more salty.* B ....?
3 Use a subject pronoun, an auxiliary verb and a question word
A *They ate it raw.* B ....?

5 **a** Write echo questions to check the information.

1
A Three men broke into the bakery last night.
B ....? Which one, the one round the corner?
A Yes, that's right. The local bakery.

2
A My brother destroyed my bike over the weekend.
B ....? How did he do that?
A He rode it into a tree.

3
A Lydia got the job, you know.
B ....? That's great, I'm so happy for her!
A Yeah, she's starting next week.

b 4.6 Listen and check.

"Responding to news"

4.6 Listen to the questions in 5a. Notice how the speaker's voice goes up on the last word. Is the speaker **a** surprised? **b** pleased? Listen and repeat paying special attention to the intonation.

Over to you

6 **a** Work in pairs. Student A, read one of the pieces of information. Student B, respond with one or two echo questions.

- My football team have just won the league!
- There's been a terrible air crash.
- There's 20% unemployment at the moment.
- We're getting a day off work tomorrow.

b Swap roles.

7 **a** Write down three pieces of exciting or surprising news (it could be personal, local or international).

b Work in pairs. Listen to each other's news and respond using appropriate echo questions.

8 Do you know of any amazing survival stories? Share them with the class.

El Cosmico – a holiday with a difference

A El Cosmico is a campground in Marfa, where you can rent trailers, teepees or just a shady place for your own tents. The trailers are beautifully restored and feature stoves, small fridges, fans, floor heating and hot water, while the owners provide bedding, bath towels, dishes, pots, and pans and all for $100 a night or less. The outdoor washing facilities include power showers, a real luxury.

B But El Cosmico is more than just a place to spend the night, or relax in a hammock all day. It's where artists can get some solitude and inspiration away from urban life. The owners organise craft workshops and a music festival. And it's all eco-friendly.

C Owner Liz Lambert has worked closely with a committed team of artists, builders and students to set up a unique community in the West Texas desert in a creative and sustainable space.

D El Cosmico offers wood-fired Dutch hot tubs, and eventually a large pool and pavilion will lie at the heart of the village to provide an oasis for guests and locals alike.

TUNE IN

1 Look at the images of the *El Cosmico* lodge. Where do you think it is? What type of lodging and facilities are shown? What kind of person do you think would like to stay there? Would you like to stay there?

2 Read the review of the lodge on the website and check your answers to 1. Are you more keen to stay there now or less so? Why?

3 **a** Match categories 1–8 to paragraphs A–D.

1 the guests
2 the owners
3 the location
4 the buildings
5 the facilities
6 the basic concept of the place
7 future plans
8 events

b What other information is given? What other information would you like to know?

4 Read the review again and <u>underline</u>

1 positive and vivid language.
2 two verbs which mean *give*.

NOTICE MAKING CONTRASTS

We can use *more than just* to contract two different ideas in an emphatic way.

El Cósmico is more than just a place to spend the night...

We use *not only... but also* in a similar way.

PREPARE FOR TASK

5 **a** Work in pairs. Think of a place to stay in your area that you both know well. It could be a campsite, a student residence or a hotel. Make notes about 1–5 in 3a.

b Think of some photos to accompany your review. Which ones would give the most positive image of the place?

6 Consider which positive adjectives you are going to use to describe your place. What makes it such a special place?

It has a unique atmosphere...

7 **a** In what context would you write a review of this place?

b Think about the people your review is aimed at. How best can you write to appeal to these people? Consider both style and content.

TASK

8 Look at your notes in 5a. Decide what information you are going to include and in what order you are going to present it. Then write a short review.

REPORT BACK

9 **a** Work in pairs. Show your review to your partner. Ask each other more questions about the place.

b Tell the class about the places you have described. Vote on the place where you would prefer to stay.

➔ Go to Review B, Unit 4, p. 68

5 BRIDGES, BORDERS AND BARRIERS

a

b

c

1 **a** Work in small groups. Look at the photos. Answer the questions.

1 What can you see?
2 What is the connection between the photos and the unit title?

b 5.1 Listen to two people answering the questions in 1a. Check your answers. In what order do they talk about the photos?

2 **a** Listen again. Match statements 1–3 to photos a–c.

1 Yeah, for example, you can find someone you've lost touch with... it provides that link...
2 Joining hands refers to establishing new links with people and how we can do <u>that</u>.
3 So that's a barrier, as well, of course, <u>something</u> that divides nations and people...

b What do the <u>underlined</u> words refer to?

3 Complete A in the KEY VOCABULARY PANEL. Can you think of any other types of connecting? Add them to the list.

4 **a** Which of the expressions in A could you use to make sentences about your life?

b Which could you use to talk about the world?

Some sporting events, like the Olympics, can unite countries.

5 **a** Read transcript 5.1 on page 163. <u>Underline</u> five verbs and expressions which mean *disconnect*.

....

b Look at B in the KEY VOCABULARY PANEL and complete 1–4 with the verbs.

1 I .... some people from seeing my Facebook page.
2 Many nations .... barriers to .... their people from meeting.
3 Sometimes language can .... people, that's what's called a language barrier.
4 You have to do something to .... everyone from seeing all the details of your private life.

6 **a** Work in pairs. How do we use different kinds of barriers on the internet to stop people accessing information? What kind of information is blocked and in what context?

You can use filters on Google to prevent kids from looking at some websites.

b What other important barriers and borders exist in the world today?

KEY VOCABULARY

Connections & prevention

A Verbs which refer to connecting

- Which of the verbs can collocate with the nouns? Use a dictionary to help you.

break down	barriers
bridge	bridges
build	borders
contact	countries
get in touch with	friends/people
join	gap
link	hands
reach across	
unite	

B Verbs which refer to preventing

to stop, prevent, deter, block someone from doing *something*
to avoid talking about *something*
to put up *barriers/walls*
to divide /separate *nations/people*

NOTICE *AVOID/PREVENT*

Avoid means to stop yourself from doing something.

I avoided going there because of the crowds.

If we want to stop somebody else doing something, we use *prevent*.

I prevented him from going there.

- PRACTISE FUTURE FORMS
- TALK ABOUT SOCIAL NETWORKING

SPEAKING & LISTENING

1 Work in groups. Discuss the questions.

- What is social networking? What do people usually use social networking sites for?
- Do you use a social networking site? If yes, which one? How long have you been using it? What do you use it for? If not, why not?

2 5.2 Listen to Jordi, Karin and Thom talking about how they use social networks. Do they mention any of the uses you discussed in 1?

3 **a** Listen again and match speakers Jordi (J), Karin (K), and Thom (T) to the topics in the box.

family photos   friends   good causes   jobs
music   news   professional development

b Discuss the question with the class.

- Which person's use of social networks is most similar to yours? In what way?

READING

1 **a** Read three status updates. In each update the writer is running a risk by sharing their information. What risk do you think they are running?

A Last day of work today – hooray!! The plane **leaves** at 6 a.m. tomorrow! **We're going away** for three whole weeks 🙂 – I hope the plants'll survive with no-one in the house to water them.

Like • Comment • Share

B I've heard that my company **is going to fire** 150 employees. I hope **I'll be** one of them. I'm sick of this old dump!

Private Message   View Friends

C I am definitely getting a pair of these! www.fabtrainers.com #fabtrainers
Jin sent me the link – she loves this brand!

b Read the article about the dangers of social networking. Check your answers to 1a and match each danger to status updates A–C.

2 Work in small groups. Discuss the questions.

- Do you know of any other possible dangers of using social networks?
- On the whole, would you say that social networks are good or bad?

Subscribe   Previous Posts

The dangers of social networking

It's all just a bit of fun, right? Keeping in touch with friends, sharing photos and jokes. I certainly remember people's birthdays better now, and I get a chance to congratulate my friends on their good luck and commiserate with them when things go wrong. I love logging in and seeing everyone's messages, finding out what clips they've been watching, the music they've been listening to, the things they've been doing.

But there's a darker side to social networks, too; dangers lurking behind every status update and every link. Here are three things to think about when you write your next status update.

Are you inviting burglars to your house?

Does your profile information contain your home address? If so, never write about the exact dates of your holiday, or tell people that your house is going to be empty. You might come back to a nasty surprise!

Are you giving away information about your friends?

Every time you press the 'like' button on a website, your tastes and your preferences are being stored to be used by marketing departments to target ads at you. Sometimes this may be useful, but it often leads to spam. Maybe you don't mind, but if you name a friend at the same time, then you're giving their information away, too. Will they be happy with that? Think about it next time you hit the 'like' button.

Have you written something you're going to regret?

Be careful what you write about online. You might think it's private and that only your friends are going to see it, but that's not always true. There was a famous case a few years ago where a teacher in the USA wrote a message to her friends complaining about her students and her school. The principal of the school saw the message. The teacher lost her job. So never write anything you're not happy for everybody to see!

Grammar

1 a Look again at the three status updates in Reading 1. Match the verbs in **bold** to the uses below.

Talking about

1 hopes
2 intentions
3 a scheduled event
4 a definite plan

b Complete 1–8 in the Grammar panel with the uses in 1a and examples from the status updates in Reading 1.

2 a Write four status updates for yourself about

a something you're doing later today
b a plan you've got for the near future
c a story in the news
d an interesting link

Use at least one of the future forms in each update.

b Compare your updates with a partner. Give more information if necessary.

3 a Work in small groups. If you use a social network, can you remember what your last update was? Did it include any future forms? Was it in English? If not, how would you say it in English?

b Write a status update from your classroom. Give it to your teacher. Your teacher will read out the updates. Guess who wrote each one.

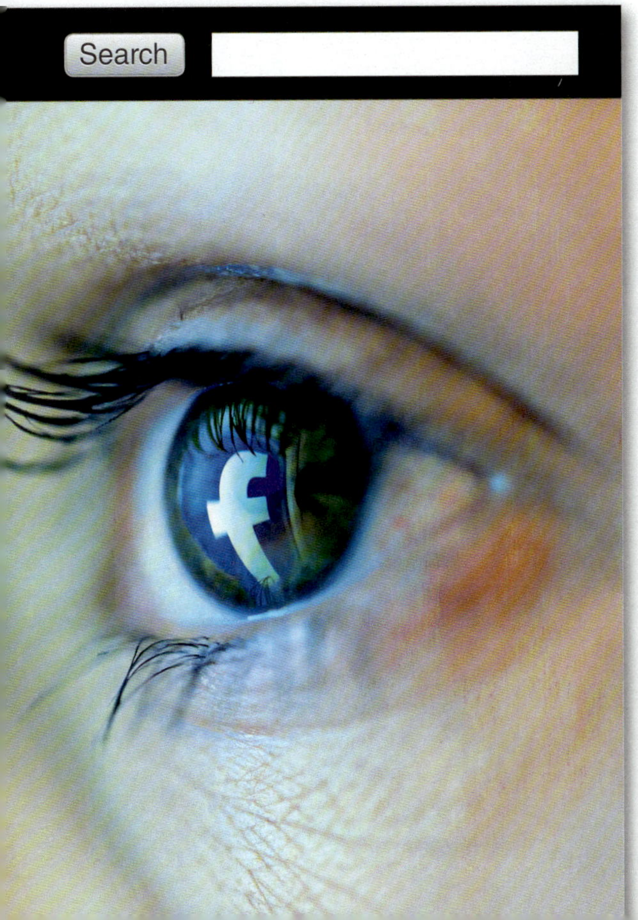

Future forms (1): plans, intentions, hopes & fears

A Present simple

We can use the present simple to talk about (1) .... in the future. We often use it to talk about timetables or to talk about the starting and end times of shows, e.g. *on TV*, *at the cinema*, etc.

The match starts at 8. (2) ....

B Present continuous

We can use the present continuous to talk about (3) .... in the future. We often use a future time expression, e.g. *tomorrow*, *next week*, *later today*.

I'm playing tennis this afternoon. (4) ....

C *Going to*

We can use *going to* to talk about future plans and (5) .... We usually use *going to* and not the present continuous when no definite arrangements have been made.

I'm not going to do any studying tonight. (6) .... (this is an intention, but no arrangements have been made)

D *Will*

We often use *will* to express our (7) .... and fears about the future.

I hope the weather'll be better next week! I hope it won't rain for the wedding! (8) ....

See page 144 for grammar reference and more practice.

Pronunciation: reduction in auxiliary verbs

1 a 5.3 Listen to three questions. Tick the version you hear. What do you notice about the pronunciation of the auxiliary verbs?

1 a Are you doing anything special this weekend?
  b Are you going to do anything special this weekend?
2 a What are you going to do after the class?
  b What are you doing after the class?
3 a When are you doing your homework?
  b When are you going to do your homework?

b Listen again and repeat the questions.

2 Work in pairs. Ask and answer the questions in 1a.

Speaking

1 Work in groups. Imagine that you are planning to put up a page for your class on a social network that is popular in your country. Discuss the questions.

- Which network are you going to use? Why?
- What kind of information are you going to show on your page? Are you going to add links? If so, what kind of links?
- What information are you not going to include in the profiles?

2 Present your ideas to the class. Do you know of any pages like this that share information about events or organisations in your local area?

- Practise words related to future plans & intentions
- Talk about engineering projects

Speaking & Reading

1 **a** This is one of the longest bridges in the world. Do you know which two countries it joins? Read about it on page 161 and answer the questions.

1 What is special about its name?
2 What does the project consist of?
3 What does it symbolise?

b Work in pairs. Do you know other well-known bridges or tunnels? What do they join? Which is the longest bridge or tunnel in your country?

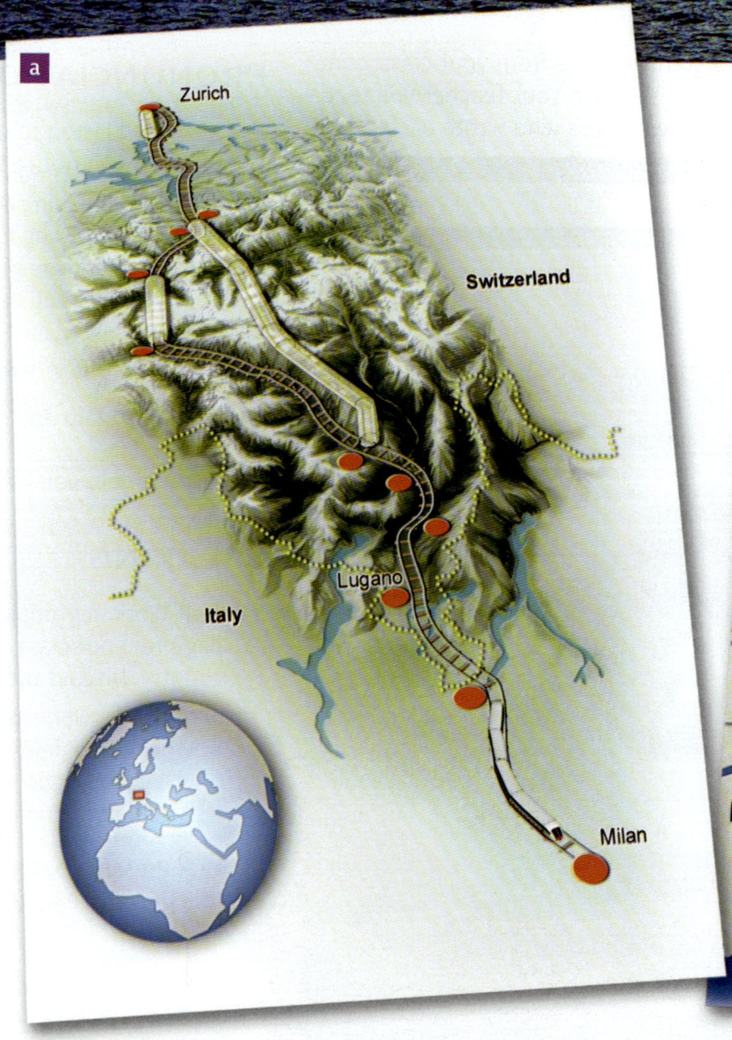

LISTENING

1 Look at the two maps. What do they show?

2 a 5.4 Listen to a news report about two engineering projects and match them to the maps. Why is each one in the news?

b Listen again and complete the information in the chart.

Zurich-Milan Tunnel	
Form of transport	
Record	*world's long rail tunnel*
Distance	
Opening to the public	
New travel time	
Problems	

Hong Kong-Macau-Zhuhai Bridge & Tunnel Project	
Form of transport	
Record	
Completion date	
New travel time	
Problems	

3 Read transcript 5.4 on page 163 and find words or phrases that mean

1 solutions can be found to these problems
2 come to an important moment in its development
3 has caused a lot of discussion
4 have given their permission

4 Which of the two projects do you think will be completed first? Why? What are the advantages and disadvantages of carrying out these projects?

5 Would you prefer to travel in the Swiss tunnel or on the Chinese bridge project? Why?

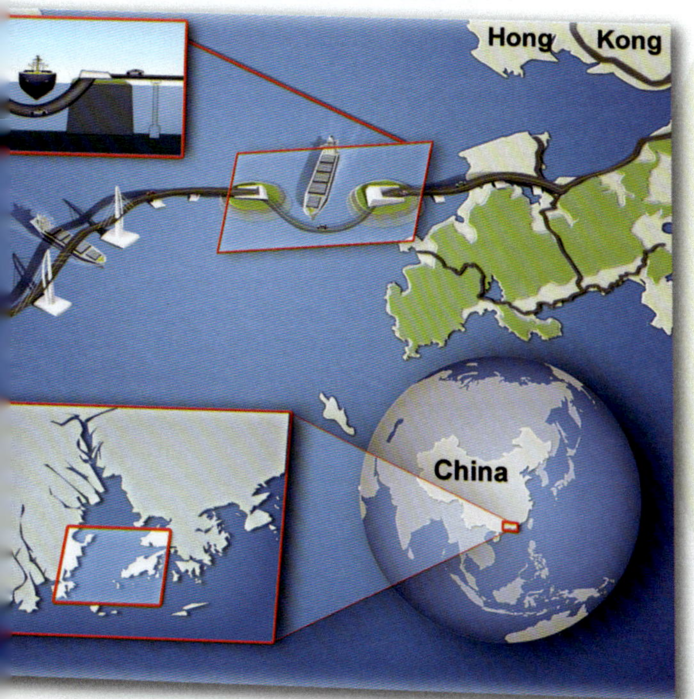

VOCABULARY: future plans & intentions

1 a Look at statements 1–4 about the projects in LISTENING 2a. What do the words in bold have in common?

1 They **intend** to open it to the general public in 2017.
2 This new network **aims** to improve finance, logistics and professional services.
3 The project **plans** to boost the construction industry.
4 The project **hopes** to cut travel time.

b Look at the Notice box. Rewrite the sentences in 1a using nouns instead of verbs.

NOTICE NOUNS & VERBS

We sometimes use a noun instead of the verb.

We're planning to leave first thing in the morning. → *Our plan is to leave first thing in the morning.*

They're aiming to get here by ten. → *Their aim is to get here by ten.*

2 a Complete the sentences with short-term plans you have made.

1 This evening, I intend to ....
2 Tomorrow, I hope to ....
3 Next week, I plan to ....
4 Next month, I aim to ....

b Work in pairs. Show your plans to your partner. Give more information if necessary and then report back on your partner's plans to the rest of the class.

3 Work in pairs. Think of three long-term plans or intentions you have. Tell them to your partner, but include one plan that is not true. Can your partner identify which story is untrue?

Next year, I plan to travel to New Zealand...

SPEAKING

1 a Work in pairs. Think of a new project that could improve the quality of life in your area and make notes in the chart.

What (bridge/sports centre/road, etc.)?	
Where?	
Why?	
Impact	

b Present your plans to the class. Which project would

- make the biggest impact?
- be the easiest to build?

- PRACTISE FUTURE FORMS
- TALK ABOUT PREDICTIONS

a

b

c

READING

1 Look at the images. What four global trends do you think they could represent? Choose from the topics. One image can match with more than one global trend.

birth rate	urban drift*
wealth distribution	women in the workplace
climate change	rise of Asia
multilingualism	m-learning

**urban drift: movement of people from rural to urban areas*

2 Read two articles from two different sources on global trends. Which of the topics from the list in 1 are mentioned? Which article has a more positive view of the future?

1

The Endless City

Urban drift is now '**unstoppable**', the director of UN-Habitat, Anna Tibaijuka, states sadly: 'The rural population **is decreasing** fast. At the moment, just over half the world lives in cities. By 2050 that figure will **rise** to 70%.'

We are going to see the world's cities merge to form an **increasing** number of urban 'mega-regions'. Some of them will stretch for hundreds of kilometres and across more than one country. This process is already happening in China. The largest of these mega-regions – the Hong Kong-Shenhzen-Guangzhou region – will be home to about 120 million people by 2030. It will certainly create more jobs, but the gap between rich and poor will **grow** as people move in from the rural areas in search of work. 'If these new cities are going to be successful, they will need to know how to reduce these inequalities,' said the report's co-author Eduardo Moreno.

3 Read the articles again and answer the questions.

Article 1

1 What exactly are 'mega-regions'?
2 What is the only advantage of these regions, according to the UN report?
3 Which cities will be the most successful when this change comes?

Article 2

4 What does the article say about the status of mobile phones?
5 Why is mobile phone use increasing more rapidly than computer use?
6 In what ways will mobile phones be used in Africa?

4 Work in groups. Which of the trends in 1 do you think is the most important? Why? Which affects you and your country the most?

2

Mobile devices take over the world

In developing nations, 57% of people now have mobile phone access and this number is going to **increase rapidly**. While internet use is also increasing, UN reports say it won't **go up** so **quickly** because of higher costs. There are currently 5 billion global mobile phone subscriptions, compared with about 1 billion in 2002. It will **gradually turn into** 'the most prolific and desirable consumer device on the planet'. The difference is that in Africa, mobile devices will be used in all aspects of life, not just to chat with friends. Mobile devices will be used, for example, for the movement of money, for finding jobs and even to follow university courses.

VOCABULARY: describing trends

1 **a** Look at the words in **bold** in the articles in READING 2. Use them to complete the chart.

Describing trends and changes		
verbs	adverbs	adjectives
rise		

b Rewrite the words in *italics* in the sentences using the expressions from 1a.

1 The movement of people from rural to urban areas *can not be stopped*.
2 The rural population is *becoming smaller and smaller*.
3 The urban population will *increase* to 70% by 2050.
4 The number of urban mega-regions is *increasing*.
5 Internet use will develop more *slowly*.
6 The mobile will steadily *transform itself* into the most desirable product.

2 **a** Look again at the original sentences in 1b. Add more verbs, adverbs and adjectives to the chart in 1a.

b Work in small groups. Discuss the question.

- Which of the trends in 1b are noticeable in your country?

There is a rapid increase in the number of smartphones... everyone has one!

GRAMMAR

1 **a** Look at these ideas from the articles in READING 2. Underline the future forms. Are they describing a) predictions? b) plans?

1 By 2050 over 70% of the world will live in cities.
2 We are going to see the world's cities merge to form enormous urban 'mega-regions'.
3 The mobile will turn into 'the most prolific and desirable consumer device on the planet'.
4 In Africa, mobile devices will be used in all aspects of life.
5 57% of people now have mobile phone access and this number is going to increase rapidly.

b Complete 1–2 in the GRAMMAR PANEL.

2 **a** Write sentences using *will*, *won't* or *going to* (and the prompts) to make predictions.

1 China / important / economic force
2 look around you / mobile technologies / everywhere / soon
3 hope / gap between rich and poor / get bigger
4 soon almost everybody / computer
5 the birth rate / probably go up in Europe / near future
6 think / equality between men and women / workplace / improve

b Compare your answers with a partner. Do you agree? Which of these predictions do you see as being positive?

3 **a** Write three predictions about you and your friends and family.

b Share your predictions with the class. Were any of them the same?

FUTURE FORMS (2): PREDICTIONS

We can use both ***will*** and ***going to*** to make predictions and talk about beliefs about the future. There is little difference in meaning between *will* and *going to*.

*World population **will/is going to** increase steadily in the next few years.* (1) ....

We often use *will* with the passive voice to talk about predictions.

*I think English **will be** spoken by lots more people in the future.* (2) ....

See page 144 for grammar reference and more practice.

SPEAKING

1 **a** Work in pairs. Read the list of predictions and decide which were made in

a the year 1900 talking about the year 2000.
b the year 2000 talking about the next ten or twenty years.

1 People will get bored with living virtual lives and there will be a return to person-to-person communication.

2 Hot or cold air will be turned on from taps to regulate the temperature of a house as we now turn on hot or cold water from taps to regulate the temperature of the bath.

3 English will be more extensively spoken than any other language. Russian will rank second.

4 Photographs will be telegraphed from any distance. If there were a battle in China, images would be published in the newspapers an hour later.

5 There will probably be a single international currency.

b Work in pairs. Answer the questions.

- Which of the predictions have already come true?
- Which do you think will possibly come true at some point in your lifetime?
- Which do you think will never come true? Why?

2 **a** Work in small groups. Write three predictions for the year 2050.

b Swap your list with another group. Decide if you think their predictions will ever come true.

3 When you have finished, swap lists again and discuss your reactions.

TUNE IN

1 a Look at images a and b and discuss the questions.

- What kind of border crossings do they show?
- What countries does your country border? Is there a check point on the borders?
- Have you crossed any of these borders recently? If yes, how were you travelling? Did you have to stop at the border control?

b Imagine you are at passport control. What kinds of questions might you be asked? Look at image c. What else do you sometimes have to do when you cross a border?

2 a 5.5 Listen to two conversations at passport control. Do the officers ask any of the questions you thought of in 1b? Which officer would you prefer to talk to? Why?

b Listen again and answer the questions.

1 Who is the person entering the country?
2 What do they do?
3 What is the purpose of their trip?
4 How long is it?
5 Is the exchange friendly or unfriendly? How can you tell?

FOCUS ON LANGUAGE

3 a 5.6 Listen and write the questions asked by the immigration officer using the verbs in brackets.

1 Where .... (*stay*) in Thailand?
2 And how long .... (*intend*) to stay here?
3 And where .... (*travel*) from?
4 Are you .... (*plan*) to visit other parts of the country?
5 Are you .... (*stay*) with him?
6 And .... (*leave*) in ten days' time, is that right?

b Listen and check.

NOTICE STATEMENTS AS QUESTIONS

Sometimes we ask questions without reversing the order of the verbs. We can do this by using question intonation or using a checking expression, e.g. *Is that right? Is that correct?*

Are you leaving in ten days' time? →
You're leaving in ten days' time? ↗
You're leaving in ten days' time ↗, *is that right?* ↗

Find another example in the second conversation.

" Sounding friendly/unfriendly "

5.7 Listen again to how each of the conversations end in 2a. What's the difference in the way the person says goodbye?

Listen and repeat, paying special attention to the pitch and intonation when saying goodbye.

OVER TO YOU

4 a Work in pairs. Student A, you work at a border control or an airport passport control. Prepare questions for B about their future plans. Are you going to adopt a friendly or unfriendly manner?

Student B, you are entering the country. Prepare to explain what you are intending to do in the country, who you are going to see and how long you are going to stay.

b Act out the conversation.

5 Repeat the dialogue in front of the class. Decide which immigration officer was a) the friendliest, b) the least friendly.

SPEAKING TASK: A CLASS DEBATE

TUNE IN

1 Work in small groups. Look at the photo and discuss the questions.

- What does it show?
- What is the connection with the unit topic?
- What is the camera doing?
- Do you see many closed circuit cameras where you live? Where?

2 Read an article about CCTV (closed circuit television). Answer the questions.

1 Where are the cameras?
2 What do you think a 'dummy' camera is?
3 Is electronic surveillance a totally new thing? How do you know?
4 What does the author say is most people's response to this issue?
5 What is his opinion about electronic surveillance? How do you know?

Walking into work one day, I began to count the CCTV cameras along the 4.3 kilometre route. The count reached 106, or one camera for every 40 metres. Some cameras are free-standing, attached to the sides of buildings or on rooftops. It seems that some are for traffic control or serve no clear purpose, others may even be 'dummy' cameras.

With approximately 4.2 million CCTV cameras in the country, the average urban Briton is said to be recorded up to 300 times each day. Yet recent studies have suggested that CCTV systems have little effect in deterring crime. The erosion of individual privacy through the use of surveillance cameras in public places began long ago, but it has accelerated enormously in recent years because of the threat of terrorism. Yet it seems to me that few people are worried. 'The world is not the same place', I was told by one security guard who had tried to stop me taking a picture. But what kind of place do we want it to be? In my opinion, that's an important question to answer.

PREPARE FOR TASK

3 a Read the text again. What reasons does the author give for criticising surveillance?

b Find two expressions in the text which the author uses to introduce his opinion.

4 Look at the sentences. Underline the expressions used to introduce the speakers' opinions. The first has been done for you.

1 As far as I'm concerned these are dangerous times and we need efficient surveillance, wherever, whenever.
2 It would appear to me that precious money is being thrown away on expensive equipment which does nothing to tackle the real reasons for crime.
3 I reckon that it's the only practical way to control urban crime.
4 I don't know about you, but I don't want to feel observed all the time.
5 You may disagree, but what I think we need is more policemen in the community, not more cameras.

5 Read the sentences in 4 again. Which are for using more surveillance cameras and which are against?

TASK

6 Work in two groups. Group A, turn to page 158. Group B, turn to page 160.

7 Work in new groups with two or three students from each of groups A and B. Take it in turns to present your reasons for or against the statement.

8 a When you have presented and explained all your reasons, write a short summary of your opponents' arguments.

b Present your summaries to the class.

REPORT BACK

9 a Discuss the questions.

- Which group do you think argued best? Why?
- Which group do you think had the most valid arguments? Why?

b Hold a class vote to see whether the statement is accepted or rejected.

6 GLOBAL AND LOCAL

a

b

d

e

1 a Work in pairs. Look at the images. What do they have in common? What are the people celebrating in each case?

b Read the descriptions of the celebrations on page 59 and match them to the images.

2 a Look at the words in **bold** in the descriptions in 1b. Complete A in the KEY VOCABULARY PANEL.

b Work in pairs. Make as many connections as you can between the festivals. Use the words from A.

Cosplay, Halloween and Carnival all involve dressing up in costumes.

3 a 6.1 Listen to the start of a radio programme. Answer the questions.

1 Which celebration does the speaker talk about?
2 Where is the festival in the image taking place?
3 Why would this event have been unlikely ten years ago?

b 6.2 Listen to the rest of the programme. Make notes on two more festivals. Complete the chart.

Name		
Origins		
What happens		
How they have evolved		

4 a Complete B in the KEY VOCABULARY PANEL. Can you add any other festivals to the list?

b Complete C in the KEY VOCABULARY PANEL.

c

f

5 Work in pairs. Discuss the questions.

- In your country, what type of festivals do you celebrate?
- Which celebrations do you least/most enjoy? Why?
- Have these celebrations changed since your parents were young?

KEY VOCABULARY

Celebrations & festivals

A Nouns

- Which words in the box are synonyms of celebrations? Which are things that a celebration could include?

concert contest costume event festival float holiday mask parade party present procession

B Words connected with festivals

- How many words in 2 can you match with the festivals in 1?

Carnival – music, seasonal, traditional

1 Festivals Carnival Chinese New Year Christmas Diwali Easter Edinburgh Festival Eid ul-Fitr Halloween Day of the Dead Hanami Oktoberfest Venice Biennale

2 Types arts, beer, local, music, national, pagan, religious, rock, seasonal (e.g. spring), traditional, youth

C Talking about change

- Read transcript 6.2 on page 164. Find four verbs which are synonyms of *change*. Complete the gaps. The first letter is given.

1. Our habits have e........................ a lot in recent years.
2. We have m........................ our behaviour.
3. We a........................ local traditions to modern times.
4. But these changes won't t........................ the way we do things, change here is gradual.

Eid ul-Fitr is a three-day Muslim celebration that marks the end of Ramadan, a month of fasting (not eating) during the daylight hours.

Halloween is a pagan **festival** held before All Saints Day. In some countries they celebrate the Day of the Dead at this time.

Carnival is usually celebrated before Lent. Street **parties** include **concerts** and dancing, **contests** for the best **floats**, **costumes**, **masks** and **processions**. However, different festivals with this name occur in other places on other dates.

Christmas is a Christian **holiday** and involves giving **presents**. Figures such as Santa Claus have become symbols of the celebration.

Cosplay is an **event** in which participants wear costumes that represent specific characters from popular Japanese culture.

The Cherry Blossom Festival is a festival which originated in Japan as a way to celebrate the start of spring. People organise special dishes and **parades**.

- PRACTISE *IF* IN REAL SITUATIONS
- TALK ABOUT FESTIVALS

Berlin is a city with a large international population. Among the 3.4 million inhabitants of the German capital, 450,000 do not have German citizenship. Many more have a mixed ethnic background. The Carnival represents the cultural and ethnic diversity of Berlin.

SPEAKING & READING

1 Look at the images of the Carnival of Cultures in Berlin. What are the people doing? Would you like to go to it? Why/Why not? Think of three adjectives to describe the atmosphere.

2 **a** Match texts A–C to the people 1–3 who wrote them.

1 event organiser 2 travel guide writer
3 a Carnival fan

b Decide which text is

1 giving instructions to participants.
2 describing the atmosphere.
3 giving advice to visitors.

3 Read the texts again. Find adjectives that mean

1 full of activity 2 very full 3 very exciting

4 Work in small groups. Discuss the questions.

- Are there any cities in your country with a similar ethnic mix to Berlin? Do they hold a similar festival?
- Do you think this type of carnival is beneficial to a country or a city? Why/Why not?

VOCABULARY: recommendations

1 6.3 Listen to four opinions about the Carnival. Are they positive or negative?

2 **a** Listen again and complete the extracts from transcript 6.3.

1 It's only .... days and there's a unique .... here. It's a **great time** to be in Berlin!
2 It's **an interesting way** to find out about ....
3 I think Berlin is **the worst place** to be at .... time.
4 Everything is so ...., it's **a good idea** to stay away.

b Look at the expressions in **bold** in 2a. What verb form is used after these expressions, *to* + infinitive or verb + *-ing*? What other adjectives can you use in each expression?

3 Work in pairs. What recommendations would you give a visitor who wanted to visit your town/city? Use the expressions in 2a and 2b.

NOTICE *A MUST*

Must can also be a noun. We use *a must* to mean something that is essential in a particular situation.

Comfortable shoes are a must if you're going to walk in the country.

A Berlin is very much a party town with a busy year-round calendar of concerts, street parties, sports events, trade shows and festivals. And the best time to visit the city? If you can choose when to go, make sure you book a trip in June for the *Karneval der Kulturen*, you won't be disappointed. If you decide to come for the Carnival, it's a good idea to book a hotel early: they can get really packed! And remember to bring a raincoat. The fun doesn't stop if it rains! And when the sun shines, the festival goers spray each other with water to keep cool.

B When you get to the Carnival, you won't know where to start. It's so dynamic, the whole atmosphere is electric. It seems like the whole city is in the street celebrating. It's a wonderful thing, everyone together in one big street party, dancing and forgetting their problems for one day. That's what Carnival should be about. Stay for the whole three days if you can, I always do!

C Before you get to the procession, make sure you know where you are going and what time your float leaves. Schedules are available online. Come with your costume, instrument, props, etc. and everything else prepared. If you arrive late, the parade won't wait ;-) And if you remember to bring ID with you, it might save time. Good luck and enjoy the Carnival!

GRAMMAR

1 Work in pairs. Match 1–6 to a–f to make sentences.

1 If you can choose when to go,
2 Stay for the whole three days
3 If you arrive late,
4 If you bring ID with you,
5 The show doesn't stop
6 When the sun shines,

a if it rains.
b if you can.
c the parade won't wait.
d make sure you book a trip in June.
e it might save time.
f people spray each other with water.

2 **a** Look at the sentences in 1 again and answer the questions.

1 Which sentences
a) refer to a general fact? *1,* ....
b) refer to a possible future situation? *3 and* ....
2 Which sentence doesn't contain the word *if*? ....
3 In which sentence could you replace *if* with *when* without changing the meaning? ....

b Look again at your answers in 2a and complete 1–6 in the GRAMMAR PANEL.

SENTENCES WITH *IF*: REAL SITUATIONS

We use *if* + present simple + present simple to talk about things that are (1) ....

The show doesn't stop if it rains.

Notice in these sentences you can replace *if* with (2) .... with no change in meaning.

If the sun shines / (3) .... *the sun shines ...*

We use *if* + present simple + future to talk about situations that are likely to happen in the (4) ....

If you remember to bring ID with you, it'll save time.

Notice that we do NOT use a future form after *if* in these sentences.

If the weather is good, we'll have a picnic.

NOT ~~*If the weather will be good,*~~ *we'll have a picnic.*

We can also use a modal verb or an imperative form in the main clause.

If you bring ID with you, it might save time... (modal)

Stay for the three days if you can. ((5) ....)

If can come at the beginning of the sentence.

If it rains, the show doesn't stop.

Or in the middle of the sentence.

The show doesn't stop if it rains.

Notice that when *if* comes at the (6) ...., we use a comma before the second clause.

We often use sentences with *if* to offer advice or to make recommendations and suggestions.

See page 145 for grammar reference and more practice.

3 Work in pairs. Choose the correct option to complete each sentence.

1 If you*'ll have / have* some free time, you can go for a walk around the city as well.
2 You *can / 'll* dress up if you want to, but there's no obligation.
3 *Don't come / Come* to the Carnival if you want to have a good time.
4 You'll forget all your problems if you*'ll go / go* to the Carnival.
5 If you *don't / won't* remember the time of the procession, you can check the online schedule.

4 **a** Complete the sentences with your own ideas.

1 If I have a holiday this year, I ....
2 If I have time today, I ....
3 If I have some extra money, I ....

b Read your sentences to a partner. Were your partner's ideas similar to yours?

LISTENING & SPEAKING

1 **a** 6.4 Listen to Eva talking about a festival. What is it? How has it changed?

b Listen again and complete the summary.

The festival is at the end of (1) .... It's at the same time as (2) .... Basically the stall holders in the market dress up their goods – meat, fish, (3) .... or (4) .... In the evening, people queue up to see the (5) .... and there's a (6) .... in the market square. Some local people are worried that the old traditions will (7) .... because more people are choosing to have (8) .... parties instead.

2 Work in small groups. Discuss the question.

- Do you think it's important to protect local traditions? Why/Why not?

6.2 LOCAL HEROES

- PRACTISE MODAL VERBS
- TALK ABOUT SUPERHEROES

SPEAKING & VOCABULARY: qualities

1 Work in pairs. Look at the images and discuss the questions.

- What do you know about these superheroes?
- Do you think they are good role models for young people? Why/ Why not?

a

b

c

2 **a** Look at the words in the box. Which qualities would you associate with a superhero? Why? Which two qualities have a negative meaning? Use a dictionary to help you.

> acceptance cooperation evil knowledge popularity
> prejudice strength tolerance wisdom

b Make adjectives from the nouns in 2a. Which word does not change? Use a dictionary to check your answers.

acceptance – accepting

3 Work in pairs. Think about two real-life heroes. What qualities do you associate with them? Tell your partner. Use the nouns and adjectives in 2a and 2b.

LISTENING

1 6.5 Listen to the first part of a podcast about a new group of superheroes, the 99. Answer the questions.

1 Who are the 99?
2 What is the significance of the number 99?

2 **a** 6.6 Listen to the second part of the podcast. Make notes about

- the origins of the Noor stones
- Dr Ramzi Razem and his mission
- Rughal and his plans
- reactions to the 99 so far

b Work in pairs. Choose the correct options to complete the sentences. Listen again and check your answers.

1 The Noor Stones are powerful because they contain *knowledge / secret qualities*.
2 Dr Razem wants to *use the powers for himself / use the powers to fight evil*.
3 Rughal wants to use the stones for *the same reason as Razem / his own personal gain*.
4 The 99 have to learn *to work together / to work alone*.
5 The series has been popular *in the Arab world / all over the world*.

3 In what way or ways are these heroes different from the ones you discussed in SPEAKING & VOCABULARY 1?

4 **a** Read the comments that were left on the radio's website. Which comment is a) the most enthusiastic? b) the least enthusiastic?

1 It sounds like more of the same thing to me. It's all been done before. But I suppose it can't be that bad if so many people are interested in it.
Reply • Like

2 I suppose it could work. There are so many negative images of Islam in the west right now, it might just help balance things out a little.
Reply • Like

3 Well, I guess Dr el-Mutawa must be pretty proud of his creation. It's got people talking about Islam in a new context – a positive context – and that must be a good thing, surely.
Reply • Like

b Work in pairs. Discuss the question.

- Do you think a cartoon series like this can really influence people's opinions? Why/Why not?

GRAMMAR

1 **a** Look at the extracts from the comments in LISTENING 4a. Underline the modal verbs.

1 It can't be that bad if so many people are interested in it.
2 I suppose it could work.
3 It might just help balance things out a little.
4 ... that must be a good thing, surely.

b Match the modal verbs in 1a to their meanings a–c.

a I think this is possible. (two verbs)
b I have no doubt that this is true.
c I don't think this is true.

Complete 1–3 in the GRAMMAR PANEL with a–c.

2 Complete 4–5 in the GRAMMAR PANEL with the appropriate modal verb.

3 Look at three characters from the series. Complete the comments using an appropriate modal verb.

His special power (1) .... be strength. Look how big he is!

Look at name. She (2) .... be Spanish, or maybe she's Latin American?

He (3) .... be one of the superheroes, he looks too old. I suppose he (4) .... be Dr Razem, or he (5) .... be the bad guy, Rughal.

4 **a** Look at the statements. Decide whether you think they a) can't be true, b) must be true, c) might be true.

1 Batman was the first superhero to appear on TV.
2 The 99 series has been translated into more than 30 languages.
3 Superman was first created as a villain.
4 A copy of the comic book in which Superman made his first appearance was recently sold for $1 million.
5 There has never been a French superhero.

b Work in pairs. Discuss your opinions.

I don't know about the first one, but I guess it might be true.

MODAL VERBS: MAKING DEDUCTIONS

We can use the modal verbs ***can't***, ***could***, ***might*** and ***must*** to give opinions and say whether or not we think something is true or possible.

must = (1) ....

could, might = (2) ....

can't = (3) ....

We don't use *mustn't* to say that something is not possible. We use (4) ....

That (5) .... *be true*, NOT *That ~~mustn't~~ be true!*

See page 145 for grammar reference and more practice.

PRONUNCIATION: modal verb stress in making deductions

1 Look at the phrases. What do they have in common? Imagine a situation where you might want to use them.

1 That can't be right!
2 I'm sorry, but that must be a mistake.
3 I suppose it might be true.
4 I suppose you could say that.

2 **a** 6.7 Listen to the expressions and underline the main stress in each expression. What are the people talking about?

b Listen again and repeat the phrases in 1.

3 6.8 Listen to four statements. Respond using the phrases in 1.

SPEAKING

1 You have been asked to create a new cartoon superhero to tackle a problem in your community. Look at the questions and think about your answers.

- What qualities do you want your superhero to represent?
- Will it be a man or a woman?
- What superpowers will he/she have?
- Will he/she have a costume? If yes, what? If no, why not?
- Who or what will your superhero fight against?
- What will his/her name be?

2 **a** Work in pairs. Discuss your ideas and present your hero to the class.

b Decide which hero you think will be most successful and why.

■ Practise future time clauses
■ Talk about changes with far-reaching consequences

Reading

1 a Look at images a–c. What does each one show? What do you think could be the link between them?

b Read the newspaper article and check your answers to 1a.

2 Match paragraphs A–D to their main message 1–4.

1. the consequences in terms of jobs and money
2. a description of something that's happening at the moment
3. detailed information about the cut-flower industry
4. detailed information about a past event

3 Read the article again. What do the numbers in the box refer to?

2010 millions 3,000 5,000
seven days 10 million 8,000

4 a Work in pairs. Find the five words or expressions in the box in the article. Which mean
a) to cause something to happen?
b) to be caused by something?

create lead to result from
stem from trigger

b Complete the sentences with the expressions in 4a. More than one answer is possible.

1. All this chaos was .... by a volcano.
2. In this way, a small incident can .... major problems worldwide.
3. Airport closures .... the size of the ash cloud.

5 Work in small groups. Can you think of any other recent events that have caused disruption and chaos? What effects did they have?

Will Kenyan farmers be hit by volcano disruption once again?

A Once again an Icelandic volcano is threatening to create travel chaos. Once again airline passengers all over the world are watching the news, wondering if they will be able to make their way home before a cloud of volcanic ash makes flying impossible. And Kenyan farmers worry as they look at their beautiful crops of colourful flowers ready to go to market. Will they have to throw them all away when the volcano erupts as they did in 2010?

B In April 2010, a volcano in Iceland, with an incredibly difficult name (Eyjafjallajökull), suddenly erupted. The eruptions themselves were not particularly serious, but they threw up enormous clouds of ash into the atmosphere and triggered travel chaos throughout Europe. The wind at the time was blowing from the north east and pushed the clouds towards Europe. The disruption that resulted from the ash cloud was incredible. Most airports throughout Europe were closed. International flights from Asia, Africa and America were cancelled. Millions of travellers could not get away or get home.

C But that was not all. The ash cloud had an effect on economies all over the world. One of the countries that suffered most was Kenya, which relies heavily on exporting fruit, vegetables and, most importantly, cut flowers to Europe. Kenya normally exports up to 500 tonnes of flowers a day. These flowers are cut and taken to the airport. There they are stored until they are ready to be sent on planes to the UK or the Netherlands. When they get there, they are distributed to retailers across Europe. Once they are on display at the florists, they stay fresh for an absolute maximum of seven days before they have to be thrown away.

D The ash cloud in 2010 closed European airspace for over a week, leading to the destruction of 3,000 tonnes of flowers. 5,000 farm workers lost their jobs and the country lost more than $10 million in exports, and all this stemmed from a natural disaster that took place 8,000 kilometres away. And today, as experts monitor the activity of another Icelandic volcano, farm workers in Kenya are hoping that this time the wind will blow the other way.

Grammar

1 Look at the extract. Choose the correct verbs to complete it without looking back at the article in READING 1b.

> Airline passengers all over the world are watching the news, wondering if they will be able to make their way home **before** a cloud of volcanic ash [(1)]*makes / will make* flying impossible. And Kenyan farmers worry as they look at their beautiful crops of colourful flowers… Will they have to throw them all away **when** the volcano [(2)]*erupts / will erupt*?

2 Check your answers in the article in READING 1b. What do you notice about the verbs? Complete 1–3 in the GRAMMAR PANEL.

3 **a** Complete the text with *will* or the present simple and the verbs in brackets.

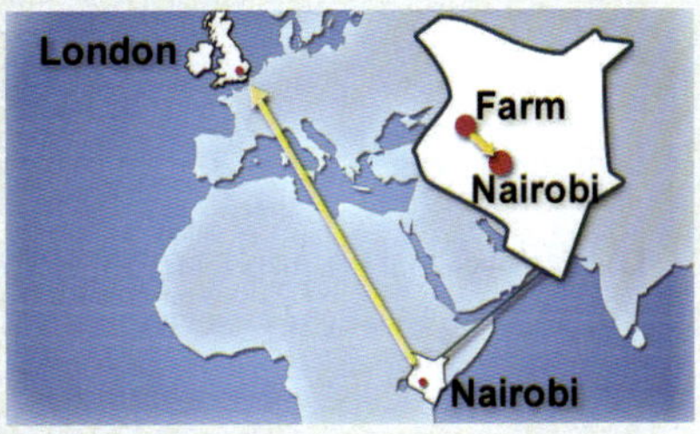

How long do you think will it take for this flower to reach your table? And how far it will have travelled by the time it [(1)] .... (*get*) there?
Early tomorrow morning, when the farm workers [(2)] .... (*start*) work, this flower [(3)] .... (*be*) cut and loaded with thousands of others in a refrigerated lorry. It [(4)] .... (*travel*) hundreds of miles until it [(5)] .... (*get*) to the airport in Nairobi. From there it [(6)] .... (*fly*) more than 4,000 miles to London. If you [(7)] .... (*live*) in London then you'll probably have to wait another day or two before it [(8)] .... (*arrive*) at your door. Before it [(9)] .... (*reach*) your door, it [(10)] .... (*go*) to a wholesale market. There a florist [(11)] .... (*buy*) it and take it to their shop. It may stay there for a day or more until a customer [(12)] .... (*choose*) it, [(13)] .... (*pay*) for it and [(14)] .... (*bring*) it to you.

b Work in pairs. Check your answers. Can you think of other products that have to travel that far?

4 **a** Complete the sentences so that they are true for you.

1 When I get home tonight, I ....
2 Before I go home, I'll need to ....
3 Once I finish this exercise, I'm going to ....
4 I won't stop studying English until ....

b Work in pairs. Compare your answers.

Future time clauses

We often use a time expression (*when, until, before, once, by the time*) + a verb in the [(1)] .... tense to talk about a sequence of events in the future.

When the airspace [(2)] .... *(open) up again, flights to London will resume.*

Farmers are going to have to wait until the airspace [(3)] .... *(open) up again.*

Notice we do not use *will* or *going to* in these future time clauses.

When normal flight schedules resume, the farm workers will be able to go back to work,

NOT *When normal flight schedules ~~will~~ resume, the farm workers will be able to go back to work.*

Remember that this is also true for clauses with *if*.

See page 145 for grammar reference and more practice.

Speaking

1 What do you think might be the link between the following phenomena?

1 The cut-flower trade in Kenya and a) farmers in the UK, b) local water supplies and c) climate change.
I imagine that flowers from Kenya are cheaper and so British flower growers may not be selling so many flowers?

2 A new tourist resort on the coast of Morocco and a) local house prices, b) cheap flights and c) local job market and economy.

2 Compare your answers with the class. Can you think of any changes in your local area or elsewhere that have had, or are having, far-reaching consequences? Use the ideas in the box to help you.

industries relocating to new countries
traditional jobs disappearing
ban on cars in town centre
cycle lanes opening
airport opening or airport closing
new housing being built
new road taking traffic away from town

TUNE IN

1 Look at the images. What type of air travel do they show? What are the advantages and disadvantages of this kind of air travel?

2 6.9 Listen to a conversation between Katya and Mehmed. Who is in favour and who is against budget air travel?

3 **a** Listen again. Which of these points are mentioned?

- convenience
- cost
- local economy
- pollution
- tourism
- treatment of passengers

b What do they say about them? Who do you agree with? Why?

FOCUS ON LANGUAGE

4 **a** Listen again and complete the gaps.

1 So, **are you saying that** .... should be allowed to travel?
2 **What I meant was that**, before we had to have a good ....
3 **What exactly do you mean**? When can you say a trip is ....?
4 **What I'm trying to say is,** .... you go, there are tourists. It's ....!
5 **So, do you mean** you won't be going .... again? Anywhere?

b Complete the chart using the expressions in **bold** in 4a.

1 Ask for clarification	2 Clarify what you want to say
are you saying that...?	....
....	....
....	

NOTICE *WHAT... IS*

We often use *what... is/was* when we want to clarify something.

1 *What I'm trying to say is...* 2 *What I meant was (that)...*

And when we ask for clarification.

1 *What I don't understand is...* 2 *So, what you're saying is...*

5 **a** Complete the conversations with expressions from 4b. Various options are possible.

1

A So, you're saying you would ban Halloween and other foreign festivals and only have local ones?
B No, ... we need to preserve our traditions, that's all.

2

A OK, sorry, I'll rephrase the question. .... would you rather eat a locally grown apple or an imported one? It's a simple question.
B It depends.
A .... you don't know?
B No, ... it depends if the local fruit is good or not. That's ....

b 6.10 Listen and compare. Are any of the answers the same as yours?

Being emphatic

6.10 Listen again to the conversations in 5b. Notice how the speaker uses the expressions to emphasise what they are saying. Do you think the speakers sound a) patient? b) irritated?

No, what I meant was...
Are you saying that...
What I'm trying to say is,...
That's what I'm trying to say...

Listen and repeat, paying special attention to the tone.

OVER TO YOU

6 **a** Look at the sentences and make notes on your opinion about them.

a The best music and cinema comes from the States, the rest of the world can't compete.
b There's no need to travel abroad, there's so much to see in my own country.
c We can learn a lot with technology, discover the world online etc., but I prefer face-to-face contact.

b Work in pairs. Student A, give your opinion on one of the topics. Student B, listen to Student A's opinion and ask for clarification. Student A, clarify your position as best you can.

7 Choose a new topic and swap roles.

Buy Global or Local?

Look around you. Where is everything from?

Subscribe Reply

Consider the clothes you put on in the morning. Check out the label. It's probably made in a country far away from where you live, isn't it? Next, sit down for breakfast... where did you buy your kitchen table? Did you put it together? OK, what about your breakfast? What are you having today? **Just imagine** where the fruit comes from and where you bought it. The tea and coffee have to travel a long way. Finally, you're ready to leave. You get into your car to go to work. Do they still make cars in your country or are they all imported? **My point is**, we need to stop and think, that's all. *Panos*

Katie: Yes, **I know what you mean**. But, **don't forget that** there's not much that's in our control. Some things are just not made here. And, if I only buy local goods, will it make any difference?

Roberta: But, Panos, **there's nothing wrong with** buying clothes from China, their economy has to grow too. And we don't all have the money to buy good quality furniture. **My view is**, we just buy what's out there.

Jamal: Thanks, **this is a good way to** make people realise something that they simply don't think about. I asked myself the same questions this morning and I saw that nothing was made here.

Natsumi: Yes, OK, **but what you don't see is** that we can't all be so fussy. The important thing is to have the choice. Well, **that's my opinion**, for what it's worth!

Tune in

1 Look at the images in the blog post. What types of products do they show? What is their connection with the topic *Buy Global or Local*?

2 **a** Read Panos's blog post. In what order are the images mentioned?

b What do you think is Panos's main message?

1 It is always better to buy local produce.
2 We need to think before we buy.
3 We should avoid buying foreign products.

3 Underline the direct questions and imperatives. What do they add to the text?

4 Look at the comments on Panos's blog post. Match the opinions to the four people.

1 people need to be able to choose
2 people need to know this information
3 people can't make that much difference
4 people have to buy what's economical and easily available

5 **a** Look at the expressions in **bold** in the blog post and the comments. Which ones are used to

1 state or introduce an opinion?
2 answer another person's opinion?
3 directly address the reader?

b Which three expressions mean 'this is my view'?

Prepare for task

6 Think of a local product (e.g. fresh fruit or vegetables, clothes or crafts, films or TV programmes). Which is better, the local or imported version? Make notes on

1 the price 2 the quality 3 availability 4 marketing

7 You are going to write a blog post about the product you chose in 6. Think about the people who you think might read your blog post. What kind of style or tone do you want to use to address them?

Task

8 Look at your notes in 6. Decide what information you are going to include and in what order you are going to present it. Then write a short description in defence of your product. Use expressions from 5a where possible.

Report back

9 Work in pairs. Student A, show your blog post to Student B. Do they agree with you or not? Student B, write back a short comment/reply. Swap roles.

➜ Go to Review B, Unit 6, p. 70

VOCABULARY

Landscapes

a

b

1 **a** Work in pairs. Look at landscapes a and b. How many features can you name?

b Compare your list with the rest of the class. Which pair has the longest list?

2 Look again at your list of features in 1a and answer the questions.

1 Which are man-made and which are natural?
2 Which landscape do you like the best? Why?

Natural disasters & extreme weather

3 **a** Match extracts 1–3 to words/phrases in the box. You do not need to use them all.

drought earthquake famine forest fire
flood hurricane tsunami

1 There's water everywhere! The torrential rain brought devastation and this village suffered the most.
2 Some of the buildings were built to withstand this kind of tremor, but others fell as if made of paper.
3 It hit the coast with tremendous force. The wind direction suddenly changed, nobody was prepared.

b Underline the words that helped you find the correct answer.

4 R7 Listen and check.

Natural world collocations

5 Match words from a and b to make collocations.

a environmental food marine ocean renewable rubbish sea
b chain damage dump ecosystem life materials pollution

GRAMMAR

Present perfect continuous or simple?

1 **a** Work in pairs. Look at the verbs in *italics*. In which sentence is the present perfect continuous incorrect?

1 How long *have you been living* here? *(for)*
2 How long *have you been knowing* your partner? *(since)*
3 How long *have you been looking* at these exercises? *(for)*
4 How long *have you been having* English classes? *(since)*

b Ask and answer the questions using the words in brackets.

Time expressions with *for* & *since*

2 **a** Complete the gaps with *for* or *since*.

1 .... I was born
2 .... a year
3 .... ages
4 .... I can remember
5 .... a few minutes
6 .... last weekend

b Write sentences about yourself using the expressions in 1a.

I've known my best friend, Pedro, since we were at school.

FUNCTIONAL LANGUAGE

Checking information

1 Complete the mini conversations by adding a phrase that checks information.

A Sorry, I'm late. I was caught in this really bad storm!
B ....
A Yeah, didn't it rain where you were?
B No, not here.

C What a disastrous holiday! We came home early you know.
D ....!
C We did! The weather was terrible and there's nothing to do on the beach if the weather's bad, is there?

2 R8 Listen and check.

3 Work in pairs. Student A, give some news to Student B. Student B, respond by checking that you heard correctly.

LOOKING BACK

- Tell a partner five different ways to describe the weather or the environment where you are.
- Think of five different sentences in which you can talk about 'how long' you have done something.

VOCABULARY

Connections & prevention

1 **a** How many different expressions could you use to describe this image? Use any of these words.

verbs: bridge, link, reach across, join, get in touch with, unite, break down, build, contact
nouns: hands, barriers, gap, borders, friends/people, countries, bridges

They are bridging the gap...

b Complete the gaps using the verbs and nouns in 1a.

1 People use social networks to ………………… friends.
2 Football is a way of ………………… barriers and ………………… people.
3 English can reach across ………………… because it's a universal language.
4 Countries should build more ………………… and tunnels to connect with other nations.

2 R9 Listen and check. What other ways do you think people can connect with each other?

Music is a way of reaching across borders...

Future plans & intentions

3 **a** Replace the words in **bold** with a noun and/or verb.

1 **I intend** to travel a lot next year. *(noun/verb)*
2 **My aim is** to speak English like a native speaker. *(verb)*
3 **I'm hoping** to take a break from work/studies soon. *(noun/verb)*
4 **My plan is** to meet lots of new people. *(verb)*

b Are the sentences true for you?

GRAMMAR

Future forms

1 **a** Choose the correct options to complete the text.

> Next week, (1)*I'm travelling / I'll travel* to Germany to start my language exchange programme. The flight (2)*will leave / leaves* at seven o'clock which is really early, so I hope I don't oversleep. When I arrive in Hamburg, (3)*I'm going to find / I'm finding* a flat to share with other students. I hope (4)*I'm finding / I'll find* a good one which is cheap enough for me, I'm on a tight budget. Then (5)*I'm enrolling / I'm going to enrol* on my course at the university. I hope (6)*I'm meeting / I'll meet* some nice people there. I think the most important thing in a new place is to make good friends.

b Work in pairs. Think of a future trip that you plan to do. What would your plans, hopes and arrangements be? Tell your partner.

2 **a** Write the sentences using *will / won't* + infinitive or *will / won't + be* + past participle.

1 Everybody / world / have / mobile phone / soon.
2 Global inequality / continue / rise.
3 Poverty / become / thing of the past.
4 Cure AIDS / find / soon.
5 Life on Mars / discover / soon.
6 Women and men / earn / same salary in my country.

b Work in pairs. Read out your predictions.

3 Work in pairs. Write some predictions about your own life. Read your partner's predictions. Report back on your predictions.

FUNCTIONAL LANGUAGE

At passport control

1 Complete the conversation at passport control at Hong Kong airport.

A (1) ……………………………………………… ?
B London Heathrow.
A (2) ………………………………………………
in Hong Kong?
B Three weeks.
A (3) ……………………………………………… ?
In a hotel?
B No, I'm going to stay with my brother.
A (4) ………………………………………………
on visiting other parts of China?
B No, I'm not.
A (5) ………………………………………………
in Hong Kong?
B No, I've been here before.

2 R10 Listen and check.

LOOKING BACK

- Write down several phrases that can describe your future plans and intentions.
- Which part of this unit would you like to know more about? Why?
- Tell your partner about current trends in the society you live in.

VOCABULARY

Celebrations & festivals

1 Work in pairs. How many different celebrations and festivals can you remember? What special features or events do you associate with each one?

Recommendations

2 a Think of a place that you know well, but is not your home or where you are from. Make recommendations.

- (1) .... is a real **must**. *(visiting a place)*
- It's a **good idea** to go (2) .... *(season)* because...
- The **worst thing** you can do is (3) .... *(activity)*
- If you have the time, **don't miss** (4) .... *(excursion)*

b Work in pairs. Read out your recommendations to your partner. Can they guess the place?

c R11 Listen to another person doing the same task. What city do you think it is?

Qualities

3 a Think of five adjectives to describe personal qualities. Are they positive/negative/neutral?

b Work in pairs. Do you know somebody personally or in the public eye who matches these descriptions? Tell your partner about them.

GRAMMAR

Sentences with *if*: real situations

1 a Complete the gaps giving advice about London with the present simple, *will*, *might* or an imperative.

1 .... *(need)* to buy sterling when you arrive, they don't use euros!
2 If it .... *(rain)*, ... *(go)* to one of the great museums.
3 You .... *(run out of)* money, if you .... *(do)* lots of different things. London's very expensive.
4 If you go to London, ... *(miss)* going on the London Eye!
5 If you .... *(understand)*, ... *(ask)* the people to repeat what they said.

b Write similar sentences about your capital city.

Modal verbs: making deductions

2 Look at the image of a city and its celebrations. Make deductions about it using *must*, *might* or *can't*.

It could be somewhere in Asia...

Future time clauses

3 a Complete the text. Add *will* to the verbs in *italics* where possible. Who do you think is speaking to whom?

> 'Just some things to bear in mind on your first day. We (1)*pick you up* from the station at ten o'clock and we (2)*take* you to your hotel to freshen up. Call us when you (3)*want* to leave and a car (4)*take* you to the conference, say at 11.30 a.m.? You'll be there until the morning sessions (5)*finish* at two o'clock and then we (6)*go* to lunch. After that, you'll be able to rest until the events in the evening.'

b R12 Listen and check.

FUNCTIONAL LANGUAGE

Clarifying

1 Look at the follow-up conversation from the situation in GRAMMAR 3a. Complete the gaps.

A Thanks for all the info. So are you (1) .... (2) .... I'm free from lunch till the evening?
B That's right.
A Great!

A And another thing (3) .... (4) .... (5) .... is what the evening events are...
B They're just for public relations...
A Sorry?
B What (6) .... (7) .... (8) .... meeting potential clients, being nice to people.

2 R13 Listen and check.

LOOKING BACK

- What was the most memorable part of this unit? Why?
- Think about a place you've been to recently. What would you (not) recommend about it?
- Think of some deductions you can make right now about the class, the weather, the news.

READING

1 **a** Work in pairs. What do you think are the five most common reasons for studying English?

b Compare your answer with the class.

2 Look at the online survey. Why are Dina, Isabel and Erik studying English? Who do you think is the most motivated? Why?

How do you think English will help you in the future?

Dina (16)
English is useful for travel and holidays, but I don't really have a clear aim in mind at the moment. I guess it'll probably help me (1) .... for a job, and, if, one day, I want to work (2) .... then obviously it'll be really important. For the moment I'm just studying it because I have to!

Isabel (25)
(3) .... English really hard over the last year or so. I'm in my last year at Med school. (4) .... The employment situation isn't too good here in my country and I know there are a lot of good jobs in English-speaking countries. I want my English to be as good as possible so I can get one of those jobs.

Erik (21)
I'm going to stay with my brother in the States for three months. I really want to make the most of the experience and (5) .... some intensive conversation classes for the last couple of weeks. I know it's going to be really difficult (6) .... English in the classroom is one thing, but in the real world it's completely different! I really want to be able to make friends and learn more about life in the States. You can't get to know people (7) ...., can you?

3 **a** Look at the survey again. Complete responses 1–7 with phrases a–g.

a if you can't speak to them
b I'm going to be graduating soon
c I've been doing
d I've been studying
e or study abroad
f when I first get there
g when I'm looking

b Look at the way phrases a–g are used in the responses. Which refer to i) the future? ii) a general truth? iii) a period of time that started in the past and continues in the present?

4 Work in pairs. Discuss the questions.

- Why are you studying English?
- How do you think English will help you in the future?

SPEAKING

motivation the desire or willingness to do something

5 Work in small groups. Look at the list of factors that can influence motivation for learning English and discuss the questions.

- you need English for your future studies or work
- you need English for your present studies or job
- you want to travel or live abroad
- you have English-speaking friends or colleagues
- your English classes are fun
- you are good at English and learn quickly
- your parents want you to learn English
- English is everywhere and its influence is growing

- Which of the factors have the biggest influence on motivation?
- Which would be negative?
- Which factors influence your personal motivation most?

6 Report back on your discussion to the class. What do you, as a class, think is the one most important factor in increasing motivation?

QUICK CHECK

Complete the checklist below.

Can you...	Yes, I can.	Yes, more or less.	I need to look again.
1 describe traditional houses and homes in your country?	☐	☐	☐
2 talk about man's influence on the environment?	☐	☐	☐
3 talk about future plans and intentions?	☐	☐	☐
4 describe changing trends?	☐	☐	☐
5 present your reasons for and against an argument?	☐	☐	☐
6 describe a local festival or cultural event?	☐	☐	☐
7 discuss the consequences of an event or action?	☐	☐	☐
8 clarify what you want to say?	☐	☐	☐

Compare your answers with a partner.

- What else do you know now after studying units 4–6?
- Do you need to look again at any of the sections?
- Do you need any extra help from your teacher?

7 IS THIS YOURS?

a

b

c

1 Work in pairs. Look at the photos. How many items can you identify? What do the photos have in common? In what ways are they different?

2 a 7.1 Listen to a photographer explaining what the three photos represent. In what order does he mention them?

b Listen again. Answer the questions.

1 Which objects were
   a) sent to somebody?
   b) lost?
   c) removed?

2 In which photos were the objects related to
   a) a natural disaster?
   b) the financial crisis?
   c) an accident?

3 a Work in pairs. Re-tell the story behind each of the photos.

b Which of the photos affects you the most? Why?

4 Complete A in the KEY VOCABULARY PANEL. Read transcript 7.1 on page 165. Use a dictionary to help you.

5 a 7.2 Listen to three people responding to 3b. Which photo are they referring to?

b Listen again. Which speaker

a doesn't know why the objects are important?
b thinks the situation is very sad?
c feels the photo is unexpected and shocking?

6 **a** Match sentences a–e to speaker 1, 2 or 3 from 5a.

a Elvis Presley and earplugs! I wonder why this man **treasured** those particular objects so much? And why did he **send them back** up to the surface?

b ... that's somebody's life that's just been **dumped** on the street there...

c They probably really want to **hold onto** their stuff... so they end up just having to **get rid of** it.

d I thought these were possessions that somebody had found and wanted to **give away** or even sell...

e Or I imagined that it was junk, items people had **thrown away**... and these are things which a family had to **leave behind** when they fled...

b Look at the words in **bold** in 6a and complete B in the KEY VOCABULARY PANEL.

KEY VOCABULARY

Possessions

A Nouns

- Match the words in the box to the categories.

articles belongings contents items
junk possessions property stuff

1 individual objects ....
2 objects in general ....
3 objects that are old and broken ....
4 objects that you own ....
5 objects that are inside something else ....

- Match the adjectives and the nouns to form expressions used in the listening texts.

Adjectives	Nouns
private	contents
treasured	items
personal	possessions
household	property

B Verbs associated with objects

- Complete the chart with the verbs in the box.

dump get rid of give away hold onto
leave behind send back throw away
treasure

Don't keep/ unimportant	Keep/important

7 Work in pairs. Discuss the questions.

- What kinds of objects do you like to keep and for what reasons?
- What possessions do you not mind throwing away? Why?
- How would you describe your home/room? Is it full of objects or quite empty?

VOCABULARY: organisation

1 Look at the photo. What does it show? Where is it? What does it tell you about the person who works at this desk?

2 Which adjective in the box can you NOT use to describe the desk in the photo? Use the definitions to help you.

cluttered disorganised inefficient messy neat untidy

clutter *(n)* – the situation created when you put too many things in one place without any particular order or care

efficiency *(n)* – the ability to work well and get good results

mess *(n)* – a situation where things are not in the right place and possibly dirty

neat *(adj)* – everything is in the right place and looking nice

tidy *(adj)* – everything is in the right place

organise *(verb)* – to put things into an order or system

3 **a** Use the words in 2 to complete 1–9 in the chart.

Noun	Adjective	Adjective + negative prefix
(1)	(2)	uncluttered
(3)	efficient	(4)
mess	(5)	-
neatness	(6)	-
tidiness	(7)	(8)
organisation	organised	(9)

b Work in pairs. Think about your home, your bedroom, your desk, your belongings, your emails and computer files. Are they tidy and organised? Tell your partner.

READING

1 Read the article. What does it say about messy desks? Are they good or bad? Why?

2 Read the article again and match statements 1–5 to paragraphs A–E.

1 Mess can be good.
2 A tidy desk makes a good impression.
3 A messy desk is difficult to work at.
4 People who work at messy desks are more efficient.
5 People who work at messy desks feel less stress.

Say YES to mess

A The desk in the photo is a classic example of a messy desk. There are so many documents and **books** and things piled in an untidy way all over it, how could anyone possibly get any work done? It's obviously someone who has too much **work** to do and too little **time** to tidy up. Could you work at that desk? Most people would say no and a lot of company managers would agree.

B How many **companies** these days have clean desk policies? Most do, especially if the desks are in public view. Most people would agree that a messy desk makes a very bad impression. It makes the company look disorganised and inefficient. A few **people** have even lost their jobs because of their untidy desks. In the US, a police chief was recently fired for not having a neat desk.

C So, mess is bad? Well, actually it seems not. The desk in the photo is actually a perfect example of creativity and flexibility. This is the desk of one of the greatest minds in modern science, Albert Einstein, who once said: 'If a cluttered desk is a sign of a cluttered mind, what, then, is an empty desk?'

D Psychologists suggest that people who can tolerate mess at their desks are less likely to be stressed by mess and disorder in life. They are likely to be more relaxed, more confident and more able to deal with unpredictability. Research also shows that they are also likely to earn more money and hold more responsible posts.

E It also seems that people with messy desks spend up to 36% more time working on their actual job than their tidier workmates. Their apparent chaos is just as efficient as a clear desk. When asked to find something it might take a little **effort**, but it'll be there. And they argue that the short time they take to find something when they need it is much less than the time the tidy desks owners spend constantly re-organising their desks.

So, is it all just a clever excuse to be lazy and disorganised? Or is a messy desk a sign of a superior mind?

Write and let us know what *you* think!

3 Work in pairs. Make a list of arguments in favour of messy desks. Do you think it is a good thing to say yes to mess? Why/Why not?

4 Read the comments that were left on the website. Do they agree with the title of the article? Do you and your partner agree with any of them?

1 It's so good to hear someone praising mess. I've never got enough **time** to tidy my desk! At last I can just enjoy my untidiness. Thank you!

2 Very few **people** I know actually enjoy mess. That doesn't mean they're boring or inflexible. They just have different priorities. Live and let live, I say!

3 I think that people with messy desks are actually very selfish. If you've got plenty of **space**, then that's fine. But when you have to share a workplace with a messy person, it can be very frustrating.

4 Have you ever worked with a messy boss? You've no idea how much **energy** I've wasted over the years tidying up after mine! Far too much, I can tell you!

5 I'm so busy, I have very little **time** to tidy my desk. Sometimes someone else will do it for me – and that's always a complete disaster. I can never find anything!

5 Write your own comment in response to the article.

Grammar

1 a Look at the expressions that are highlighted in yellow in Reading 1 and 4. Decide if the nouns in **bold** are

a) countable (have both a singular and a plural form e.g. *desk/desks*)

b) uncountable (only have a singular form and cannot be counted e.g. *space*)

b Complete 1–4 in the Grammar panel with *a few*, *a little*, *many* and *much*.

2 Look again at the highlighted expressions. Complete 5–12 in the Grammar panel with the words in the box.

enough few how little plenty so too many too much

3 a Choose the correct options to complete the text.

I've got (1) *a lot of* / *so much* books and magazines. I don't have (2) *enough* / *too much* space for them at home. So recently I've brought (3) *a few* / *a little* of them to work. I've got (4) *plenty of* / *too much* space in my office. I think the bookshelves look great with (5) *so many* / *so much* books on them. But my boss disagrees. She says there are (6) *not enough* / *too many*. She says they make the office look cluttered and untidy.

b Compare your answers with a partner. What causes the most clutter in your home/workplace/school?

Quantifiers

We use the quantifiers *much*, *many*, *a little*, *a few*, *a lot of* and *lots of* to talk about general quantities without giving a specific number or value.

	Countable	Uncountable	Both*
Large quantity	(1)	(2)	lots of, a lot of
Small quantity	(3)	(4)	–

* We also use *plenty of* and *(not) enough* with both countable and uncountable nouns.

Much & many

We do not tend to use ***much*** or ***many*** on their own in affirmative sentences. We prefer to use *a lot* of or *lots of*.

I have lots of space in my room. NOT *I have ~~much~~ space in my room.*

We often use *much* and *many* in combination with (5) .... in questions and (6) .... to emphasise a large quantity.

How much time do you spend tidying your desk?

I've got so many clothes I don't know where to put them.

Few & little

We use ***very few*** and ***very little*** to say that we think a quantity is not sufficient.

I have very (7) .... *opportunities to stop and tidy my desk.*

I have very (8) .... *free time during the day.*

Enough, plenty, too much & too many

We use (9) .... and (10) .... to say that a quantity is more than is necessary. We often use it to criticise or complain.

We use (11) .... to say that we have a large quantity and it is more than sufficient.

We use (12) .... to say that we have sufficient quantity.

See page 146 for grammar reference and more practice.

Speaking

1 a Work in pairs. Look at the image. What can you see? What does it tell you about the person who sleeps in this bed? Where do you think the bed belongs?

b 7.3 Listen and find out more about the bed. What surprised you about it?

2 Work in pairs. Do you agree that this bed is a 'wonderful work of art'? Why/Why not?

7.2 GAMES AND STUFF

- PRACTISE USING *ONE* & *ONES*
- TALK ABOUT TOYS & GAMES

VOCABULARY: toys & games

1 a Work in pairs. Look at the toys and games in the image. How many can you name? Turn to page 160 to check.

b Look again at the image and answer the questions.

1 Which are
   a) digital? b) traditional? c) educational?
2 Which are
   a) board games? b) ball games? c) video games?
   d) puzzles? e) other?
3 Which appeal mainly to younger children? Which appeal to adults as well as children?
4 Do you have any of these games in your home? Do you use them often or do they just add to the mess in your home?

LISTENING

1 a 7.4 You are going to listen to the first part of a podcast about a museum which is dedicated to toys and games. Tick the information you hear.

1 what it's called
2 what it is
3 where it is
4 when it opened
5 how many people visit it
6 what kind of toys it includes
7 what you can do there

b Compare your answers with a partner. Listen again and make notes about the information given.

2 Compare your notes and discuss the museum in 1a. Would you like to visit this museum? Why/Why not?

3 a 7.5 Listen to the second part of the podcast. Which toy is the presenter most interested in, a, b or c? Why?

a

b

c

b Listen again. Which statement does the presenter NOT make?

1 Sticks are everywhere.
2 They encourage the use of your imagination.
3 Some animals play with sticks.
4 They can be big or small.
5 They can sometimes be dangerous.
6 They can represent a lot of different things.

4 Compare your answers in 3b with a partner. Can you remember how many different uses the presenter mentioned? Read transcript 7.5 on page 165 and check your answers.

5 a Look at the other two toys in 3a. Think of three reasons why each one should be included in the National Toy Hall of Fame.

b Compare your reasons with the class. What other everyday objects would you include in the National Toy Hall of Fame?

GRAMMAR

1 **a** Look at the extracts from the whole podcast in LISTENING 1a and 3a. Which refer to a) toys in general? b) sticks in general? c) a specific toy? d) a specific stick?

1 ... **new ones and old ones**,... all much loved by adults and children alike.
2 Choose **your favourite one** and sit right down...
3 Here in this box is **one of my favourites**.
4 ... **big ones, small ones, straight ones, bent ones**...
5 ... **the one in the corner** is a sword, **this long one** is a horse and **this other one** is an aeroplane.
6 ... someone's drawing with **one** on the sand...
7 ... come and find out **which one** you like best.

b Work in pairs. Complete the GRAMMAR PANEL with some of the words in **bold** in 1a.

2 **a** Replace the words in **bold** with *one* or *ones* where appropriate.

1 I used to love those old **video games**, you know, the **video games** with the little dot that jumped around the screen.
2 We played lots of **board games** when I was a kid. Me and my brother always used to argue over which **board game** to play.
3 My favourite toy was **a train set**, you know, **a train set** with a station and bridges and crossings.
4 I think the best **toys** are the **toys** that you can make yourself.

b Look again at the sentences in 2a. Are any of them true for you? Compare your answers with a partner.

USING ONE & ONES

We use *one* and *ones* to refer back to something that has already been mentioned in a conversation or text.

... the most popular games and toys of all time, (1) ...., *... all much loved...*

We often use *one* or *ones* with
- ***the***: (2) .... *is a sword*
- ***other***: *this* (3) .... *is an aeroplane.*
- ***this/that/these/those***: (4) .... *is a horse*
- ***an adjective***: *Choose* (5) .... *and sit down.*
- ***which***: *find out* (6) .... *you like best.*

Notice we also use *one* to talk about one member of a group of people or things: *Here in this box is* (7) ....

See page 146 for grammar reference and more practice.

NOTICE *ONE OR TWO?*

Notice how we use the expression *one or two* to mean a *few*.

I've spotted one or two of my childhood favourites.
Have you had any problems with your computer recently?
Yes, one or two.

Do you have a similar expression in your language?

PRONUNCIATION: *one / ones*

1 7.6 Listen to three short conversations. Match them to the words in the box.

a child's bike   a cupcake   a cushion

2 **a** Look at the extracts. Which conversation do they come from?

a I think the first one looks better, the rainbow one.
b Can I have another one, please?
c Look, that's the one!
d No, one is enough, thanks!
e So which one is it going to be?
f The one with the chocolate bits, please.
g What, the red one in the corner?

b Listen again and underline the main stress. The first two have been done for you. In which case is *one* used to stress the number?

3 Listen again and repeat.

SPEAKING & LISTENING

1 **a** 7.7 Listen to two people talking about a childhood game they used to play. What were the rules? What was it called?

b Listen again and complete the sentences. Did you play the same game, or a similar game, when you were a child?

1 It was a very .... game.
2 There was .... who went off to hide.
3 We had to shut .... and count to ....
4 When you found them, you had to .... them.
5 And the last person to find us all was the one who had to ....

2 **a** Think of a game you used to play with your friends. Think about the questions and prepare to describe the game.

- What was it called?
- Did everybody play it?
- What were the rules?
- Why did you enjoy it?

b Work in pairs. Tell your partner about your game. Did you both play the same games? If yes, were the rules exactly the same every time or were there variations?

7.3 A HISTORY OF THE WORLD IN 100 OBJECTS

- PRACTISE ARTICLES
- TALK ABOUT OBJECTS

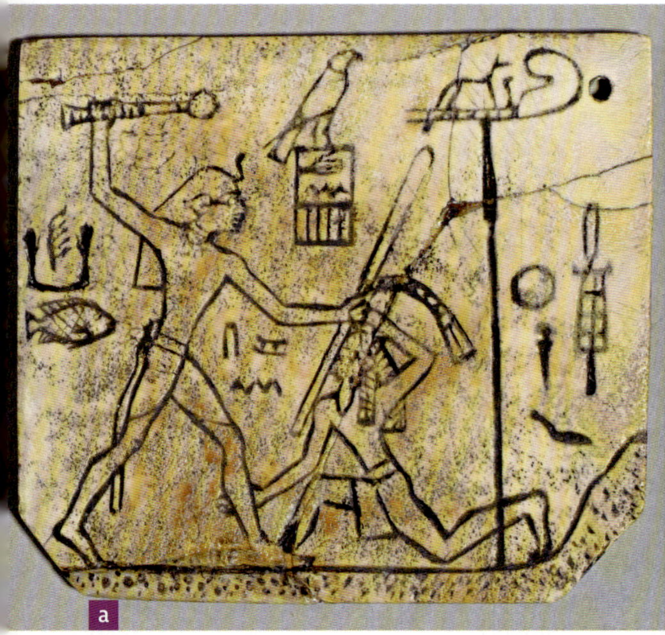

a

b

c

SPEAKING

1 Work in pairs. Look at the three objects in the images. Where would you expect to find them? What is the link between them and the lesson title? Check your answers on page 160.

READING

1 Read the texts describing the history of the objects. Match objects a–c to texts 1–3.

2 Read the texts again and match descriptions 1–6 to objects a–c.

1 It's a sophisticated piece of technology.
2 It was only used after the owner's death.
3 It represents two distinct ideas.
4 Its use is more symbolic than practical.
5 It has been used by people from several different religions.
6 It tells us a lot about its owner.

3 Find words in the texts that mean

1 a person who has studied a lot (1)
2 come from a particular time in the past (2)
3 the material taken from an elephant's tusk (2)
4 a competitor (2)
5 guns and other instruments used for fighting (3)
6 is a symbol of (3)

4 Work in small groups. Discuss the questions.

- Which object do you think is the most interesting? Why?
- Can you think of any objects from your own town or family that tell an interesting story?

1 The astrolabe is an amazing instrument. It can tell you the time, the date and your exact geographical position using the sun or the stars. It can do mathematical calculations and even work out your horoscope. In its day, it was a high status object, very much like a modern day smartphone or tablet computer. It's the same size and shape as a pocket watch, but it's much more complicated. The first astrolabes were made in Greece around 150 BC. They were further developed by Islamic scholars and were often used for finding the exact direction of Mecca. This astrolabe was owned by a Jewish scholar living in the south of what we now know as Spain in the thirteenth century – a time when Jewish, Islamic and Christian communities lived together in relative harmony.

2 This object dates from 2985 BC. It is about 5 cm squared, it's very thin, it's made of ivory and it looks and feels a bit like a modern-day business card. In fact, it's a label that was once attached to a pair of sandals, just like a modern day name tag on a pair of school shoes. The sandals belonged to an Egyptian pharaoh (King Den) and they were just one of the many things that would accompany the pharoah to the afterlife. The label would identify him to those he met and the picture engraved on it would tell them what kind of leader he'd been. On the label we see the king attacking and beating a rival in a clear demonstration of force: an image and a message that has often been repeated throughout history.

3 This object doesn't have a practical purpose, but it does have a very powerful message. It is made from weapons from the Mozambique civil war (1977–92). Almost 1 million people died during the war and 5 million people were left without homes. This sculpture represents both the tragedy of that war and the human triumph of those who succeeded in creating lasting peace. It was made by the Mozambican artist Cristóvão Canhavato (Kester) in 2001 for the *Transforming Arms into Tools* project. In this project approximately 7 million guns were voluntarily exchanged for useful tools and hardware.

Grammar

1 a Work in pairs. Complete the extract from Reading 1 text 2.

In fact, it's **a** label that was once attached to **a** pair of (1) .... **The** sandals belonged to **an** Egyptian (2) .... (King Den) and they were just one of the many things that would accompany **the** pharaoh to the after life. **The** (3) .... would identify him to those he met...

b Check your answers in Reading 1 text 2.

2 a Look at the articles (*a*, *an* and *the*) in **bold** in the extract in 1a. Which article is used to

a) talk about an object for the first time?
b) refer to an object that has already been mentioned?

b Complete 1–4 in the Grammar panel with *a/an* or *the*.

3 a Work in pairs. Add *the* to the sentences where necessary. There are five missing.

1 *The* Astrolabe is an amazing instrument.
2 It can do mathematical calculations and even work out your horoscope.
3 It's same size and shape as a pocket watch, but it's much more complicated.
4 First astrolabes were made in Greece around 150 BC.
5 They were further developed by Islamic scholars.
6 This astrolabe was owned by a Jewish scholar living in south of Spain in thirteenth century.
7 It was a time when the three communities lived together in relative harmony.

b Check your answers in Reading 2 text 1. Use examples from 3a to complete 5–11 in the Grammar panel.

4 a Choose the correct options to complete the text.

This is my favourite object in (1)*a / the / –* whole collection. It's (2)*a / the / –* very simple object, (3)*a / the / –* penny, but it's (4)*a / the / –* writing on (5)*a / the / –* penny that I find interesting. Can you read it? It's (6)*a / the / –* protest. At (7)*a / the / –* time, women were asking for (8)*a / the / –* right to vote. This penny is interesting for two reasons: it represents (9)*a / the / –* money and its importance in (10)*a / the / –* society, but it also symbolises (11)*a / the / –* fight for (12)*a / the / –* independence and (13)*a / the / –* democracy.

b 7.8 Listen and check.

Articles

A *The or a/an?*

We use (1) .... to talk about an object, person, thing or place in general terms. We often use (2) .... when someone or something is mentioned for the first time. *It's a label.*

We use (3) .... to talk about a specific object, person, thing or place. We often use (4) .... when someone or something has already been mentioned in the text.

The label would identify him to those he met.

B Other uses of *the*

We also use *the*

- to talk about a thing, or group of things, that are unique in your world. *the moon* (it is the only one) *the internet, the sun*
- with a singular noun to talk about one object as an example of a group. (5) ....
- with *same*, superlative adjectives (e.g. *best*) and ordinal numbers (e.g. first, nineteenth). *the best example,* (6) ...., (7) ...., (8) ....
- with *north, south, east* and *west* to describe the position of something or someone. (9) ....

C No article

We use **no article** when we talk about a concept in general terms, and not a specific or unique example of that concept.

It can do mathematical calculations... (in general)

I found the mathematical calculations we did in class yesterday very difficult. (specific example)

Other examples where no article is necessary.

(10) .... (11) ....

See page 146 for grammar reference and more practice.

Speaking

1 a Look at the image. What does it show? Why do you think it was nominated for the list of 100 objects?

b 7.9 Listen to someone describing his object and compare your answer.

2 a Work in pairs. Think of an object you would like to nominate for the collection. You should choose an object that shows some particular aspect of your country, community or time.

b Present your object to the class. Tell them why you chose it and why you think it should be in the collection.

3 Vote on the three most interesting objects to add to the collection.

7.4 Functional language: Using vague language

Tune in

1 **a** Work in pairs. Think of different situations where you would give someone a present.

b Compare your answers with another pair and then with the rest of the class.

2 Look at your class list. Discuss the questions.

- When did you last receive a present? What was the occasion? What was the present? Did you like it?
- When did you last give a present? What did you give?
- Was it difficult to choose? Why/Why not? Do you think the person liked it?

3 **a** 7.10 Listen to two people talking about choosing a gift and answer the questions.

1 Who is the present for?
2 What's the occasion?
3 What presents do the two people decide to get?

b Listen again and make a list of the five suggestions that are made and rejected, and why.

Suggestions	Reason rejected
flowers	wants to give something different/ more personal

c Which suggestion is accepted in the end?

4 Work in pairs. Discuss the questions.

- Who do you find it difficult to buy presents for? Why? What do you usually get for them?
- Have you ever bought or received an 'experience' as a present?

Focus on language

5 Look at the expressions in bold in the extracts. Are they a) referring to a specific object? b) talking in general about a group of things or objects?

1 **something** for her, **something she can enjoy**
2 **something through the post**
3 **something different, something** a bit more personal
4 **some sort of** kitchen appliance
5 I can't buy her a painting or an ornament or **anything like that**
6 **stuff like** tickets to concerts
7 **something like** a dinner for two
8 or a day in a spa... **that kind of thing**

6 **a** Complete the sentences with ideas for presents.

1
A What would you like for your birthday?
B I'd like something different like a .... or a ....

2
A We really should get a thank-you present for the neighbours.
B Yes, you're right. I think we should get something small, just a token, maybe some sort of ....

3
A Have you got any ideas what I can buy for your sister for her birthday?
B She really loves ethnic stuff, you know, incense, ..., ..., that kind of thing.

b 7.11 Listen and compare your answers.

Stress

7.12 Listen to the extracts. Underline the main stress.
I'd like something different...
We should get something small...
... maybe some sort of cake.
She really loves ethnic stuff, you know incense, candles, ornaments, that kind of thing.
Listen again and repeat with the correct stress.

Over to you

7 Work in pairs. Look at the list of people and occasions. Choose three. Discuss what you think would be the best present for each one. Use the expressions in 5 and 6.

- your father's birthday
- a classmate is moving to a new town
- a thank-you present for a friend who helped you with your exams
- your grandparents' golden anniversary
- a present for your new-born niece or nephew
- a surprise present for someone you love

8 Report back on your decisions to the class. Which pair had the most original present ideas?

TUNE IN

1 Look at the images of two objects. Why do you think they could be important for their owners?

a

b

2 a 7.13 Listen and answer the questions.

1 Why is the object so important for the person?
2 How long have they had this object?

b Listen again and match the facts to the speaker.

1 The object has sentimental value.
2 It forms an essential part of their life.
3 It's relatively new.
4 It's embarrassing for the owner to talk about this object.
5 The object reassures the owner.

PREPARE FOR TASK

3 Look at the extracts from 7.13. Match expressions a–g to 1–3.

1 say that something is special
2 say that something is necessary
3 say that something has sentimental value

a I can't live without my glasses...
b ... they're an absolute necessity.
c It's terrible to be so dependent on something.
d It's not something valuable or precious or anything like that, but it has great sentimental value.
e ... it has some very special associations for me.
f It's like a reminder of home, something familiar amongst the unfamiliar.
g I know it's stupid, but there's something reassuring about having it with me.

4 a Think of an object that is important to you. Tick the reasons why.

- [ ] its sentimental value
- [ ] its financial value
- [ ] its age/history
- [ ] the service it provides for you
- [ ] its uniqueness – how difficult it is to replace
- [ ] the story attached to it

b Answer the questions and make notes.

- What is it? What does it look like?
- Do you have it with you in class?
- Did you buy it or did someone give it to you?
- How long have you had it?
- What do you do with it?
- Where do you keep it?
- What associations does it have for you?
- How would you feel if you lost it?

TASK

5 Work in pairs. Describe your important object to your partner. Use your notes from 4a and b.

I can't live without my laptop. It has so much information on it that I need. It's like part of me.

REPORT BACK

6 Listen to other students' stories about their objects. Which is the most interesting story? Do you have an object or a story similar to anybody else's?

➜ Go to Review C, Unit 7, p. 102 ➜ Go to Writing bank 4, p. 155

8 TELLING A DIFFERENT STORY

a

b

1 Work in pairs. Look at the images. What form of popular culture is shown in each? Do they have positive or negative associations for you?

2 Read two opinions about the images. Which text makes these points? In some cases more than one answer may be possible.

1 it can be a way to meet people
2 it is more creative than people imagine
3 both men and women enjoy it
4 it's a way to express your identity
5 you don't need to associate it with violence

3 Find words in the texts which mean *story*. Complete A in the KEY VOCABULARY PANEL.

1

The media's version of this sport is typical – male football fans in a battle with the police. But not all men are hooligans, and women love and enjoy football too! It brings people together, it breaks down barriers but you don't hear media reports about that.

2

My favourite music is hip hop. There's a myth that only gangs listen to it, it's racist and sexist, the lyrics are violent. That's not true. This image shows the other side. All sorts of people rap about things that are important to them, about who they are. The raps are like anecdotes, personal tales of what life is like, and that can be very creative.

4 **a** 8.1 Listen to two different opinions about football and hip hop. Does each person a) agree? b) partly agree with the opinions expressed in the texts?

b Listen again. What points do they make? Note down the two expressions with *story* that you hear. What do you think they mean?

5 Complete B in the KEY VOCABULARY PANEL.

6 Work in pairs. Discuss the questions.

- Are either of these examples of popular culture important in your life? If yes, in what way? If no, which do you like or consider important? Why?
- Do you agree with the opinions expressed here? Why/ Why not? Give examples from your personal experience.

KEY VOCABULARY

Storytelling

A Types of story

- Complete the sentences with the words in the box. You will need to use the plural in some cases. Use a dictionary to help you.

anecdote myth report tale version

1 A newspaper can have stories or .... on any subject.
2 His .... of events was different from mine.
3 Some people are very entertaining, they can tell good jokes and ....
4 A .... is a story that people wrongly believe to be true.
5 Another word for a traditional story; we can read fairy .... or folk ...., for example.

NOTICE *SAY & TELL*

Notice how we use *say* and *tell*.

She said that she loved stories.

I told him that I loved stories.

Say is followed directly by the words that were spoken.

Tell is followed by the person who is listening.

Note: *I told him.* NOT *I told ~~to~~ him.*

B Expressions with *story*

- Match the words in **bold** with the synonyms in the box. Think about the context.

authorised complicated main real well-known

1 It's moving because it's based on a **true** story.
2 That's a **familiar** story. How many times have we heard this tragedy repeat itself?
3 That's the **official** version, but nobody knows what really happened that night.
4 The **top** story today is football violence.
5 Sorry, it's a **long** story, you'd better not hear it now.

- In what context do you think you would see or hear these sentences?

- PRACTISE REPORTED SPEECH
- TALK ABOUT STEREOTYPICAL IMAGES

a

b

READING

1 Work in pairs. Look at images a–c and answer the questions.

- Where are they from? What do they show?
- What do they tell you about this place?
- Do you think they tell you the whole story? Why/Why not?

2 **a** Look at the blog title and the image, and read the first paragraph of the blog post. Answer the questions.

1 What is the place in the image?
2 What is the blog post about?

b Read the rest of the blog post. Answer the questions.

1 Who was Rosa?
2 What did the writer learn when she visited Rosa's village?
3 In what way did she have a similar experience in the United States?
4 What did her experience in the United States teach her?

3 Read the blog post again. Mark the statements true (T) or false (F). Correct the false statements.

1 The writer came from a poor family.
2 Rosa lived in a poor village.
3 English isn't spoken in Kenya.
4 The writer knew a lot about the United States before she went there.
5 The writer learned very little about the United States while she was there.
6 The writer believes that every country has one story to tell.

4 Work in small groups. Discuss the questions at the end of the blog post. Share your answers with the class.

Not the whole story

I was born and brought up in Kenya, in a happy, wealthy family. We had servants to look after us and we had everything we could ever want or need. As a child I took all this for granted. I didn't even know there was another side to the story. **Read more**.

One of our servants was called was Rosa. When she first came to live with us, we were both eight. When she wasn't working, we used to spend hours playing together. She was my best friend. My mother told me that she came from a very poor family. But it wasn't until I visited her family in their village three or four years later that I realised exactly what poor meant.

Her house was a simple hut, one room shared by the whole family. Their lives were very simple, too. For the first time in my life I saw people who had less than me. For a moment I was an outsider, like a curious tourist with a camera. It was like visiting a new world. Once I got over that initial shock, what really stayed with me wasn't the poverty, but the smiles and the warm welcome. And my view of my home, of my country, of Africa, had changed.

When I went to study at university in the United States, the opposite happened. Most of the people I met knew just one story about Africa: a story of poverty and war. They were surprised by my clothes and my taste in music. They asked me where I had learned to speak English so well. When I explained that it was my first language, they said they didn't know that English was spoken in Africa. I told them that in Kenya, English was an official language. When they asked if they could see photos of Africa, I showed them photos of my home and my family and my school. I told them about my best friend Rosa, too. I wanted them to know that Kenya has a thousand truths, a thousand stories to tell.

And I realised that I was just as guilty. Before I arrived in the United States, I had only known one story, fed by images from Hollywood, showing beautiful people leading beautiful lives. When I arrived, I saw so many other stories – needy people living on the street, high unemployment, incredible crime rates, and beautiful landscapes that took my breath away. It reminded me that we have to try and see all the different stories that every country has to tell.

What about you? What about your country? Does the world only see one side of the story of where you come from? If so, what is that story? How would you like people to see your culture?

C

Reported speech

To report and summarise what someone said in the past we use a past reporting verb (*said, told, asked*). We often report the words in a past tense, too.

'People like Rosa have nothing,' my mother said.
→ *My mother told me that people like Rosa had nothing.*

Notice how the verbs change from present to past.

'I don't know.' → *She said that she* (1) .... *know.*
'I can read.' → *He told me that he* (2) .... *read.*
'I've never visited New York' → *I explained that I* (3) .... *never visited New York.*
'I'm studying Literature.' → *I told them that I* (4) .... *studying Literature.*

To report a question, we use the word order of an affirmative sentence. Do not use a question mark at the end of the sentence.

'What language do you speak in Kenya?' → *She asked me what language we* (5) .... *in Kenya. NOT She asked me what language ~~did we speak~~ in Kenya?*

To report a *yes/no* question, use *if*.

'Is English the official language in Kenya?'
→ *She asked me if English* (6) .... *the official language in Kenya.*

See page 147 for grammar reference and more practice.

Pronunciation: word stress – three- and four-syllable words

1 **a** Match the words in the box to the stress patterns.

beautiful curious incredible initial official
opposite outsider poverty

Ooo *beautiful*
oOo
oOoo

b 8.2 Listen, check and repeat.

Grammar

1 **a** Look at the extracts from Reading 2a. Who do the pronouns and possessives refer to?

1 My mother told **me** that **she** came from a poor family.
2 **They** asked me where I had learned to speak English so well.
3 When **they** asked if they could see photos of Africa,...

b Look again at the extracts. Write the actual words you think the person used.

1 'She comes *from a poor family*.'
2 'Where did ....?'
3 'Can I ....?'

2 Look again at the extracts in 1a and the sentences you wrote in 1b. Notice how the verbs change tense. Complete 1–6 in the Grammar panel with a verb in the past.

3 Work in pairs. Report the statements and questions.

1 'I've never been to Africa.' She told me that she...
2 'I love watching films in other languages.' He said that he...
3 'Have you travelled a lot?' He asked me...
4 'Where did you learn to speak English?' She asked him...
5 'Why are you studying English?' They asked her...

4 Work in pairs. Ask and answer questions 3–5 in 3. Write out your partner's answers as reported speech. Share your answers with the class.

Speaking

1 **a** Work in pairs. Think of five positive, non-stereotypical images of your country.

b Choose the one image you like most. Prepare to present it to the class. Explain what it shows about your country and why you think it is both representative and positive.

This is a significant image because...
What I like about this one is...

2 **a** Present your choice to the class. Use the language to help you.

We chose this image because...
We feel it gives a really positive image because...
It shows...
It represents...
We think it's the best image because...

b Have a class vote on the three best images (you cannot vote for your own image).

- PRACTISE REPORTING REQUESTS & INSTRUCTIONS
- TALK ABOUT ALTERNATIVE TOURS

b

SPEAKING & VOCABULARY: travel activities

1 a Look at the images. Discuss the questions.

- Which image shows independent travellers and which shows a guided tour?
- Do you prefer to go on organised trips or to travel independently? Why?

b Look at the words in the box. Answer the questions. Use a dictionary to help you.

1 Which activities do you associate most with
  a an organised holiday or trip?
  b independent travel?
2 Can you add any more activities to the box?
3 Which activities do you enjoy most when you're on holiday?

taking a guided tour
taking a trip on a tour bus
bargain-hunting
enjoying the atmosphere
exploring the backstreets
people-watching
sight-seeing
window-shopping

LISTENING

1 8.3 Listen to a podcast from Abdou, a Moroccan visitor to London. Answer the questions.

1 How long has he been in London?
2 What has he done so far?
3 What was so special about today?

2 a Look at the list of activities. Which two activities did Abdou not mention?

1 a ride on an open-top bus
2 seeing Big Ben and the Houses of Parliament
3 going on a guided tour of the Tate Gallery
4 taking it easy over coffee
5 window-shopping on Oxford Street
6 bargain-hunting in Camden Market
7 eating some Indian food
8 a walking tour with *Unseen Tours*

b Listen again and check your answers. Which did he think was the most interesting?

3 a 8.4 Listen to the second part of the podcast where Abdou tells us more about the *Unseen Tours*. Make notes about

1 the stories that the guides told them.
2 the advice that the guides gave them.
3 how Abdou felt at the end of the tour.

b Compare your answers with a partner. Would you like to go on an *Unseen Tour* of London? Why/Why not?

Grammar

1 a Match 1–6 to a–f to make sentences.

1 They told us to
2 We asked them to
3 They told us how to
4 They told us where to
5 We asked
6 They told us

a avoid pickpockets.
b bring a camera.
c get the best cup of tea.
d show us where they slept.
e so many questions.
f their personal stories.

b Look again at the sentences in 1a. Which are talking about
a) making a request?
b) giving instructions?
c) giving information or advice?
Complete 1–4 in the Grammar panel.

2 Look at the reported statements. What do you think were the actual words the people said?

1 She told me to come back tomorrow.
2 They told us not to worry about pickpockets.
3 They asked us not to eat in the church.
4 They told us how to get to the station.
5 They told us where to catch a taxi.
6 He asked me to pay $5.

3 Report what was said using *ask* or *tell* + person + (*not*) *to* + infinitive.

1 'Can you please be quiet?'
2 'Turn left at the end of this road.'
3 'This is the best pizza place in town.'
4 'Please don't close the door.'
5 'Could you please not use your mobile phones during the tour?'
6 'This is the quickest way to get into town.'

4 Think of three requests that you have made today. Report them using *ask* + *to* + infinitive.

I asked my son to brush his teeth.

5 a Think of the last time someone gave you some orders or instructions. Report them using *tell* + infinitive.

My workmate told me how to use the photocopier.

b Work in pairs. Compare your sentences. Explain the context for each one.

Reporting requests & instructions

We use ***ask*** **+ person + *(not) to*** + **infinitive** to report [1] requests / instructions.

'Can you show us where you sleep?' →
We asked the guides to show us where they slept.
'Please don't take photos.' →
They asked us not to take photos.

We use ***tell*** **+ person + *(not) to*** + infinitive to report [2] requests / instructions.

'Bring a camera!' →
They told us to bring a camera.
'Please don't be late.' →
They told us not to be late.

We can also use ***tell*** **+ person + question word + *to*** + infinitive to report information or advice.

They told us [3] .... *to avoid pickpockets.*
They told us [4] .... *to get the best cup of tea.*

See page 147 for grammar reference and more practice.

Speaking

1 Work in pairs. Discuss the questions.

- Are there any walking tours or bus tours for visitors and tourists in your town?
- If yes, have you ever been on one?
- What do they usually show?

2 a You are going to organise an alternative tour of your town. The aim is to show a different side of your town, as the *Unseen Tours* do in London. Look at the questions and make notes.

- What part of the town or city would you choose? Why?
- How long would the tour last?
- Would it be a walking tour or a bus tour?
- Where would it begin and end?
- Who would the guides be?
- What stories would they tell?
- How much would you ask people to pay?

We could do a guided tour of the port and fish market... most tourists don't see that and it's really interesting.

b Compare your answers with a partner. Then present your tours to the class.

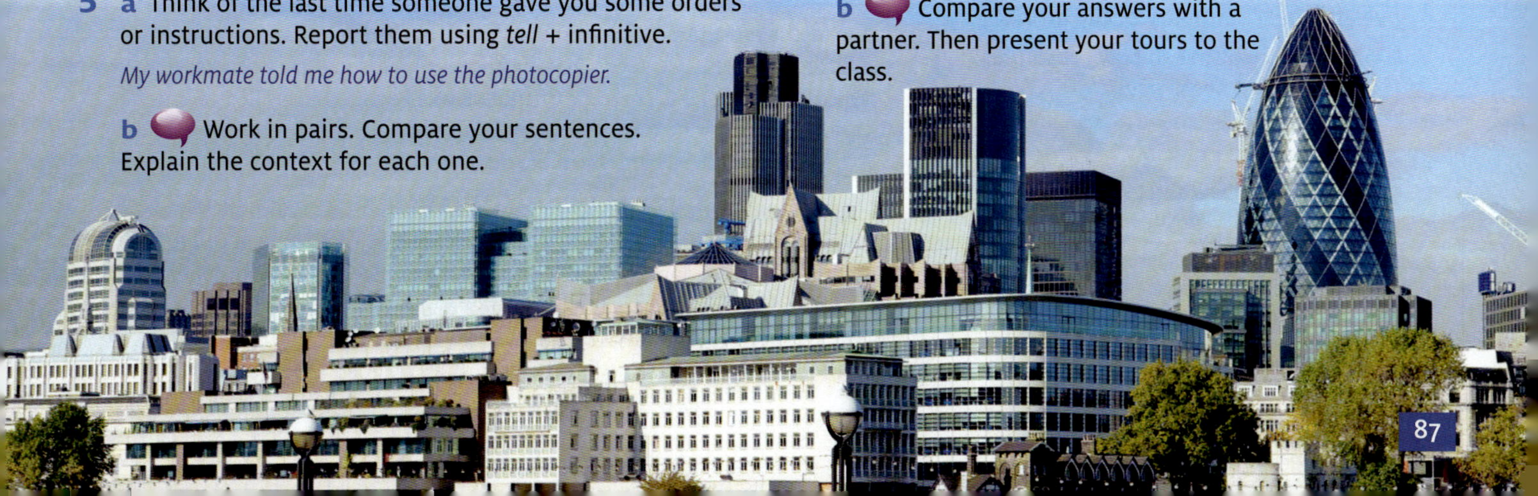

a

b

READING

1 Look at photos a and b and answer the questions.

1 What do the photos show?
2 What is the difference between them?
3 Who do you think took the photos, a professional news photographer or person standing nearby? Why?

2 **a** Photo b was taken by a citizen journalist. What is the difference between a citizen journalist and a professional journalist? Read the article and check your answer.

b Who do you think wrote the article? Who does 'we' refer to?

3 Read the article again. Which sentence gives the best summary of the article?

1 Citizen journalism can now substitute for traditional news media.
2 Citizen journalists have a new and important role in society.
3 Citizen journalism provides the best news in today's world.

When the Buncefield oil depot near North London blew up, the BBC received more than 6,500 emails and **tweets** from the general public that contained shots and video **footage** of the fire. The first arrived at 6.19 a.m. just minutes after the explosion happened. This was a long time before the police, ambulances and fire engines arrived, and of course the journalists, too.

Reporting like this shows that we now have a new role in society. As amateurs, we can publish information when and where we like. We can send our images to the press or publish them ourselves on some of the 150 million blogs that now exist. The information that we provide may be better and quicker than that of our professional colleagues. We can supplement and compare what we get from conventional media sources with other voices, telling different stories.

One of the most famous examples of this was the Egyptian uprising in 2011. Bloggers, tweeters, amateur photographers and **eye-witnesses** provided unique **news coverage** of the event. The videos travelled around the world. The **clips** were not professional, but they produced more vivid and immediate broadcasts and **breaking news**.

That doesn't mean the end of conventional journalism, as Jimmy Wales, the founder of Wikipedia said: 'Everybody makes jokes, but we still need professional comedians'. That's true, we can't replace news media, but we can offer a fresh alternative that they can't ignore. We can collaborate and write the news together. Now, they have to listen to our side of the story.

4 Choose the correct answer to complete the sentences.

1 The amateur images of the Buncefield explosion were important because they were
   a) the best images the press had.
   b) the first ones that arrived.
   c) shocking and unexpected.
2 The author suggests that citizen journalists
   a) don't realise their potential.
   b) have many possibilities to publish their work.
   c) have to compete with the professionals.
3 The amateur footage from the Egyptian uprising was powerful because
   a) everything seemed more real and spontaneous.
   b) there weren't any other images available.
   c) everybody in the world watched it.
4 Citizen journalism is
   a) not changing the way news is reported.
   b) replacing old ways of presenting information.
   c) all about collaborating with others.

5 Work in small groups. Discuss the questions.

- Do you agree that citizen journalists play an important role?
- Where would you go to find details of the latest news story? Why?

VOCABULARY: the media

1 a Match the media words in **bold** in the text in READING 2a to definitions 1–6.

1 film of a particular subject or event
2 short part of film, programme or news story
3 people who have seen something happen (often a crime)
4 news about an event, it can also refer to the amount of attention given to something
5 a news story which is often unexpected and develops quickly
6 short messages sent via Twitter

b Choose three words from 1a to complete the sentences. Continue the sentences to make them true for you.

1 I watched a .... of my favourite group on YouTube, it was...
2 Did you see the .... just now on TV? It was about...
3 I don't like the .... on that channel. I prefer to watch...

LISTENING & SPEAKING

1 a 8.5 Listen to two people talking about the article. What example of citizen journalism do they discuss?

b Listen again. Make notes on the differences between the news reported on the newspaper website and the news on Twitter. Which did the speakers think was more effective? Why?

2 a Complete the extracts from 1a with the words and expressions in the box.

first thing internet minute-by-minute reports story

1 the ....I heard was from my flatmate
2 we looked it up on the ....
3 There was a story there, with a photo and some eye-witness ....
4 the .... said there were 40 people stuck on the roof
5 it was fascinating... so much detail, and a .... commentary

b Read transcript 8.5 on page 165 and check your answers. Look again at the extracts in 2a. Underline all the language connected to news.

3 a Work in pairs. Think of a story that has been in the news recently. It could be local, national or international. Answer the questions.

- What happened?
- How did you first hear of it?
- Did you follow it closely? Why/Why not? If yes, how?

b Report back on your discussion to the class. Did anyone else discuss the same story?

4 a Work in pairs. Imagine that one of you was an eye-witness to the story. Decide exactly what the role of the eye-witness was.

b Act out an interview between a news reporter and the eye-witness.

5 Report back to the class on the interview.

8.4 Functional language: Phone messages

Tune in

1 a 8.6 Look at the images and listen to three phone conversations. Match conversations 1–3 to the topics a–c.

a travel problems
b work arrangements
c time to meet

b Listen again. What is the message in each case? Which person is able to speak to a real person?

Focus on language

2 a Work in pairs. Match expressions a–h to conversations 1–3 from 1a.

a It's Marc here.
b Who's speaking?
c Hold the line, please.
d Hi, this is Damian.
e Do you want me to take a message?
f Can I speak to Peter Moorcroft, please?
g Could you ask him to call me, please?
h ... do you think you could call Petra?

b Which expressions are used to

i introduce yourself? ....
ii ask to speak to someone? ....
iii ask for the caller's name? ....
iv ask somebody to wait? ....
v take a message? ....
vi leave a message? ....
vii make a request? ....

3 Work in pairs. Act out conversation 1 in 1a. Student A, you are the caller. Student B, answer the phone and take a message.

4 Read transcript 8.6 on page 165. What do you think will happen next in each conversation?

5 a 8.7 Listen to what happened next. Is it the same as you imagined in 4? Why/Why not?

b Listen again and complete the exchanges.

1 Natalie Martin has just phoned. She told me that .... an important file. Can you .... that you received it okay?
2 Marc just called. He said he .... tonight... so don't wait for him at the airport.
3 I told you that .... 5.15.

"Stress"

8.8 Listen to the extracts from 8.6 and 8.7. Underline the stressed words. Why does the speaker choose to stress these words?

I told you that we were meeting at 5.15... not 4.15...
Tell her not to wait for me at the airport.

Listen again and repeat with the correct emphasis.

6 a Work in groups of three. Read the instructions and write the three conversations.

1 Giovanni phones Claire to confirm their meeting for tomorrow at 11.30 a.m. Claire is not in. He has to leave a message with her flatmate, Monica.
2 Claire comes home from work and Monica tells her that Giovanni has called and passes on the message.
3 Claire calls Giovanni.

b Act out the conversations.

Student A, you are Giovanni.
Student B, you are Monica.
Student C, you are Claire.

Over to you

7 a Work in a new group of three. Act out three conversations. Turn to page 160 and follow the instructions.

b Check that the original message got through correctly to student C.

8 Discuss the questions with your classmates.

- When was the last time you had to leave a message on the phone? Who was it for? What was it about?
- Do you ever need to speak in English on the phone?
- If yes, who do you speak to and what about? If not, who do you think you might need to talk to in the future?

a

b

c

d

TUNE IN

1 **a** Look at the images of people taking notes. Where are they? What do you think they are taking notes about?

b In what other situations do you often take notes? Do you take notes on paper or use another device? Why?

2 **a** 8.9 Listen to a short phone conversation between two people organising a business meeting. What is the relationship between the two people? Who is taking the notes?

b Listen again and correct the notes.

Meeting 10 Dec

Tasks:

1 prepare & send agenda by tomorrow a.m.
2 ask Sue for publicity material
3 Cocktail party (15 max.) – decide on caterers

Other business:

Call de Freitas re shipment Arg. asap

PREPARE FOR TASK

3 **a** Look again at the notes in 2b. Underline examples of

1 abbreviations
2 symbols
3 headings/subheadings
4 numbering

b What do the abbreviations mean?

4 **a** In small groups, look at the abbreviations and symbols. What do you think they refer to?

etc	b4	e.g.	km	≠
☺	+/–	tel.	✖	∴
&	✓	p.m.	w/	re

b Look at a short note. Write out the information in full sentences.

Prof. Thomas Mankowitz (TM) Office Meeting Tues. 21st @2pm → *There was a meeting on Tuesday 21st at two in the afternoon.*

Present: TM, PhD students: Dave, Antonia & Jamal:

1 deliver exam results b4 end of week (TM)
2 organise grant application asap (→ D)
3 interviews w/ new candidates, etc. (→ J)
4 plan next meeting & book restaurant (→ A)

TASK

5 8.10 Listen to another phone conversation between a boss and an employee. Imagine that you are the employee. Take notes on what you have to do. Remember to use the suggestions in 3a and 4a.

REPORT BACK

6 Work in pairs. Compare your notes. What is the difference between them? Look at other sets of notes from your classmates. Who do you think wrote the best/clearest notes? Why?

➔ Go to Review C, Unit 8, p. 103

9 RULES AND REGULATIONS

1 **a** Work in pairs. Look at the signs and answer the questions.

- What do the signs have in common?
- What exactly is each one telling us?
- Where would you expect to see these signs?
- Why do you think the action is being prohibited in each case?

b Complete A and B in the KEY VOCABULARY PANEL.

2 9.1 Listen to two people talking about two different signs and answer the questions.

1 Where was each sign?
2 Do the people think they are
a) a good idea? b) a bad idea?

3 Listen again and draw the signs the people saw.

4 **a** Work in pairs. Look at the signs again and discuss the questions.

- Which actions are **illegal** where you live?
- Which actions are simply **irresponsible**?
- Which signs would be **unusual** where you live? Why?
- Do you think any of the signs are **unnecessary**?

b Look at the adjectives in **bold** in 4a and complete C in the KEY VOCABULARY PANEL.

5 **a** Complete D in the KEY VOCABULARY PANEL.

b Work in pairs. Do you think there are a lot of rules where you live? Do you agree with the rules?

KEY VOCABULARY

Permission & prohibition

A Actions

- Find actions in the box to describe each of the signs. Which two actions are not represented?

bathing carrying firearms disturbing the wildlife
feeding the pigeons flash photography
skating or scooting trespassing
using a mobile phone walking through a building site
wearing a helmet wheelchair access

- What signs could you use to show that the two extra actions are prohibited?

B Public places & prepositions of place

- Match signs a–i to the most likely places 1–8 where you might see them. There may be more than one answer.

1 at the entrance to a bar or restaurant
2 in a square or a park in the middle of a town
3 in a courthouse
4 on the banks of a river
5 on the gates of a building site
6 at a viewpoint
7 at the bottom of an escalator
8 on a door

- Underline the prepositions *in*, *at* and *on*. What prepositions do you use in your language?

C Negative prefixes

- Complete the chart with the words in the box.

common legal legible logical necessary
possible relevant responsible usual

il-	im-	ir-	un-

D Talking about prohibitions & obligations

- Find four pairs of synonyms in the box. Use a dictionary to help you.

allowed banned compulsory limited obligatory
permitted prohibited restricted

- Think of two actions to match each pair of synonyms.

banned/prohibited: riding a motorbike without a helmet

■ PRACTISE PRESENT PERMISSION, PROHIBITION & OBLIGATION
■ TALK ABOUT INTERNET RESTRICTIONS

SPEAKING & VOCABULARY: internet

1 a Work in pairs. Match the words and expressions in the word cloud to the questions.

1 How and where do you usually access the internet?
2 What do you use the internet for?

chattingwithfriends athome 4G atschool cybercafé 3G atwork doingschoolprojects formalcorrespondence gettingthefootballscores inclass makingtravelarrangements inmeetings onmyPC shopping onthephone sharingphotos watchingTV wifi onmylaptop onthebus keepingupwiththenews downloadingmusic

b Underline all the prepositions used in the answers to question 1. What prepositions do you use in your language? What do you notice about the verbs in the answers to question 2?

2 a Work in pairs. Ask and answer the questions in 1a. Add your answers to the lists in 1a if they are not already included.

I usually use my laptop. My mobile doesn't have internet access. I use the internet for news, shopping and downloading music.

b Share your answers with the rest of the class. How do most people in the class usually connect with the internet? What are the most common uses?

LISTENING

1 a 9.2 Listen to two people discussing internet restrictions at their school. Who is speaking each time: a teacher or a student? Are they talking about the same school?

b Listen again. Who says the following statements?

	Speaker 1	Speaker 2
1 Internet access is possible on the school computers.	✓	✓
2 There are some restrictions to internet use.		
3 Mobile phones are generally not allowed in class.		
4 Mobile phones are often used in lessons.		
5 Mobile phones can be distracting.		
6 It's important to know about the dangers of using the internet.		

2 a Look at the words in the box. How do they relate to the issues discussed by the two speakers?

banned blocked chatrooms cyber-bullying firewall safety security

b Read transcript 9.2 on page 165 and check.

3 a Work in small groups. Discuss the questions.

- What have your experiences, or those of people you know, been of using the internet for school, further studies or training? In what way can it help?
- Do you think restrictions can protect young people from the potential dangers of the internet? Why/Why not?

b Report back on your discussion to the class.

GRAMMAR

1 **a** Complete the extracts with words from the box. Some words are repeated.

chatrooms computers internet laptops mobile phones music sites WiFi

1 We have .... that we **can** use to access the internet.
2 We **can't** access YouTube or Facebook and a lot of .... and .... are blocked.
3 Students **aren't allowed to** access .... or chatrooms on the school ....
4 Students **are allowed to** bring their .... to class.
5 We **don't have to** rely on the school ...., which isn't always very efficient!
6 They **mustn't** misuse the ....
7 They **have to** learn about good and bad .... use – and I think that's something we really **must** help them with.
8 Our general studies teacher **lets us use** our .... to access sites that are blocked on the computers.
9 Most of the teachers hate ....! They **make us switch them off** as soon as we enter the class.

b Match each sentence in 1a to functions a–d.

a permission b prohibition c obligation d lack of obligation

2 Complete 1–7 in the GRAMMAR PANEL with some of the verbs in bold in 1a.

3 **a** Choose the correct options to complete the sentences. Where do you think you might find these signs?

1 All residents *must / mustn't* sign in and out.

2 Visitors *can / can't* park their cars in the car park, but only if they are in possession of a temporary permit.

3 Owners of bicycles and motorbikes *mustn't / don't have to* have a permit.

4 Children *don't have to / must not* play in this area.

5 All dogs *can / must* be kept on a lead.

6 Customers *cannot / have to* consume their own food on the premises.

b Think of a sign you have seen recently. Write the text of the sign in English. Show it to a partner. Can they guess where you saw the sign?

4 **a** Rewrite the sentences with *make* or *let*.

1 We're allowed to use our phones in class.
They ....
2 I can't stay out after 11 p.m. at the weekends.
They don't ....
3 I sometimes have to work extra hours in the evening.
They sometimes ....
4 We don't usually have to pay to use the tennis courts.
They don't usually ....

b Who do you think *they* refers to in each sentence?

5 Write three sentences about yourself using *they* and *make* or *let*. Read them to the class. Can your classmates guess who *they* refers to?

PERMISSION, PROHIBITION & OBLIGATION (1): PRESENT

A Modal verbs & phrases

Permission	Prohibition	Obligation	Lack of obligation
(1) ...., is/are allowed to	mustn't, (2) ...., isn't/aren't (3)	must, (4)	(5) ....

We usually use ***must*** on signs or when giving direct orders. We tend to use ***have to*** to talk about obligations in general.

B *Make/let* + object + infinitive

We use ***make*** to talk about obligation.
(6) ....

We use ***let*** to talk about permission and prohibition.
(7) ....

They don't let us use our mobile phones in class.

See page 148 for grammar reference and more practice.

PRONUNCIATION: *are / aren't* in permissions and prohibitions

1 **a** 9.3 Listen to the sentences. Notice the pronunciation of *are/aren't*. Is the word stressed in the affirmative sentence or in the negative sentence? Why?

Students **are** allowed to bring their phones to school, but they **aren't** allowed to bring them to class.

b Listen again and repeat.

2 **a** 9.4 Listen to six more sentences. Write them down.

b Compare your answers with a partner. Are any of these sentences true for where you live? Do you know of anywhere where they might be true?

- Practise past permission, prohibition & obligation
- Talk about laws

a

b

Speaking & Listening

1 **a** Work in pairs. Where would you expect to see these two signs? Write two lists.

b Compare your lists with the rest of the class.

2 **a** Match the words in the box to the signs. Use a dictionary to help you.

> a smoking ban   designated smoking area   heavy fines   non-smokers   smoke-free zone   smokers   smokers welcome

b Work in small groups. Discuss the questions.

- What exactly are the smoking laws in your country?
- When did they last change?
- Were people happy about the change?

3 9.5 Listen to a short news story. What is the link between the man in the photo and the signs?

4 **a** Listen again and make notes about

- conditions under the old law
- conditions under the new law
- the bar owner's protest
- the final result.

b Work in pairs. Compare your notes.

5 **a** Are the sentences true or false?

1 Under the old law larger bars and restaurants could choose whether to be smoking or non-smoking.
2 Under the new law all bars and restaurants have to follow a non-smoking policy.
3 Smoking has also been banned in children's parks.
4 You can still smoke at the entrance to schools and hospitals.
5 The bar and restaurant owner's customers didn't support him in his protest.
6 Neighbouring bars and restaurants sympathised with his problem.
7 The authorities closed his restaurant.
8 The bar and restaurant owner stopped his protest immediately.

b Read transcript 9.5 on page 166 and check.

6 Look at the extracts from transcript 9.5. Explain the words and phrases in **bold**.

1 Bars, restaurants and cafés are **coming to terms with** the new smoking ban.
2 Some **grumbled** and complained, but on the whole it was seen as being inevitable.
3 He refused to accept that he wasn't allowed to choose what to do in his own **establishment**.
4 He decided to **make a stand against** the new law.
5 He claimed that banning smoking would **ruin his business**.
6 The rebel bar and restaurant-owner **stuck to his guns**.

7 Work in pairs. Do you have any sympathy for the bar owner? Why/Why not? Are there any laws in your country that you disagree with? How would you like to change them?

Grammar

1 **a** Look at the statements. Which apply to a) the new law? b) the old law?

1 Small establishments **could** choose whether to be smoking or non-smoking.
2 Larger establishments **had to** designate a special, sealed-off area for smokers.
3 Bars **weren't allowed to** choose.
4 The smoking area **couldn't** be more than one third of the total area available.
5 Smoking **was allowed** in this area.
6 Customers **didn't have to** go outside to smoke.
7 Everybody **had to** go out on the street to smoke.

b Complete 1–4 in the Grammar panel with some of the verbs in **bold** in 1a.

2 **a** Look at the sentence from transcript 9.5. What are the verbs in **bold** describing? Match them to two of the categories in the chart in A in the Grammar panel.

He **let** his customers continue to smoke over their food and **didn't make** them stand out in the street.

b Write the first verb in 2a in the negative form and the second verb in the affirmative form. How does this change their meaning? Complete 5–8 in the Grammar panel with examples.

3 **a** Choose the correct options to complete the text.

My parents were very strict. When we came home from school we (1)*had to / could* take our shoes off at the door and change out of our uniforms so as not to get them dirty. Then we (2)*had to / made* do our homework. We (3)*couldn't / were allowed to* go out to play until we'd finished. We were (4)*only allowed to / only let us* watch half an hour's TV a night, and we (5)*didn't have to / had to* take it in turns to choose which programme to watch. They (6)*let / made* us watch an extra hour on Saturdays, but only if we had done all our chores. I (7)*could / had to* wash the car and they (8)*let / made* my brother cut the grass and clean the windows. We (9)*didn't have to / were allowed to* do any chores on Sunday, but my mother always (10)*let / made* us sit and read for at least an hour.

b Work in pairs. Compare your answers. Were any of these rules true for you when you were younger? What rules did you have to follow?

We didn't have to do chores, somebody came to clean the house...

Permission, prohibition & obligation (2): past

A Modal verbs & phrases

Permission	Prohibition	Obligation	Lack of obligation
(1) ...., was/were allowed to	couldn't, wasn't/ (2) .... allowed to	(3)	(4) .... have to

B *Make* & *let* in the past

We use ***made*** to talk about obligation.
(5) ....

We use ***didn't make*** to talk about lack of obligation.
(6) ....

We use ***let*** to talk about permission.
(7) ....

We use ***didn't let*** to talk about prohibition.
(8) ....

See page 148 for grammar reference and more practice.

Vocabulary: verbs with *law*

1 Match the verbs that combine with *law* to the people who do them: general public, politicians, the police.

break challenge change/amend enforce introduce make make a stand against obey pass

2 **a** Complete the gaps with the best verbs from 1.

1 It was hard for the police to .... the law at first.
2 Politicians .... many laws that we don't find out about.
3 It's not always easy to .... a law you don't like, but in the end you have to .... it.

b What laws would match descriptions 1–3?

Speaking

1 **a** 9.6 Listen to a short news report. What law has been changed? How has it changed? Why? Has the change been popular?

b Work in pairs. Compare your answers. Would the change be popular in your country?

2 Work in small groups. Think about a law that has changed recently in your country or community. What was the law before? And now? Do you agree with it?

3 What new laws would you like to introduce? Why? Make notes on your ideas. Report back to the rest of the class. Which is the most popular law? Why?

■ Practise talking about ability
■ Talk about mobility

a

b

c

d

Speaking

1 **a** Look at the images and answer the questions.

- What do the images have in common?
- Where do you think these facilities are?

b Match captions 1–4 from a government brochure on assisting people with mobility problems to images a–d.

1. Lifts from the streets are now in operation in most stations.
2. Temporary facilities are available, some are wheelchair accessible.
3. Special seats can lower disabled people into the pool.
4. Ring the bell if you want the driver to lower the ramp.

2 **a** In your daily routine, how many of the facilities in 1a do you see? Can you think of other places which have access for people with mobility problems?

There are usually special seats in theatres and cinemas.

b What other facilities can help disabled people live a normal life? Consider at work/free-time activities/sports/routine.

Some disabled people can drive with specially adapted scooters.

Reading

1 Look at images e–f. What solutions are they offering to problems of disabled access? Read anecdotes 1–2 and check your answers.

e

f

1 Rachel

I couldn't go to the beach before because there were few with disabled facilities or wheelchair access. I could only ride on pavements and flat surfaces. But now a family business in Spain has come up with a solution and my life has really been transformed. You can see it here in the photo... yes, that blue and yellow machine is a wheelchair carrier. It can help me to get to places I couldn't dream of going to before – beaches, dunes or footpaths in parks. It's based on a pretty simple principle – caterpillar tracks. Those are tracks that you see on a tank or a bulldozer. They're very strong, they can go anywhere. Now what the company has been able to do is adapt the tracks to power a simple wheelchair carrier. It moves at walking pace and is guided by someone walking alongside on foot. I can go for walks along the beach with my friends and family now and that's great. Two ramps extend out in front so we can lower the wheelchair to the ground or lift it onto the vehicle on our own without any additional assistance needed.

2 Ryuichi

Travelling with my brother by plane is difficult sometimes. Once, the airline lost his wheelchair and now we insist that he travels with his own wheelchair at all times. But the other day, we were travelling to Paris and the airline authorities told him that because of new security regulations he couldn't take his own chair on the plane. They said he had to use one from the airport. Just imagine, taking away somebody's chair – it's like taking away your legs or something. In the end, we managed to convince the authorities that he could travel with his own wheelchair to the plane, but that meant we couldn't go through the normal security channel. We had to put the chair through a special, extra large security scanner. I couldn't understand it, but we had to cross to the other side of the airport to get to a much larger scanner which they use to scan the containers transporting animals. So, in the end, my brother succeeded in boarding the plane with his own chair, but only after being scanned with everybody else's pets. We were relieved, but it was really humiliating.

2 Read the anecdotes in 1 again and answer the questions.

1 Why couldn't Rachel go to the beach?
2 How does the carrier work?
3 How does the wheelchair come off the carrier?
4 Whose wheelchair did Ryuichi's brother use on his Paris trip?
5 Why did they have to use a different scanner?
6 How did they feel about the experience?

3 Match 1–5 to a–e to make collocations.

1 airline	a access
2 security	b facilities
3 family	c business
4 disabled	d regulations
5 wheelchair	e authorities

NOTICE *ON MY OWN*

We use the expression *on* + possessive pronoun + *own* to mean *alone, with no help or assistance*.

I can ride the bike on my own. She can ride it on her own.

We can also use *by myself* as an alternative.

GRAMMAR

1 a Look at the extracts from READING 1 and think back to the anecdote. What does the pronoun in **bold** refer to in each case?

1 You *can* see **it** here in the photo...
2 **It** *can* help me get to places I *couldn't* dream of going to before...
3 **They're** very strong, they *can* go anywhere.
4 ... so **we** *can* lower the wheelchair to the ground...
5 I *couldn't* understand **it**...

b Look at the modal verbs in *italics*. Do they refer to the past or the present? Complete 1–2 in the GRAMMAR PANEL.

2 a Work in pairs. Complete the chart for your partner. Ask questions using *can* or *could*.

Could you (walk) when you were (one)?
Can you (play the guitar) now?

	1 year	5 years	10 years	Now
Talk				
Ride a bike				
Speak English				
Swim				
Play the guitar				
Cook an egg				

b Think of three more actions to add to the chart in 2a and continue the exercise. Can you think of anything you could do in the past that you can't do now?

3 Look again at the sentences from READING 1. Which sentence/s refer to general ability and which to the ability to do something at a specific time? Complete 3–5 in the GRAMMAR PANEL.

1 In the end, we **managed to** convince the authorities.
2 We **succeeded in** boarding the plane.
3 I **could** only ride on pavements and flat surfaces.

4 a Rewrite the sentences with the same meaning with the verbs in brackets.

1 I did all my homework this week. (manage)
2 I couldn't go to class. (manage)
3 I've passed all my exams this year. (succeed)
4 I still haven't found a good replacement for my old phone. (succeed)

b Are any of these sentences true for you?

TALKING ABOUT ABILITY (PAST & PRESENT)

A General ability

We use (1) .... to express ability in the present and (2) .... in the past.

The machine can help me get to places that I couldn't go to before.

B *Manage & succeed*

We use *manage to* + infinitive and *succeed in* + verb + *-ing* to refer to the ability to do something (3) ....

We (4) .... *to convince the authorities.*

We (5) .... *in boarding the plane.*

Notice we use both *manage* and *succeed* to talk about something which is difficult and requires skill or effort.

See page 148 for grammar reference and more practice.

SPEAKING

1 a Work in groups. Has mobility changed in your city/town in recent years? Think of a few examples.

*Before, you **couldn't** find many ramps; now they are everywhere.*

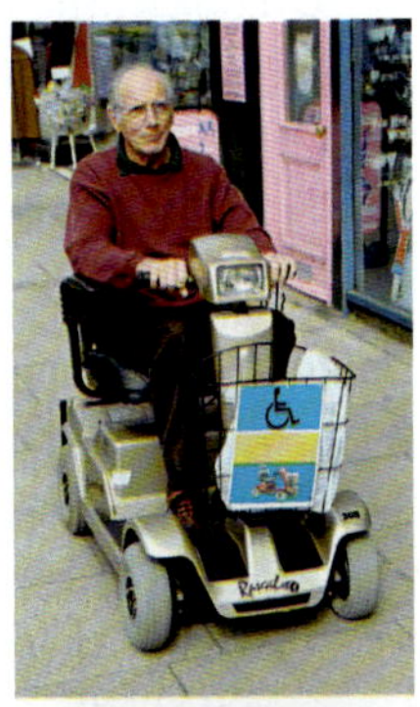

b Report back on your examples to another group.

*You still **can't** access the subway in a wheelchair; most stations don't have a lift going down to the platform.*

2 a Think of a few specific ways that the authorities could improve wheelchair access where you live.

b Report back to the rest of the class. Which ideas were the most popular?

a

b

c

TUNE IN

1 **a** Work in pairs. Look at the images. Where does each situation take place? What do you think the people are saying? Write a short exchange for one of the images.

b Read it out to the class. Can your classmates guess which image it is?

2 **a** 9.7 Listen to six short exchanges. Match them to the images. There are two for each image.

b Listen again. In which exchanges does someone a) ask for help? b) offer help? Were any of the exchanges similar to the one you wrote in 1a?

FOCUS ON LANGUAGE

3 **a** Listen again. Match the requests and offers to the situations in 1a.

1 *I was wondering if you* ***could*** *help me with this, please?*
2 ***Do*** *you need any help with that?*
3 ***Do*** *you want a hand?* ***Can*** *I take the pushchair for you?*
4 *Do you think you* ***could*** *help?*
5 *Here,* ***let*** *me help you.*
6 ***Would*** *you mind helping me pick them all up again?*

b Look at the modal verbs and auxiliaries in **bold**. Which are used in

a) polite requests?
b) offers of help?

4 **a** Match responses a–f to the requests and offers in 3a.

a Oh, thank you, if you don't mind, that'd be wonderful.
b Sure thing, no problem.
c No, of course not, no worries, here you are.
d Thank you for offering to help – not many people do you know.
e Yes, of course. Here, let me do it.
f Thank you! They're all over the place!

b Underline the three expressions used to say *yes* to the request for help.

5 **a** Work in pairs. Write polite requests for situations 1–3. Use a different expression each time.

Excuse me, I was wondering if you could give me a hand with this?

1 You are in the car park of a shopping centre. You have just bought a new TV set and you can't lift the box into the boot of your car.
2 You are waiting at the bus stop. You don't have the right change to pay for the bus ticket. You need to ask someone if they can give you some change.
3 You are in a queue at the supermarket, and you only want to buy two things. The person in front of you has a large trolley full of food. You are in a hurry.

b Pass your requests to another pair.

6 Respond to the requests. You can say *yes* or *no*. If you say no, you have to give a reason why.

Using *please*

9.8 Listen to the request. Notice how the speaker's voice goes up on the last word.
Underline the main stress.
I was wondering if you could help me with this, please?
Listen again and repeat.
Look at the requests. Practise reading them out aloud using *please* to make them sound more polite.
Could you open the door for me?
Sorry, do you think you could move over a little?

OVER TO YOU

7 **a** Work in pairs. Discuss the questions.

- When was the last time someone asked you to help them? What did they ask you to do?
- When was the last time you asked someone for help? What help did you need?

b Choose one of the situations from 7a. Act out the situation with your partner. Student A, ask for help. Student B, offer your help.

8 Swap roles and act out a second situation from 7a.

9 Report back to the class on your situations. Were any of them similar? Which was the strangest request?

a

b

c

TUNE IN

1 Look at the images. What type of rules and regulations can apply to these forms of transport?

You can't drive and speak on your mobile phone at the same time.

2 a 9.9 Listen to three monologues about travelling by plane, car and train. Match monologues 1–3 to images a–c. Who is the angriest?

b Listen again and answer the questions.

1

1 What was the change to the rules?
2 How does it affect the speaker?

2

3 What did the speaker have to pay for? Why?
4 What other complaints does he make?

3

5 What was the change to the law and why were the changes introduced?
6 What happened to the speaker? Why was he angry about it?

PREPARE FOR TASK

3 a Complete the extracts from 2.

1 **What** .... **angry about** this is that the trains…
2 **I just don't** .... they had to change it.
3 … the thing was **I had** .... **about** that change so, yes, I had to pay there and then.
4 **What are you** .... **do if** you don't have a printer?
5 … **it wasn't my** ...., I just didn't see the signs.
6 **I mean how was I** ....? I was really annoyed about that.

b 9.10 Listen and check your answers. How would you describe the speaker's tone?

4 Work in pairs. Have you ever complained about similar things? Tell your partner.

5 a Look at a–e and note down any unacceptable rules/regulations that might apply in each case.

a parking regulations
b in a block of flats
c on a train/bus
d at a concert/in the cinema
e pets

a *We've got parking meters outside the office, which is OK even if they're expensive, but then after two hours you've got to move your car and you can't come back to the same parking zone for another hour!*

b Work in pairs. Why are the rules in 5a unacceptable?

1 too strict
2 too demanding/difficult to fulfil
3 unnecessary
4 irrelevant

parking regulations: you come back five minutes too late and you still get a parking ticket… that's just too strict.

TASK

6 Work in pairs. Read the model below. Do you agree with the opinion? Have you, or has anyone you know ever experienced something similar? What happened?

What really annoys me is the security checks at airports these days. You can't carry liquids in your hand luggage or you have to carry them in tiny 100 ml bottles. I just don't understand why they have to enforce that. I don't think a shampoo poses a risk to air safety, do you? The checks just waste time and add to stress. What is a liquid anyway? I once had some soft cheese taken away from me! I mean, have you ever heard of anything so stupid? I'm going to try and avoid flying in future.

7 a Think of a rule (or a series of rules) that you feel is unnecessary, irrelevant or simply too difficult to keep. Think of as many reasons as you can why you dislike the rule.

b Work in small groups. Tell each other your complaints. Which is the most frequent complaint? Whose complaint is the most/least valid. Why?

REPORT BACK

8 Tell the class about the complaints in your group. What is the most common complaint in the class?

➔ Go to Review C, Unit 9, p. 104 ➔ Go to Writing bank 5, p. 156

VOCABULARY

Possessions

1 a Change the words in *italics* for one of the words in the box. More than one answer may be possible.

belongings contents item junk
property possessions stuff

1 Only one *piece* of hand luggage is permitted on board the plane.
2 When you leave the plane, don't forget to take all your personal *things* with you.
3 Every year I try to clear out all the *useless things* from my house.

b In what context would you hear sentences 1–3?

Organisation

2 a Complete the text with words related with organisation. The first letter of each word is given.

(1)T.................. is not exactly my strong point; everybody says that I'm really (2)m.................. , and my flat is a disaster I have to admit. But that's only really related to objects. I'm much more (3)e.................. when it comes to my work. All the files on my computer are really (4)o.................. , for example, and my desktop is really (5)n.................. and (6)t.................. .

b Change any parts of the monologue so that the information is true for you.

GRAMMAR

Quantifiers

1 a Look at these sentences describing the place in the image. Which type of place do you think it is? Why?

1 There are too many tourists in winter.
2 There aren't many jobs for people.
3 There are a few places to visit.
4 There are plenty of places to ski.
5 You need a lot of money if you want come here.

b Change the sentences so that they are true for you and your town.

There are not many tourists here in winter, but there are a lot in summer.

Using *one* & *ones*

2 a R14 Listen to two short conversations. What do you think *one* and *ones* refer to in each case? Where do you think the speakers are?

b Listen again and complete the gaps. Which one/ones do the people like in each case?

1 A Would you like to try .... ones?
B I'm not sure, I think those would suit me better...

2 A I've already had ...., thanks.
B You can have .... one, you know...

Articles

3 Insert *a/the* where appropriate in the following text. There are two examples each of *a* and *the*.

Most valuable possession I own is sixteenth century painting that I inherited from my great aunt. But my favourite possession is simple silver watch. I don't normally like valuable things, but it's special to me because it was my father's and when I look at time I always think of him.

4 Talk to your partner about either a valuable object or one that has sentimental value for you.

FUNCTIONAL LANGUAGE

Using vague language

1 Work in pairs. Make the sentences vague using words in the box.

something something a bit more somewhere
stuff that kind of thing things like that

1 I'm looking for a present for my nephew; he likes model trains.
2 I want to go on holiday to a place where I can relax and have a good time.
3 Before I start the job, I need to know my schedule and other conditions.

2 R15 Listen and compare.

LOOKING BACK

- Think of your family's most treasured possessions. Explain why they are so important.
- Think of five things that you use everyday and different ways that you can describe them and what they do.
- What was the most memorable part of the unit? Why?

VOCABULARY

Storytelling

1 a Work in pairs. Think of

1 a well-known myth.
2 a common anecdote.
3 the top news story of the moment.
4 an interesting sports report.
5 an unlikely tale someone has told you recently.

b Compare with the class. Did you have any in common?

Travel activities

2 a Look at the four images. What activities are they showing?

b When was the last time you did these things? Did you enjoy it? Why/Why not?

I last went window-shopping yesterday – I loved it!

The media

3 a Match the news media expressions in the box to the categories in the chart.

breaking news   citizen journalists   eye witnesses
footage   news coverage   Twitter   video clips

People	Type of news	Way of broadcasting news

b Add words of your own to each category.

GRAMMAR

Reported speech

1 a Write down three things people have said to you today.

'I'll see you later.' (a friend)

b Work in pairs. Report the three things you wrote in 1a to a partner.

My friend said she'd see me later.

Reporting requests & instructions

2 a Look at the requests, questions and instructions asked by the police to a citizen journalist. Report what was said.

1 'Give us your name and address, please.'
They asked me to give them my name and address.
2 'Can you show us the photos you took?'
....
3 'Did anybody see you take them?'
....
4 'How many people did you see looting the shop?'
....
5 'Please don't leave the police station.'
....

b What type of event did the person witness?

FUNCTIONAL LANGUAGE

Phone messages

1 a R16 Listen to two phone conversations. Report the information by completing the gaps.

1
Dr Baron called and said that he (1) .... the appointment. Can you (2) .... to fix a new time? He (3) .... sorry.

2
Somebody else called and (4) .... to phone this number: 0489 230388. They (5) .... urgent. Can you (6) .... as soon as possible? No, they didn't give a name.

b Listen and check.

2 Work in pairs. Think of a conversation that you have had recently in which you had to report a message to somebody. Tell your partner what it was.

LOOKING BACK

- Think of five different stories you have heard recently. How many different ways could you tell them?
- Can you describe a favourite story to your partner? Why is it your favourite?
- Describe to your partner the breaking news of the moment.

UNIT 9

VOCABULARY

Permission & prohibition

1 **a** Work in pairs or small groups. Think of five actions that are prohibited in or around the area where you live. Do you think these prohibitions are fair?

b Can you think of any other prohibitions you would like to impose?

2 **a** Complete the sentences with *at*, *on* or *in*.

You can find signs...

1 .... the entrance to a garage.
2 .... the front door of a classroom.
3 .... the bottom of an escalator.
4 .... a museum.
5 .... the gates of a building site.
6 .... the beach.

b What signs could you find in these places?

Internet

3 **a** R17 Listen to three people talking about the internet. Complete the chart.

	Information/Activity	Device/Place
Speaker 1		
Speaker 2		
Speaker 3		

b Work in pairs. Which of the speakers do you identify with? Why? Ask your partner about his/her online habits.

Verbs with *law*

4 **a** Complete the gaps with verbs in the box in an appropriate tense. One does not apply.

break defend introduce respect

1 The government .... a very controversial new law.
2 People who download music illegally don't always realise they are .... the law.
3 Sometimes you have to .... a law even though you think it's stupid, like those in airports.

b Think of other verbs or phrases to replace the verbs in the gaps in 4a.

5 Work in pairs. Which of the statements in 4a do you think are true? Explain why/why not.

GRAMMAR

Permission, prohibition & obligation (1): present

1 **a** Choose the correct options to complete the sentences.

1 You're not allowed to chew gum in here.
You *mustn't / don't have to* chew gum here.
2 The boss or teacher forces us to do our work everyday.
The boss or teacher *lets / makes* us do our homework.
3 We can drink water here but not other drinks.
We *are / aren't* allowed to drink water.
4 You can come in with a dog but only on a lead.
Dogs *are / aren't* allowed but they *can / have to* be on a lead.

b Which sentences are true for you?

Permission, prohibition & obligation (2): past

2 Work in pairs. Think of a place where you used to go regularly in the past (e.g. an old school or place of work). Write down five rules and regulations for that place.

Talking about ability (past & present)

3 **a** Complete the gaps in the conversations.

A I was very bad at first, but somehow I (1) .... to pass the test and now I can cope fine. It's all practice.
B I know what you mean, I (2) .... park at first. It was awful!

C I was terrible at this subject at school, I (3) .... in passing a single exam. I was convinced I (4) .... do it, but now I love it.
D It's strange, isn't it? You even write your own songs now.

b R18 Listen and check.

4 Work in pairs. Talk about your experiences.

FUNCTIONAL LANGUAGE

Making polite requests

1 R19 Make the request more polite in three different ways. Then listen and check.

Give me a hand with this bag, will you?

1 I was ....
2 Do you ....
3 Would you ....

2 Work in pairs. Think about requests you have made in your language. Make polite requests in English.

LOOKING BACK

- Which laws do you consider fair/unfair where you live?
- Think of five different ways of describing your abilities.

LISTENING

1 Work in small groups. Look at the images of two language classrooms and answer the questions.

1 What do you think the students are doing in each image? How can you tell?
2 What kind of teaching equipment can you see?
3 How are the classrooms similar to, and different from, the classrooms you've known?

2 R20 Listen to David talking about two classrooms he has studied in. Answer the questions.

1 What equipment does he mention?
2 What similarities and differences does he describe?

3 **a** Complete the text by adding ONE word in each gap.

When I first started studying English it was in a classroom very much like the (1) ………… in the photo. At (2) ………… time we thought this was cutting-edge, state-of-the-art technology – our teacher always told us how lucky we (3) …………! We used to do a lot of work in this mini language lab. The teacher would ask us (4) ………… listen to dialogues on a tape that she played on her cassette player. The individual headphones were great. We (5) ………… record our voices too and then listen to them. We were (6) ………… to listen to them as many times as we wanted. Hearing my own voice really helped my pronunciation. I thought the lab was really cool! But the rest of the time we (7) ………… to do grammar exercises and vocabulary tests and we didn't get much chance to speak.

The course I'm doing now is so totally different! As is (8) ………… classroom. We have (9) ………… projector and WiFi access. We (10) ………… watch videos and other clips on YouTube. I think that really helps, though I actually prefer to do it at home when I (11) ………… decide what to watch. But they're great for starting (12) ………… conversation and we get a lot of opportunity to talk and learn through talking. I still love recording my voice though and playing it back and listening to it. The only difference is that now I don't (13) ………… to be in a classroom to do it – I do it on my mobile phone – so I can do it when I want, where I want. That's (14) ………… one thing I love most about new technology – it's all so portable!

b Listen again and check.

SPEAKING

4 Work in pairs. Discuss the questions.

- How long have you been learning English?
- Have things changed at all during that time?
- Do you use mobile technology or web tools to help you study and practise outside the classroom? If yes, what do you do?
- What else do you do to practise English outside the classroom? What do you find is the one thing that helps you most? Why?
- Are there any mobile applications, websites or other activities that you could recommend to your classmates?

QUICK CHECK

Complete the checklist below.

Can you...	Yes, I can.	Yes, more or less.	I need to look again.
1 talk about your personal possessions?	☐	☐	☐
2 discuss childhood games and toys?	☐	☐	☐
3 talk about the different sides of a story?	☐	☐	☐
4 report what someone has said to you?	☐	☐	☐
5 take and pass on a message on the phone?	☐	☐	☐
6 talk about rules and regulations?	☐	☐	☐
7 discuss new laws and legislation?	☐	☐	☐
8 talk about mobility issues in your area?	☐	☐	☐

Compare your answers with a partner.

- What else do you know now after studying units 7–9?
- Do you need to look again at any of the sections?
- Do you need any extra help from your teacher?

10 INSIGHTS AND INNOVATIONS

a

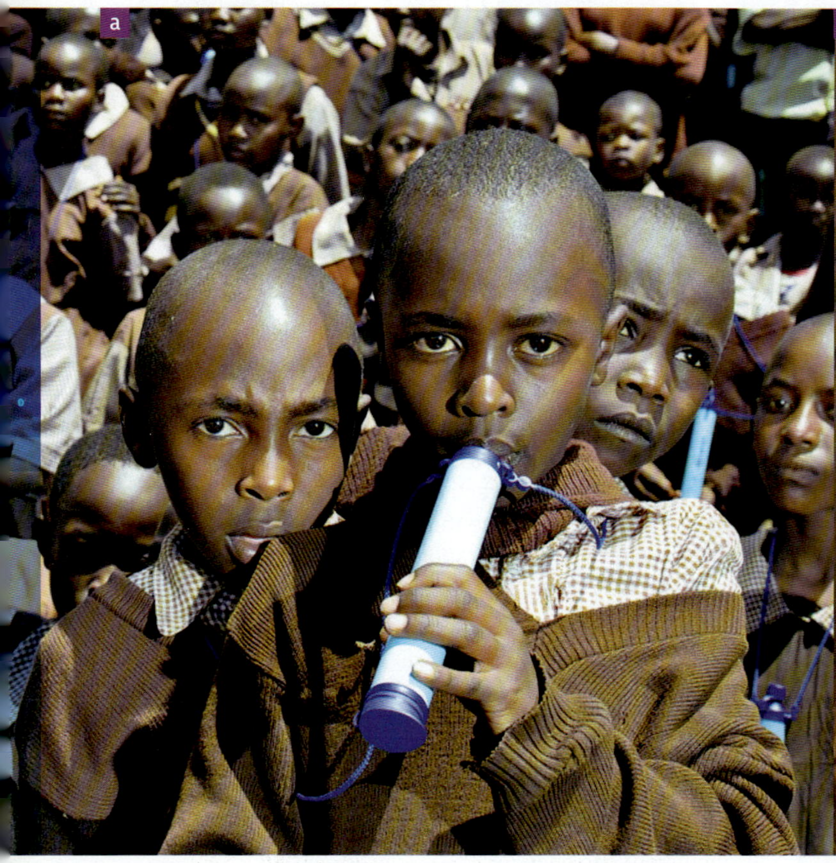

b

1 **a** Work in pairs. Look at the images of three innovations. They feature in an exhibition called *Design for the other 90%*.

- What do you think the title of the exhibition means?
- Match the images to the names of the innovations in the box.

LifeStraw®	Portable Light Bag	Pedal Cell Charger

b What do you think each innovation is for?

2 **a** 10.1 Listen to the descriptions of the innovations and check your answers to 1b.

b Listen again and answer the questions.

1 What three basic things are needed by 'the 90%'?
2 Which two of these do the above innovations help with?
3 What does the Portable Light Bag include?
4 How can it help support local industries?
5 What kinds of water can people drink from using the Life Straw?
6 How can the LifeStraw® save time?
7 How long do you have to cycle to get 30 minutes' talking time on the phone?
8 Which countries is it particularly useful for?

3 **a** Complete A in the KEY VOCABULARY PANEL.

b Read transcript 10.1 on page 166. Find adjectives used to describe

a all three
b the Portable Light Bag
c the LifeStraw®
d the Pedal Cell Charger

NOTICE *LIGHT*

What other meanings of *light* can you think of?

4 Choose the best options with words from B in the KEY VOCABULARY PANEL. More than one answer may be possible.

1 Here are three unique ideas that we hope will *help / support* people to live their lives more happily.
2 The bags are of great *beneficial / benefit* to local industries.
3 The Life Straw will be *help / helpful* to rural communities.
4 ... *enabling / benefitting* people to access drinking water without having to walk miles to find it.
5 The exhibition explores these low-cost, innovative solutions to *enable / support* the other 90%.
6 A lot of people *can't afford / affordable* to charge the battery on their phones.

C

5 **a** Work in pairs. Discuss which you think is the most interesting/worthwhile/important invention in 1a. Why?

b Do you think any of the solutions in the images could be useful in your community or in other communities in your country? Why/Why not? What solutions does your country offer in the area of energy, water or shelter?

We use a lot of wind and solar power. This is good because it's a very green, low-cost option.

Key vocabulary

Ideas & solutions

A Describing ideas & solutions

- Match the adjectives in the box to their meanings 1–8.

affordable	beneficial	essential
innovative	personal	portable
temporary	unique	

1 for individual use
2 economically priced
3 new, original and advanced
4 easy to carry around
5 very special and/or unusual
6 not for permanent use
7 of great help
8 really necessary

- Can you use all the adjectives to describe all the innovations in the images?

I think they're all affordable and beneficial. I'm not so sure they're all essential.

B Describing help & benefits

- Adjectives & nouns

We can use adjectives and nouns to talk about helping others.
We can say these inventions are *beneficial* / are of *benefit* **to**... and they are *helpful* / are a great *help* **to**...
We can also say people can *benefit* **from** these inventions.

- Verbs

We also use verbs.
benefit somebody
help someone to do something
enable someone to do something
allow someone to do something
support someone
These inventions benefit people.
The Life Straw™ enables people to drink fresh water safely.

Notice *AFFORD*

The verb *afford* is often used with *can't* and in questions with *can*.
I can't afford a new bike.
They can't afford to spend money on expensive chargers.
Can we afford the expense?
How do you use *afford* in your language?

10.1 Biking

- Practise passives
- Talk about alternative uses for items

a

b

c

Speaking

1 a Work in pairs. What are the bikes in the photos being used for? Match photos a–d to the words in the box. More than one answer is possible.

to earn a living	to get to work	to have fun	to keep fit

b Discuss the questions.

- Have you got a bike? If yes, what kind of bike is it? What do you use it for?
- If no, would you like one? Why/Why not?

Reading

1 Read the opening paragraph of a blog post. Why has this blog post been dedicated to bikes?

> In a recent poll the bicycle **was voted** the number one invention of the last 200 years. It was chosen for its simplicity of design and enormous versatility. Throughout their history, bikes have been used for much more than just transport. Here are some links to recent blog posts about how bikes are used to <u>create jobs</u>, <u>to save energy</u>, <u>to save lives</u>.

2 a Read texts A–C. Match them to the links in the blogpost in 1 and to three of images a–d.

b Read the texts again. Which text

1 talks about how the idea came about? ....
2 compares the bike service with another similar service? ....
3 explains how using a bike saves energy? ....
4 explains how using a bike is faster and more efficient? ....
5 describes how a bike can be transformed into something else? ....
6 talks about how the bike is being used to spread a message? ....

3 Work in pairs. Which idea do you think is the most interesting? Why? Do you know of any other interesting uses for bikes?

A The Cycle Response Unit

Ambulances on two wheels are on the increase. Throughout London, and other cities in the UK, more and more emergency calls **are being answered by cycling paramedics**. Their specially-fitted mountain bikes are like mini-ambulances, carrying all the medical equipment needed to save lives. Bikes can get through heavy city traffic and down pedestrian streets much faster than ambulances. The fully-trained paramedics can assess injuries and administer emergency first aid. Patients who need further treatment **will be taken to hospital by conventional ambulances**. The cycle response unit is saving time, saving lives and saving money. And as it also helps the ambulance service to reduce exhaust fumes, it may also be helping to save the planet!

B Coffee to go

Coffee-to-go has taken on a new meaning on the streets of New York where bikes are being used to run a portable coffee stand. Two friends recently discovered that their bicycles **could be used** for more than just cycling to work. Inspired by their love of coffee and of cycling, they combined the two and created *Kickstand* – a portable, fold-away coffee bar completely powered by bicycles. Two carts are attached to the back of their bikes. When they want to set up the bar, the carts are unfolded and linked together to create a three-metre long bar. The coffee **is ground by hand**, each cup is made with freshly ground coffee, just enough for one cup. There's no waste and a great taste!

C An e-bike adventure

What is an e-bike? It's an electric bike, a conventional pedal bike which also has a small engine. Most e-bikes run on rechargeable batteries, but Catalan Guim Valls's e-bike is charged by solar power. And the solar power is supplied by a panel on a trailer that's attached to the back of the bike. Clean, green, sustainable energy wherever you go! And Guim has decided to go a long way – all the way round the world, in fact! He wants to persuade people all over the world that there's an alternative to fossil fuels. More than 120 million e-bikes **have been sold** in China – now if Guim can persuade them all to convert to solar power, that's a lot of energy saved!

d

Grammar

1 **a** Look at the verbs in **bold** in the texts in Reading 1 and 2. What is the subject of each verb? Who is responsible for the action?

b Underline the verb *to be* in each of the expressions. What tense is it in? Complete A in the Grammar panel with the correct form of *to be*.

2 Look again at the expressions. Underline the expressions with *by*. Complete B in the Grammar panel with the expressions.

3 **a** Rewrite the sentences using a passive verb form. Do not use *by*. Start each sentence with the words that are underlined.

1 Somebody stole my bike. *My bike was stolen.*
2 The police have arrested the thief.
3 Thieves steal thousands of bikes from the city centre every year.
4 The local authorities are introducing a bike registration scheme.
5 They will give each bike an electronic registration number.
6 That way the police can track and find the stolen bike.

b 10.2 Listen and check. Are your answers the same?

4 Look again at the sentences you wrote in 3a. Match them to the uses in C in the Grammar panel.

5 **a** Choose the correct options to complete the text.

> The first Brompton folding bikes (1)*made / were manufactured* in their inventor's bedroom. Andrew Ritchie, an engineering graduate, (2)*built / were built* the bikes for his friends. These first prototypes (3)*made / were made* by hand and were quite heavy. But the concept was good and the bikes (4)*folded / were folded* cleanly and easily into the size of a small backpack. Selling the first 30 bikes (5)*gave / was given* Ritchie enough money to start a small production line. And now more than 200,000 bikes (6)*sell / are sold* each year.

b What are the advantages of a folding bike? Do you know anyone who has one?

Passives

A *Be* + past participle

Present simple: *The solar power* (1) .... *supplied by a panel.*
Past simple: *It* (2) .... *chosen for its simple design.*
Present continuous: *Bikes* (3) .... *used to create jobs.*
Present perfect: *Coffee to go* (4) .... *given a new twist.*
With modals: *More e-bikes will* (5) .... sold.
More lives could (6) .... *saved.*

The object of an active verb becomes the subject of the passive verb.
Active: *A panel supplies the solar power.*
Passive: *The solar power is supplied by a panel.*

B *By*

We use *by* + noun

- to emphasise who or what is responsible for an action.
(7) ....
- to emphasise how an action is performed.
(8) ....

C Without *by*

We use the passive without *by*

- when we don't know who/what is responsible for an action. *The police were informed.*
- when it's obvious who/what is responsible for an action. *The stolen bikes were sold to second-hand bike shops.*

Note: We often use the passive to describe a process. *Stolen bikes are returned to their owners.*

See page 149 for grammar reference and more practice.

Speaking

1 **a** Look at the pictures. What are the tennis balls being used for?

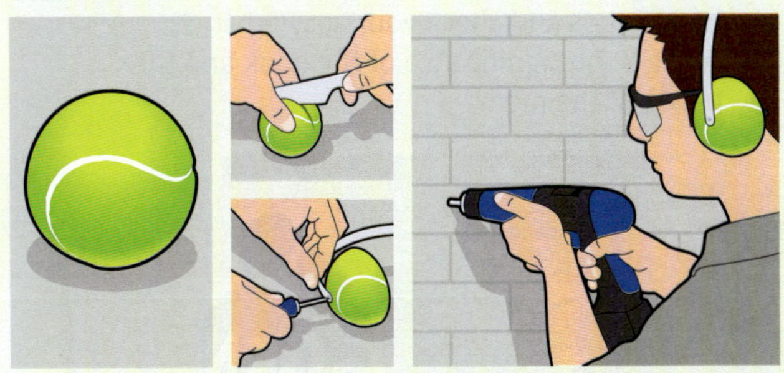

b Work in pairs. Look at the items in the box. Think of alternative uses for at least three of the objects.

a fork	a loaf of bread	a mobile phone
a pair of gloves	a plastic bag	a potato
a sheet of paper	an umbrella	

2 Share your ideas with the class. Who came up with the most original idea?

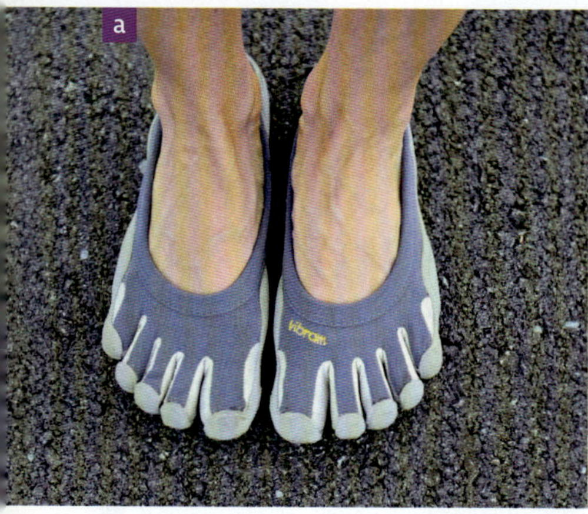

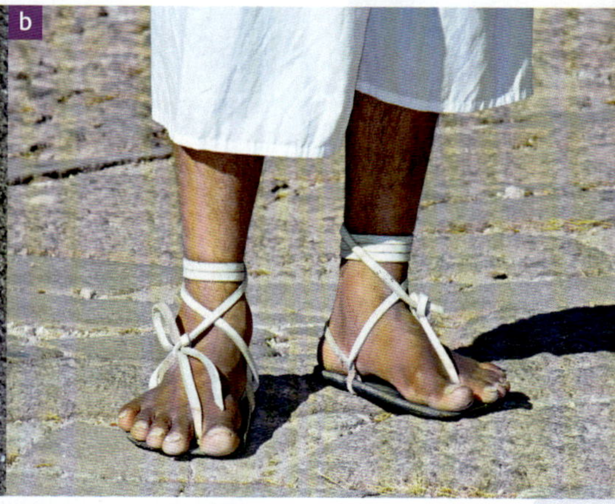

Speaking & Listening

1 **a** Look at images a–d. What do they show? Which do you see most often where you live?

b Work in pairs. Discuss the questions.

- Is running a popular sport in your town?
- Where do people usually go running?
- Do you like running? If yes, where do you go? How far and how often do you run?
- If you don't like running, why not? Do you do something else to relax and keep fit?

2 **a** Look again at images a–d. What do you think might be the advantages and disadvantages of running in each way?

b What relationship could the words in the box have with the topic?

> barefoot glove ground impact injuries support

3 **a** 10.3 Listen to a conversation between two friends and check your answers in 2. What is the significance of the book and the photo of the men?

b Listen again and choose the correct answer.

1 What most surprised Chris McDougall was that the runner
a) didn't get an injury. b) was over 50 years old.
2 Running for the Tarahumara is
a) a fun activity. b) integral to their lives.
3 Most people think that conventional running shoes give you
a) more support. b) less support.
4 The local people inspired Chris to
a) learn a whole new way of running. b) hate normal running shoes.
5 Anyone can run barefoot
a) almost immediately. b) after a few attempts.
6 Bogdan thinks that running is
a) an art form. b) hard work.

4 Work in pairs. What would you consider the best footwear for running? Why?

Vocabulary: phrasal verbs (1)

1 Look at phrasal verbs 1–6. Find them in transcript 10.3 on page 166 and match them to meanings a–f.

1 try out	a continue
2 keep up	b stop doing something
3 burn out	c start an activity
4 give up	d experiment doing
5 carry on	e move at the same speed
6 take up	f stop because you have done too much and are tired

2 Complete the sentences with the correct form of the phrasal verbs in 1.

1 I'd like to .... barefoot running, it sounds fun.
2 When you start running, the problem is .... with everybody else.
3 I .... running because I thought it was boring.
4 If you .... a new hobby like running, it can make you feel better.
5 Be careful – if you train too hard, you can .... and never want to run again.
6 I believe in 'No pain, no gain'. It means you have to .... even if you are tired and suffering.

3 Work in pairs. Which of the sentences in 2 do you agree with? What was the last sport or hobby you took up or gave up? Why?

GRAMMAR

1 **a** Remember the information in transcript 10.3. Match 1–6 to a–f to make sentences.

1 There are people
2 There are events
3 There are a number of runners
4 They have thin, flexible soles
5 This was a runner
6 There are companies

a *that* had won a 100-mile race through the mountains wearing only a pair of sandals.
b *who* have got rid of their shoes.
c *which* require special preparation and equipment.
d *that* make a lot of money from running products.
e *which* are really comfortable.
f *who* say that shoes give you more support.

b Look at the words in *italics*. Which are used to refer back to a) people? b) things? c) both people and things?

2 Complete 1–3 in the GRAMMAR PANEL.

3 **a** Complete the sentences with *who* or *which*.

1 Only use shoes .... I recommend.
2 I don't understand people .... run marathons.
3 It was the Tarahumara people .... influenced Chris.
4 There are many things .... you can do barefoot.
5 It's the Five Fingers shoes .... resemble feet.
6 Runners .... I know don't like being barefoot.

b Read B in the GRAMMAR PANEL. Look again at the sentences in 3a. In which sentences can you omit *who* or *which*?

4 10.4 Listen and check.

5 Complete the sentences with *who* or *which* so that they are true for you.

1 I really like sports...
2 I don't understand people...
3 I can't stand people...
4 I only watch sports...

I really like sports which you can do with other people – I don't like doing sports on my own.

WHO, WHICH, THAT

A Relative clauses

We use relative clauses to give more information about a person or thing.

He was the person *who told me about barefoot running.*
These are the sandals *that he ran in.*
I ran in shoes *which were really uncomfortable.*

We use *who*, *which* and *that* to introduce the relative clause.

We use *who* to refer to (1) ....
We use *which* to refer to (2) ....
We use *that* to refer to (3) .... or ....

B Omitting *who, which, that*

We can only omit *who*, *which*, *that* if it is not the subject of the verb that follows.

The shoes (which) I want are like gloves for your feet.
(*I* is the subject of the verb, so we can omit *which*)
I want shoes which fit me like a glove.
(*shoes* is the subject of the verb so we can't omit *which*)

See page 149 for grammar reference and more practice.

SPEAKING & VOCABULARY: footwear

1 **a** Look at the images of footwear on page 160 and label them with the words in the box. Use a dictionary to help you.

boots flip-flops high heels sandals slippers trainers walking boots work shoes

b Work in pairs. Which footwear do you consider to be

a more formal?
b more informal?
c more comfortable?
d more uncomfortable?

2 **a** Work in pairs. Discuss the questions.

- What kind of shoes are you wearing at the moment? Have you had them for a long time? Do you remember where you bought them?
- Do you have a favourite pair of shoes? Do you like shopping for shoes? Why/Why not?
- What do you like to wear on your feet when at home? Do you prefer to go barefoot or wear slippers? Why?
- Do you take your shoes off when you visit friends' homes? What is the attitude to bare feet where you live?

b Share your answers with the class.

■ PRACTISE METAPHORS
■ TALK ABOUT MAKING DIFFICULT DECISIONS

READING

1 Work in pairs. Look at images a–c. What do you think they show? Can you think of a story about them? Share your answers with the class.

2 **a** Read the first paragraph of the blog post and check your answers to the questions in 1. Underline the three sentences that best match the images.

b Read the rest of the blog post. Match headings a–e to paragraphs 1–5.

a Describing the moment of change
b Summing up
c Flashback to a past event
d Addressing the reader
e The present situation

3 Read the post again. Mark the sentences true (T) or false (F)? Correct the false sentences.

1 Mariam thought she might lose her job.
2 Mariam says that the decision to leave her job was easy to make.
3 She thinks that the company will help others, but not herself.
4 The company has helped her meet some creative people.

4 Find expressions in paragraphs 1 and 2 which means

1 a time of economic difficulty
2 going up quickly
3 repeating again and again
4 at a decisive moment
5 a time when an important change takes place

My Epiphany Moment by Mariam Khan

1 Let's go back to about a year ago. We're in the middle of a recession, there are salary cuts and unemployment is rocketing. It dawns on me – what if something happens to *me*? To *my* job? I work in an employment consultancy specialising in the arts. But what if I'm left with *no way* to pay my bills or buy groceries? This scenario kept playing over and over in my head. Would I have to move back in with my parents? What would I do? How could I stay healthy, happy and secure without a job or the means to live my life the way I want and like to? It was like I was at a crossroads and somehow I had to choose a new direction.

2 It wasn't easy, but then I suddenly had a flash of inspiration – and that moment would be my turning point... my epiphany moment, if you like. I saw the light! I understood what I had to do and I decided to set up my own company. Yes, I set up *Creative Consulting*. I realised that there were many other well-qualified professionals who might be out of work and needing help finding an opening, so I decided to set up my own consultancy and help these people find the work that satisfies them. It's called *Creative Consultancy* because I want to help people who work in the arts – film, dance, music, painting – you name it!

3 I've come to find that my work can offer so much. It also allows me to meet really talented people and develop a network of contacts I could not have imagined. Suddenly, I feel I have a role in the community. I'm not only helping myself, but also others. And everyday, I feel I understand people better, both their personal and professional needs. My job is to find them a creative solution, an outlet for them to be what they want to be.

4 So, that was my epiphany moment. Not everyone's had one, but I'm glad I have. Starting my own company was the best decision I've ever made because for the first time I am in charge, I'm my own boss.

5 Has there been a moment in your life when it all clicked? When it all came together and everything made sense? When you overcame a great obstacle? A defining moment when everything changed?

If the answer is yes – I want to hear your story! Please take a moment to share your 'Epiphany Moment' by leaving a post on my website.

LISTENING

1 10.5 Jenny and Marco sent audio messages to Mariam about their epiphany moments. Listen and make notes about what they discovered about their lives.

2 Listen again. Choose J (Jenny) or M (Marco) to complete the sentences.

1 *J / M* describes how hard the decision was to make.
2 *J / M* realised they didn't enjoy a particular part of their work/studies.
3 *J / M* felt a sense of liberation.
4 *J / M* described what their father thought of the change.
5 *J's / M's* 'moment' is related to a childhood hobby.

3 What do Jenny and Marco's stories have in common?

4 What are these stories all about? Whose story do you find the most interesting – Mariam, Marco or Jenny's? Why? Can you identify with any of their 'moments'?

VOCABULARY: metaphorical language

1 a Complete the expressions with the words in the box.

crossroads	direction	flash	light

1 Suddenly, I saw the ....
2 I had a .... of inspiration.
3 I was at a .... and didn't know which way to go.
4 I had to choose a new ....

b Check your answers in the blog post in READING 2.

2 a Look again at the sentences in 1a. Which sentences

a compare life to a journey?
b compare understanding with seeing a light?

What does *light* symbolise in these sentences?

> **NOTICE** *THE BIG PICTURE*
> *Suddenly I was aware of the big picture.*
> We use the expression to refer to the whole situation, not just part of it.

b Do you use similar metaphors in your language?

PRONUNCIATION: sentence stress

1 10.6 Listen to the sentences in VOCABULARY 1a and mark the stressed syllable.

1 Suddenly, I saw the light.

2 a Look at the sentences and mark the main stress.

1 Suddenly everything clicked – I realised what I wanted to do.
2 Then, at that moment, it dawned on me that that was the right decision.
3 Then I realised I was at the crossroads; I had to make a choice.

b 10.7 Listen and check.

3 Listen again and repeat.

SPEAKING

1 a Work in pairs. Look at difficult decisions 1–3. Think of reasons for making these decisions. Add some of your own.

1 leaving your job
2 moving to a new town or country
3 changing course/career/degree

b Do you know of anyone who has had to make one of the decisions in 1a? Tell your partner about them and their decision.

2 Think of a difficult decision that you have had to make. Answer the questions.

- What was the decision?
- What caused you to make the decision?
- Do you think it was the right decision? Why/Why not?

3 Work in pairs. Listen to your partner's story and report back to the class. What are the stories mainly about? Which story is the most surprising?

a

b

c

TUNE IN

1 Work in pairs. Look at images a–c and discuss the questions.

- What is the problem?
- Where would you go to get it fixed?

2 **a** 10.8 Listen to six short conversations. Match conversations 1–6 to images a–c. There are two conversations for each image.

b Listen again. Which conversations are

a) asking where the problems can be solved?
b) asking someone to solve the problem?
c) both?

FOCUS ON LANGUAGE

3 Look at the extracts from 2. Match extracts 1–8 to functions a–c.

a asking for information
b giving information
c asking someone to do something

1 Is there anywhere near here where I can get my bike fixed?
2 There's a new bike shop in the street opposite the station. I think they do repairs.
3 Do you know where I can get a key cut?
4 There's a heel bar on the ground floor – you can get it fixed there.
5 I'd like two copies of this key, please.
6 Hi, can you fix this for me, please?
7 How long will it take?
8 We can get it fixed for you by tomorrow morning.

NOTICE *GET SOMETHING DONE*

Notice how we use ***get*** **+ noun + past participle**.

I need to get my bike fixed.

Where can I get a key cut?

Are we saying a) I'm going to do it? b) I'm going to ask someone else to do it for me?

How do you say this in your language?

4 **a** Complete the conversations with the verbs in the box.

cleaned cut painted printed renewed taken

1 A Can I make an appointment to get my hair .... tomorrow?
B I'm sorry, we're booked up. Can you do Thursday?
2 A Can I get this document ....?
B Of course, how many copies would you like?
3 A Can you get my coat .... by this evening?
B Sorry, the Express Service is only until 4 p.m.
4 A I'd like to get my nails ...., please.
B Let me see... yes, we have a free slot in half an hour.
5 A I really need to get my passport ....
B I think you can get the form online.
6 A I have to get some photos .... for my driving licence.
B There's a machine over there.

b When did you last get any of these things done? Where did you go?

Saying *thanks*

10.9 Listen to the extracts and notice how the speakers stress the word *thanks*.

That's great. Thanks!

OK, thanks. I'll give that a go.

Yeah, that'll be fine, thanks!

Listen and repeat, paying special attention to the stress.

OVER TO YOU

5 **a** Work in pairs. Choose one of the places in the box. Student A, think about the service you need. Student B, think about what problems or delays there might be.

beauty salon cybercafé dry cleaners garage hairdresser heel bar petrol station photo studio

b Act out a situation.

6 Choose another situation and swap roles.

7 Report back to the class. Which service was the most difficult. Why?

Tune in

1 Look at the images and answer the questions.

- Do you drink bottled water or water from the tap? Why?
- Where does your drinking water come from?

Prepare for task

2 Look at the infographic explaining how a LifeStraw® works. What can you remember about the LifeStraw® from page 106? What do you think happens to the water as it passes through the straw?

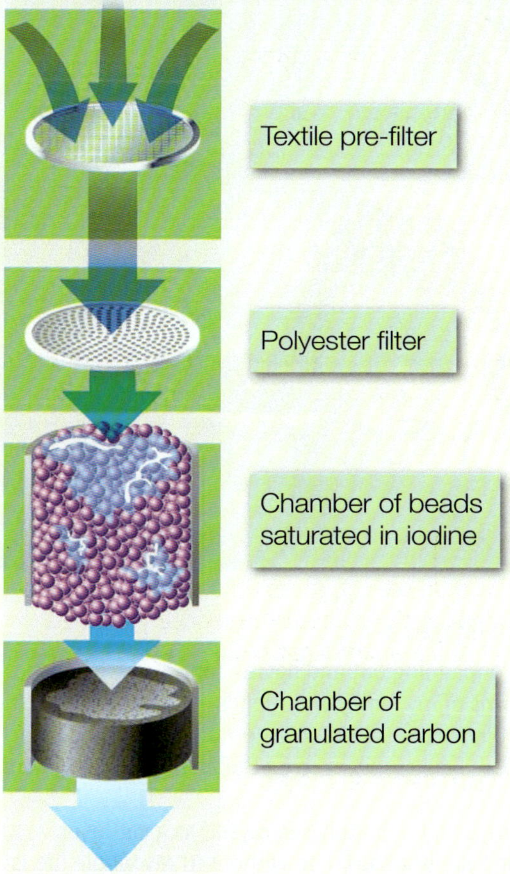

3 a 10.10 Listen and check your answers. At what stage are these things filtered from the water?

bacteria dirt parasites sediment viruses

b Listen again and complete the text.

First, the water passes through a filter and the big pieces of dirt and sediment are removed. The holes in the filter are about (1) .... microns in diameter. Next, the water passes through another filter; this time the holes are much smaller, only (2) .... microns in diameter. That's really small, each hole is just a tenth of the size of a human (3) .... This catches the bacteria that can spread diseases. In the next stage, the water is sent through a chamber of beads which are covered with iodine. Parasites and over (4) ....% of bacteria and viruses are killed by the iodine. Finally, the water passes through a chamber of carbon filter. This improves the (5) .... and (6) .... of the water and should kill any remaining parasites.

4 Look again at the text in 3b. What do you notice about the tenses? Underline four link words or expressions.

5 a Read the text describing how something else works. Can you guess what the process is? Check your answer on page 161.

First, put some water in the bottom half of the machine. Fill it up to the valve and no further. Then, place the grains in the filter. Next, place the filter carefully on top of the bottom half of the machine. It should not touch the water. Close the top tightly before putting it on the cooker. The cooker heats the water in the bottom of the machine. The water is pushed up through the filter and the grains into the top of the machine. Finally, when the top half of the machine is full of liquid, it is ready to drink.

b Underline the verbs and link words.

Task

6 Work in pairs or small groups. Choose an everyday process and write an explanation of how it works for the *How Stuff Works* website. Write the steps in a short paragraph like the models in 3b and 5a.

Report back

7 Read out your text. Can the other students guess what the object or process is?

→ Go to Review D, Unit 10, p. 136

11 A SENSE OF IDENTITY

1 **a** Work in pairs. Look at the image collage. What do you think is the connection with the unit title?

b The collage was put together by one person to show the people and things that are most important to him. Discuss the questions.

- What can you guess about this person by looking at these images?
- What do you think are his interests or likes?

2 Match descriptions 1–9 with images a–i.

1 I enjoy feeling part of a group, going out and having fun.
2 I think of my identity in terms of my family and friends – I like to support them.
3 Food plays an important role for me – I like to entertain!
4 I like to race against others – I always want to be the first! I like to think of myself as a winner.
5 I like spending time with my cat. I definitely see myself as a cat-lover.
6 *Barça* is my passion... I don't know what I'd do without it! My whole life is centred on it.
7 My life is based a lot around computers. I like to think of myself as someone who can help with problems.
8 I think what defines me most is my love of music and I love to have an audience!
9 Sometimes I need to get away from the stress and noise of the city and feel part of nature.

c

f

i

3 **a** Complete A in the KEY VOCABULARY PANEL.

b Do you identify with any of the roles in 3a? Which and why?

4 **a** Underline the different ways of describing identity in 2. Check your answers in B in the KEY VOCABULARY PANEL.

b Work in pairs. What roles do you play with different people? Decide on six different roles and explain why you chose them.

5 Work in pairs. Think of six images to create your own identity collage. Describe the images.

I'm a dog-lover, so I'd definitely include an image of my dog.

KEY VOCABULARY

Identity

A Roles

1 Match the roles to images a–i.

cat-lover competitor computer whizz
follower/fan
good listener/friend/colleague
host nature-lover party-goer
performer

2 Match the roles in 1 to the verbs. There may be more than one.

care enjoy entertain escape fix
play relax support win

3 Which of the phrasal verbs have similar meanings to the verbs in 2? Use a dictionary to help you.

calm down get ahead get away
look after stand by

B Describing identity

I think of my identity in terms of...
I feel part of...
My life is based a lot around...
My life is centred on...
What defines me most is...
I like to think of myself as...
I see/view myself as...
X plays an important role for me...

11.1 Virtual identities

- Practise present or future imaginary situations
- Talk about video games & virtual worlds

a

b

c

Reading

1 Look at the images of people and their avatars. What do you think they use them for?

2 Read the review of the book *Alter Ego: Avatars and Their Creators* and check your answer to 1. Which avatar looks most like its creator?

3 a Read the review again and change the sentences so that they are true.

1 The blogger likes the book because it's attractive to look at.
2 She likes the fact that the double identities of the people are on separate pages.
3 Most people don't change their real selves much when they create their avatars.
4 The people created the avatars for fun, but they don't symbolise anything.

b Match statements 1–6 to people K (Kimberly), Y (Young), S (Serge), R (Rainbow), C (Camilia), P (Petros).

1 Their avatar is similar to their real selves.
2 They wouldn't create an avatar.
3 Their avatar is an image of their ideal self.
4 They'd like to maintain a part of their real selves.
5 Their virtual self represents a sense of liberation.
6 They'd enjoy being a well-known person.

4 a Work in small groups. Discuss the questions at the end of the review.

b Read the comments at the end of the review. Whose answer is most similar to yours?

I've just come across this book called *Alter Ego* with these incredible images of real people and their avatars. It looks at the whole issue of identity and how we present ourselves in video games, how anonymous **users** create new identities to inhabit these alternative worlds. It's fascinating!

I love the format of the book. You see photos of **gamers** and Second Lifers in real life next to their **avatars**, with a short text about what their avatar means. Some are replicas of their creators, but most have no relation to their real-life appearance: people can change their height, gender, even species! And each person relates to their avatar differently:

Young Ki-Jang: 'I designed my avatar for the Lineage II game. His name is Knight Lummis. I enjoy the game because it's a place where I can control my own destiny. My off-line self has to conform to the expectations of my parents, teachers and peers.'

Kimberly: 'Most of the time, my avatar – Kim Anibus – looks like my real self only 20 years younger. I'm jealous of some of her clothes. I wish I could export them into real life. She doesn't have a separate persona, she's just an extension of myself in this **virtual** space. Although I did once give her a tail!'

Serge: 'My avatar is Megatox. Megatox is all that I would like to be: strong, famous, respected, daring, feared by some… My avatar and I complement each other.'

And what about me? I don't have an avatar. I'm not really that interested in **role-playing games**! But if I decided to create an avatar one day, I wouldn't create an extension of myself. I'd choose somebody that I liked looking at – maybe I'd prefer to be a guy, in fact. What about you? Do you have an avatar? If not, would you like one, and what would it be like? Let me know.

Rainbow says:
I wouldn't design an avatar – I'm happy enough with myself in the real world.

Camilia says:
I'd like to be a hero, save people's lives, be important for other people. Yes, I'd really enjoy that.

Petros says:
I'd try to be myself on the inside, but more attractive on the outside ☺

VOCABULARY: gaming

1 a Look at the words in **bold** in the text in READING 2 which have a connection with online games. Match them to definitions 1–5.

1 someone who plays computer games in which you often pretend to be a character
2 a type of game in which you adopt a different persona
3 existing in cyberspace or on a computer
4 a picture that represents a person
5 a person who uses/plays with a piece of equipment

b What other words can combine with *virtual* or *online*? Underline examples in the text in READING 2. Use a dictionary to help you.

virtual/online – world, community, character...

2 Work in pairs. Discuss a game you know using as many of the words in 1 as you can.

GRAMMAR

1 a Work in pairs. Look at the sentences.

__I'd choose__ somebody that I liked looking at – maybe __I'd prefer__ to be a guy in fact.

If I decided to create an avatar one day, __I wouldn't create__ an extension of myself.

1 Look at the verbs in **bold**. Do they refer to a) real actions? b) imaginary actions?
2 Underline the verb that follows *if*. What tense is it? Does it refer to the past, present or future?

b Check your answers in the GRAMMAR PANEL.

NOTICE *WOULD* + VERBS OF *LIKE/DISLIKE*

We often use *would* with verbs of like/dislike: *prefer, like, love, hate, enjoy*.

I'd prefer to be a guy = I'd rather be a guy

I'd rather = *I'd prefer*, but doesn't take *to* + infinitive.

2 Write sentences for the situations, using *would* and *if* + past simple.

1 I don't have much money, so I can't buy that game. If I had...
2 I don't understand anything about virtual worlds, so I don't take part in them.
3 I am very busy, so I can't always do what I want to do.
4 I don't have many friends, so I don't go out that often.

3 a Finish the sentences so that they are true for you.

1 Tonight, I'd prefer to...
2 If I could take a holiday now, I'd...
3 It'd be nice if...
4 I'd never...
5 I wouldn't like to...

b Work in pairs. Compare your answers. Do you agree with each other's sentences?

IMAGINARY SITUATIONS: PRESENT OR FUTURE

A *Would*

We use ***would*** to talk about an imaginary action or response.

I'd enjoy that...

I wouldn't design an avatar.

B Sentences with *if* + past simple

We can use ***if*** **+ past simple** to introduce an imaginary situation.

If I decided to create an avatar, I'd...

The past simple here does not refer to the past – it refers to the present or the future.

Notice when we use the verb *to be* with *if* + past simple, we can use both *was* and *were* with *I*, *he*, *she* and *it*.

If I was/were... If he was/were... If she was/ were...

See page 150 for grammar reference and more practice.

PRONUNCIATION: *I'd, it'd, wouldn't*

1 11.1 Listen to the sentences in GRAMMAR 3a. Make notes of the endings. Are any of them similar to yours?

2 a Listen again. Notice the pronunciation of *I'd*, *it'd* and *wouldn't*. Listen again and repeat.

b Read out the sentences you wrote in GRAMMAR 3a, focusing on the pronunciation of *'d* and *wouldn't*.

LISTENING & SPEAKING

1 11.2 Listen to different parents giving their opinions about video games and virtual worlds. Who is in favour of them and who is against them?

2 a Work in pairs. Which of the people do you agree with? What do you think of video games? Have you ever played them? When do you think children should be allowed to play them?

b Report back on the main points to the class.

11.2 Two sides of myself

- Practise *if only / I wish*
- Talk about wishes

a

b

c

d

Vocabulary & Listening: personality adjectives

1 Look at the images. What do you think each person is doing? Can you identify with any of them? If yes, in what way?

2 **a** Which personality traits do you think the images express?

b Find four pairs of adjectives in the box with similar meanings. Which adjective is not a pair? Match the adjectives to the images. Use a dictionary to help you.

> absent-minded careless clumsy distracted extrovert indecisive introverted out-going shy unsure

Notice adverbs as quantifiers/intensifiers

We often use adverbs as quantifiers/intensifiers when we describe someone. The stars indicate a scale from *very much* (****) to *a little* (*).

She's	*incredibly shy.*	****
	really	***
	quite	**
	a bit	*

3 11.3 Listen to an expert, Nicola Toteva, talking about a survey on the personality traits that people most dislike in themselves. Put some of the personality traits in 2b in the order that they are mentioned.

4 Listen again and answer the questions according to Nicola.

1. Why are people more distracted these days?
2. Which are the two opposites that Nicola describes?
3. Where did the survey take place and why is this important?
4. Why is being clumsy different from the others?

5 Work in pairs. Discuss the questions.

1. What examples does Nicola give of people being indecisive?
2. Where do some people find they can be less shy?
3. What makes people more clumsy?

6 Read the statements made by people who took the survey. Which of the personality traits are they talking about?

Gabriel: *I find it difficult to talk to people I don't know; if only people made it easier for me...*

Kaya: *At the office, sometimes it's hard to keep your mind on things; if only there wasn't so much noise here. I find it's really hard to concentrate and I often forget things.*

Alina: *I love going out with my workmates for a drink at the end of the day. I wish more people came with us; some quieter people just go straight home.*

Salim: *I usually make a decision and then I change my mind and decide something different. I wish I wasn't like that, it drives me crazy.*

Bruno: *It's quite easy for me to have an accident if I have something on my mind... I can't do anything about it. It's a shame that happens sometimes...*

GRAMMAR

1 a Work in pairs. Look at the words in *italics* and answer the questions.

a *If only there wasn't* so much noise.
b *I wish I could* concentrate better.

1 Which speaker expresses a desire? What is the problem in each case?
2 What does the speaker want in each case: for the situation to be the same or different?
3 Are the desired situations in the past, present or future?

b Complete 1–5 in the GRAMMAR PANEL.

2 a Rewrite the sentences using the words in brackets.

1 I don't have much time. *(I wish)*
2 I have to get up early tomorrow morning. *(if only)*
3 We're leaving tomorrow. *(I wish)*
4 I have an exam tomorrow. *(if only)*
5 The view from my room is not very nice. *(if only)*
6 It's not Friday today. *(I wish)*

b Compare your sentences with your partner.

3 a Complete the poem with the nouns in the box. Use a dictionary to help you.

dreams grass nap summer
teeth time wand weekends

I wish I had three-day (1) ....
I wish I had a (2) .... at noon
I wish I had more (3) .... to play
I wish I had greener (4) ....
I wish I had whiter (5) ....
I wish I had (6) .... all year round
I wish I had six-pack abs*
I wish I had a magic (7) ....
to make all my (8) .... come true.

**six- pack abs*: a set of well-developed abdominal muscles

b 11.4 Listen and check your answers.

4 a Work in pairs. Make a list of your wishes. Choose six to eight wishes which would work well in a poem. Write your own poem.

b Check with another pair. Were any of your wishes similar?

IF ONLY / I WISH

We use ***I wish*** or ***if only*** to talk about how you would like a situation to be (1) .... from reality.

*I'm shy → I wish I (2) .... like that.**

People make it difficult → If only they (3) .... it easier.

We use the (4) .... simple to describe the imaginary situation. This tense does not refer to the past – it refers to (5) .... or the future.

* We can say *I wish I was* and *I wish I were*. *I wish I was* is more informal.

See page 150 for grammar reference and more practice.

SPEAKING

1 Work in pairs. Look at your poems from GRAMMAR 4 again. Which things seem to be most frustrating for people in the class? Summarise the points.

Some people complain about having too much work.
A lot of us wish that we had more free time.

2 Discuss what you can do to try and make your wishes reality.

A three-day weekend is not possible, but we could work a half day on Fridays!

a

b

c

d

READING

1 Look at the photos. Who do you think took each one? Why? What success could they be celebrating?

2 Read the first paragraph of the online article. What is Positive Visualisation?

3 Read the rest of the article and match headings a–e to paragraphs 1–5.

a Do it on the move
b Brain training
c How is it used?
d What is it exactly?
e Mental pictures

4 **a** Without looking at the article, match the words to make collocations.

concentration	outlook
confidence	power
optimum	building
positive	method/tool/technique
training	performance

b Check your answers in the article.

5 Complete the definitions with the collocations in 4a.

Positive visualisation

1 can lead to *optimum performance* in sport
2 is a .... that we can apply to other skills outside sport
3 works when combined with a ....
4 can help in .... for athletes
5 can help increase ....

6 Work in pairs. Discuss the question.

- Think of a skill that you have had to learn. Do you think positive visualisation could have helped you do it better?

Positive Visualisation

1 ....

Positive Visualisation is a training technique that has been used in fields as diverse as medicine, management and sports psychology. There is a powerful relationship between mental and physical performance in sport. For sportsmen and women, visualisation is used primarily to improve the quality of athletic movement, increase concentration power and reduce the pressures of competition through confidence-building.

2 ....

Visualisation occurs when athletes create an image or a series of images, such as a diver imagining himself at the point he enters the water. Without any external prompts or stimulation, the images are mentally generated by the athlete alone. Visual images are only one part of the technique; sounds, sensations, muscle movements and emotions also play an important part.

3 ....

Visualisation is a skill that needs practice. When familiar with the technique the athlete can immediately access an image that conveys a representation of perfection. The brain is directing the muscles to work in a desired way creating a neural pattern in the brain, a pattern identical to the one created by the actual physical performance of the movements.

4 ....

During organised athletic training, psychologists and athletes will practise and perfect the visualisation techniques in a quiet area to eliminate distractions. The technique can be used as a mental rehearsal or practice of the specific techniques required in a sport (e.g. the footwork of a high jumper before take-off).

5 ....

It can be used during the athletes' off hours, during training, rehabilitation or just before the performance. These visualisations, when combined with a positive outlook, help athletes reach optimum performance. Now this technique is being applied to other skills, such as language learning, giving presentations and live performing, too.

Listening

a

b

c

d

e

f

1 11.5 Listen to two people talking about using English in the future. Match images a–f to their future visions. More than one answer may be correct. What is the difference between their visions?

2 Listen again and answer the questions.

1 What problems do the speakers imagine? What's the reason for this?
2 What kinds of positive visualisation do you think might help them with these problems?

3 **a** Read transcript 11.5 on page 167 and complete the sentences. What expressions do Rashid and Louise use to talk about this imagined future?

1 I hope to ....
2 I like the idea of meeting ....
3 I can see myself ....
4 .... really appeals to me.
5 I'd like to live ....
6 It'd be great to ....

b Rewrite the answers in 3a so that they are true for you.

Speaking

1 Read the example of another student's vision. What is the difference between this vision and those in Listening 1? How does the speaker make it more effective?

'I close my eyes and I imagine my life three or four years from now. I'm speaking in English as well as I speak in Spanish or Basque now. In my dream I live in London. I work in a hospital looking after my patients. I talk with them fluently and I understand everything that they tell me. I am very self-confident. I'm aware of the importance of language in my job, because a nurse works with people. I have to talk with my patients to know how they are and I should be sensitive to their needs. I have to talk to the doctors too to understand the treatment and diagnosis. A small mistake can have enormous and terrible consequences, so I am always very careful.'

2 What specific images from Edurne's vision in 1 come into your mind as you read the text?

I can imagine her standing next to a bed in a hospital ward.

3 Imagine yourself speaking English as vividly as possible. Try to imagine particular details. Use the questions to help you.

- Where are you? Who are you with?
- Is it a place related to work or pleasure?
- What exactly are you saying? How long do you speak for?
- What is the reaction of the people around you? How do they respond? Are there any sounds or movements that you are aware of?
- Is there any moment when things go wrong? If so, what do you do to sort it out?
- Does the vision end? Is it a one-off scene or one that is repeated?

4 Work in pairs. Once you have 'captured' your vision, tell it to your partner and discuss similarities and differences.

5 Listen to other students' visions. Are there any visions which recur? Which are the most vivid and memorable?

a

b

c

TUNE IN

1 **a** Look at the images. What problems do you think the people are having? Use the words in the box to help you guess.

> attention span computer concentrate contract crash distracted erase noise schedule

b Look at the problems on page 161 and check your answers.

2 **a** Look at statements 1–3. Which of the problems in images a–c do you think they are addressing?

1 You should always save a copy of your files.
2 If I were you, I'd read the small print first before you sign.
3 In your position, I'd set myself deadlines.

b Underline the different expressions for giving advice.

FOCUS ON LANGUAGE

3 11.6 Listen to three people giving advice about the problems in 1. Which of images a–c are they talking about? Tick the words in 1a that you hear.

4 **a** Listen again. Which speaker talks about

1 setting an objective?
2 focusing on one thing at a time?
3 doing something different?
4 isolating yourself?
5 taking a break?

b Which person do you think gives the best advice?

5 Look at some ways of responding to advice. Which accept the advice and which reject it?

1 That's a good idea.
2 That doesn't normally work for me.
3 OK, I'll try that.
4 You know, I'd prefer not to.
5 Yes, that could work, thanks.

> **Intonation**
>
> 11.7 Listen to the responses in 5. Mark the words which are stressed. What is the difference between the intonation in the positive responses and the negative responses?
> *That's a good idea*. (voice rises)
> Listen and repeat paying special attention to the intonation.

6 Look at some more pieces of advice. What do you think could be the problem in each case?

1 Have you thought about getting a new look?
2 If I were you, I'd end the relationship.
3 In your situation/position/shoes, I'd move house.
4 You could always change jobs.
5 You should/ought to start saving some money.

7 **a** Work in pairs. Student A, choose a problem on this page and ask Student B for advice. Student B, give advice. Student A, respond, by either accepting or rejecting the advice.

b Swap roles.

8 Act out the conversation with other students. Can they guess which problem you are talking about?

> **NOTICE** REGISTER
>
> It is possible to give advice using an imperative, but using this direct form means you may know the person well. *If I were you/in your situation* is more formal and indirect.
> Compare:
> *Just end the relationship!* and *If I were you, I'd end the relationship.*

OVER TO YOU

9 Think of your own problem. Go around the class, explain your problem and ask different students to give advice. Listen, decide on the best advice and accept it. Reject the other pieces of advice.

10 Report back on your decision to the rest of the class.

a

b

c

TUNE IN

1 Look at images a–c. In what different contexts do you think these people are presenting themselves or being presented?

2 **a** Match the pieces of advice 1–3 to images a–c. More than one answer may be possible.

1 After the first few minutes you won't be nervous, so remember to stay calm.
2 You should offer the card when you say hello.
3 A firm handshake is a good start.

b 11.8 Listen to three people in different situations. What do you think they are doing wrong? Match mistakes i–iii to situations 1–3.

i The tone is too informal and familiar.
ii The person shouldn't make a joke.
iii The speaker shouldn't say how they are feeling.

3 In which of the situations in transcript 11.8 would sentences 1–6 fit well?

1 Well, I feel I'm well-qualified for the post because of my previous work experience.
2 Please don't hesitate to contact me if you need any further information.
3 I'd like to thank X for inviting me to speak to you all today.
4 Today I'm going to speak about the field of...
5 I look forward to hearing from you when it's convenient.
6 Pleased to meet you, too. Many thanks for giving me this opportunity.

4 11.9 Listen to the improved versions of the situations in 11.8 and check your answers. What other differences did you notice? Read transcript 11.9 on page 167. In what ways is formality expressed?

PREPARE FOR TASK

5 Work in pairs. Have you ever been in one of the situations in the images? How did you handle it? What went wrong or right?

6 Choose one of the situations and plan other ways in which you could present yourself in a positive light (not necessarily through language). Rank the suggestions in order of importance. Is it all good advice?

1 Appear confident.
2 Establish eye contact with audience/interlocutor.
3 Wear smart clothes.
4 Smile in a friendly way.
5 Be in control of your topic.
6 Answer a question even if you don't know the answer.

TASK

7 Work in pairs. Act out one of the situations in the images. Practise it in a formal and an informal way. Remember to use body language.

REPORT BACK

8 Listen to other students' conversations. Which was the best formal and informal conversation? Why?

➜ Go to Review D, Unit 11, p. 137 ➜ Go to Writing bank 6, p. 157

12 MEMORIES

1 a Work in pairs. Look at the image and discuss the questions.

- Who wrote the message?
- Who was it written for?
- What do you think he/she forgot?
- What do you think happened next?

b Share your ideas with the class. When was the last time you said *Sorry, I forgot*? Who did you say it to and why?

2 a 12.1 Listen to three people answering the question in 1b. What did they forget? Are any of the answers similar to yours?

b Listen again and complete the sentences.

1 I **forgot** to buy .... yesterday... on the way home from ....
2 He even .... me up to **remind** me to bring it with me.
3 But I did **remember** to .... it to him today!
4 I completely **forgot that** it was ....
5 ... I just didn't **remember** to ....
6 I've set my .... to **remind** me!

3 Look again at the sentences in 2b and complete A in the KEY VOCABULARY PANEL.

4 Work in pairs. Answer the questions.

1 Do you ever forget any of the things in the list?
   - people's names
   - important dates (birthdays, anniversaries, Mother's Day)
   - appointments (at the doctor/dentist/hairdresser)
   - your phone, your sunglasses, your umbrella
   - online passwords and PIN numbers
2 What methods do you use to help you remember? Think about the ideas in the box and add your own.

   calendar   diary   lists   mobile phone   post-its

3 Do you think you have a good memory?

5 12.2 Listen to three people answering the questions in 4. Which question is each person answering?

1 Ana   2 Pete   3 Eli

6 a Look at the sentences. Which person from 5 is speaking?

1 I have a photographic memory. I found it really easy to memorise things at school.
2 Sometimes I think I have a really bad short-term memory!
3 I have a really bad memory for names!
4 I usually ask someone else to remind me.
5 I forget other things too, like umbrellas, my sunglasses.
6 And when it comes to distant memories, childhood memories and things like that, then they get really vague.

b Work in pairs. Are any of the answers similar to yours?

KEY VOCABULARY

Remembering

A Verbs

We use
***remember*, *forget*, *remind* + *to* +** infinitive (NOT verb + *-ing*) when there is something important that you need (or needed) to do.
Use (1)*remember / remind* + *to* followed by the thing you need to do.
Use (2)*remember / remind* followed by the person who needs to do it.
I remembered to call her.
Please remind me to call her.

We use
remember*, *forget* + *-ing (NOT *to* + infinitive) when we are thinking about actions, events and feelings in the past.
*I remember **hearing** that music at a party recently.*

- Complete the sentences so that they are true for you.

I always forget to (3) ....
I'll never forget (4) ....ing (5) ....

NOTICE

We usually use *forget* + verb + *-ing*.
I'll never forget Barça winning the European Cup.

B Adjectives

childhood   clear   distant   early
happy   long-term   photographic
precious   selective   short-term
vague   visual   vivid

- Look at the words in the box. Which can be used to describe
  a) memory (ability to remember things)?
     long-term
  b) memories (things we remember about the past)?
     childhood

7 a Complete B in the KEY VOCABULARY PANEL.

b Work in pairs. Discuss the questions.

- Do you think you have a selective memory? Give examples.
- Which is more important do you think: short-term memory or long-term memory? Why?

- PRACTISE PAST IMAGINED SITUATIONS
- TALK ABOUT HOW LIFE WOULD BE DIFFERENT

a

b

c

d

READING

1 Work in pairs. Look at the images and discuss the questions.

- What do the images have in common?
- What are the people doing in each of the images?
- Can you remember doing any of these things when you were a child? If yes, who did you do them with?

2 a Work in pairs. Read the blog post. Which of the images best matches the blog post? Why? Think of a title for the blog post.

b Read the blog post again. Answer the questions.

1 Why did the writer write this blog post?
2 The writer imagines her grandfather's reaction. Does she think it would have been positive or negative?
3 The writer speaks about changes that have taken place since her grandfather died. What changes does she mention?
4 The writer doesn't tell us why she chose the photo at the end. Do you know what this photo is about? Why do you think the writer likes this photo?

3 Find words in the text that mean

1 to make a mental connection between two separate things or ideas
2 started (a business)
3 perfect
4 told someone they had done something wrong
5 someone who buys new technology as soon as it is available
6 progress

4 Work in groups. Discuss the questions.

- How do the writer's childhood memories compare to yours?
- Who were the people who influenced you most as a young child? Why?

Thanks, Grandad!

Today is the birthday of the great internet search engine, Google. It's also the anniversary of the death of my grandfather. It may seem strange to associate the two things, but I've just found out that my grandad died on the very day Google was first launched and it's set me thinking about all the things that have changed in the world since then. And it's made me wonder what my grandad would have thought of it all.

When I was a kid we used to spend summer holidays at my grandparents'. It was great fun. They lived in the country and those holidays are full of idyllic childhood memories. We used to go fishing, we'd help out with the hens and the pigs, we'd swim in the river and eat the strawberries as we picked them in the garden – and grandma always told us off!

And we also spent hours in front of my grandad's computer. He was an early adopter… he was fascinated by all things technical. He'd worked as a news photographer and he loved digital photography and all its potential. I wonder what he'd have thought of the advances in digital photography today. What would he have said about the 'age of the image'? Would he have approved? I like to think he would. He was always one for sharing and I think if he'd been alive today he'd have appreciated the way Google and the internet and sites like Flickr and YouTube have made it so easy to find – and to share – images across the world.

So, in loving memory of a great man who filled me with enthusiasm for everything that's new and exciting, I'd like to share my all-time favourite photo. Thanks, grandad!

GRAMMAR

1 **a** Complete the extract from the text in READING 2a using *approved*, *said*, and *thought*. Check your answers in the text.

> I wonder what **he'd have** (1) .... of the advances in digital photography. What **would he have** (2) .... about the 'age of the image'? **Would he have** (3) ....? I like to think he would.

b Look again at the extract in 1a and answer the questions.

1 Who is 'he'?
2 Is the writer asking about something that really happened or is she imagining it?

2 Complete 1–7 in the GRAMMAR PANEL.

3 **a** Put the words in *italics* in the correct order. Check your answer in READING 2a.

I think (1)*he alive if been 'd* today (2)*appreciated have 'd he* the way Google and the internet have made it so easy to find – and to share – images across the world.

b Look at the sentence in 3a and answer the questions.

1 What does *'d* stand for in (1)?And in (2)?
2 Which verb phrase, (1) or (2), describes
   a) the imaginary reaction or result?
   b) the imaginary situation?

4 Complete 8–10 in the GRAMMAR PANEL.

5 **a** Complete the sentences using the past perfect or *would have* + past participle.

1 If I .... *(go)* to bed earlier last night, I .... *(not be)* so tired this morning.
2 If I .... *(not be)* so tired this morning, I .... *(get)* out of bed earlier.
3 If I .... *(not get)* up late, I .... *(not miss)* the bus.
4 If I .... *(not miss)* the bus, I .... *(get)* here on time.
5 If I .... *(get)* here on time, you .... *(not be)* so angry with me!

b When was the last time you were late for something? Why were you late? Write three sentences using *if* + past perfect + *would have* to explain the situation. Then share it with the class.

IMAGINARY SITUATIONS: PAST

A *Would have*

We use **would have** + (1) infinitive / past participle to talk about (2) imaginary / real situations in the past.

My grandfather would have approved of the advances in digital photography. (The writer imagines her grandfather's reactions and uses *would have* to show this.)

Complete the chart below using *'d*, *would* or *wouldn't*.

Contracted forms	*+ He* (3) .... *have approved.* *– He* (4) .... *have approved.*
Questions	(5) .... *he have approved?*
Yes/no answers	*Yes, he* (6) .... *No, he* (7) ....

B *If* + past perfect

We use *if* + past perfect to describe an imaginary situation in the past. Complete the examples using *'d*, *had* or *hadn't*.

\+ *If my grandfather* (8) .... *been alive...*
If he (9) .... *lived longer...*
– *If he* (10) .... *died...*

See page 151 for grammar reference and more practice.

PRONUNCIATION: contractions with *had / would have*

1 **a** 12.3 Look at the sentence. Listen and notice how the words in **bold** are contracted in speech.

*If he **had** been there, he **would have** done the same thing.*

b Listen and repeat.

2 **a** Write out sentences 1–3 with their full forms. Practise reading them out loud with the contracted forms.

1 If they'd asked me, I'd've said no.
2 I'd've paid less if I'd waited.
3 If she'd known, she'd've done something about it.

b Work in pairs. Think of a context for each of the sentences in 2a. Share your ideas with the class.

SPEAKING

1 **a** Work in small groups. Discuss this question.

- If you had been born 20 years earlier, how would your life have been different?

b Compare your answers with the rest of the class. Which difference would have been the most important? Why?

a

b

c

d

e

SPEAKING & LISTENING

1 Work in pairs. Look at the photos. Discuss the questions.

- What sense or senses does each image appeal to?
  coffee: the sense of smell, the sense of taste
- What sensations do they evoke?
  coffee: waking up in the morning ...
- Do any of them trigger any memories for you? If yes, what?
- Which image do you prefer? Why?

2 12.4 Listen to three people talking about one or more of the photos. Which photos a–e do they talk about? What memories do they describe?

3 a Listen again. Answer the questions. There may be more than one answer. Who talks about

1 a place where they lived in the past? ....
2 a place they visited? ....
3 seeing something for the first time? ....
4 sounds they associate with their memories? ....
5 the thing that triggers their memory? ....

b Work in pairs. Compare your answers and make a list of the sights, smells and sounds that are mentioned by the three people. Read transcript 12.4 on page 167 and check your answers.

4 Which sense is the strongest in triggering memories for you? Give examples.

VOCABULARY: phrasal verbs (2)

1 a Work in pairs. Complete the extracts without looking at the transcript.

1 I love the smell of fresh .... It really **takes me back**.
2 I had just started working for a ...., **looking after** their three ....
3 I just stood there and looked at the ...., trying to **take** it all **in**.
4 Once I actually got in the ...., they just couldn't **tear** me **away**!
5 I love this .... It **brings back** great memories of our ....
6 It's a great place to just **soak up** the ....

b 12.5 Listen and check.

2 Look at the phrasal verbs in **bold** in 1a. Match them to definitions a–f.

a absorb and understand information
b being responsible for someone or something
c to trigger feelings or memories
d remind somebody of the past
e spend time enjoying an experience
f take someone from a place using force

3 a Complete the questions with the verbs in 1a.

1 Can you think of any special sights or sounds that .... you .... to your childhood?
2 Was there any special game or activity you loved so much as a child that your parents had to .... you .... from it?
3 Have you ever had to .... young children? If yes, what are your main memories?
4 Do you have any favourite songs or music that .... particular memories?
5 When was the last time you sat back and .... the sun? Where were you? Who were you with? What else can you remember about the moment?
6 Do you find that we are offered too much information these days? Do you sometimes find it difficult to .... it all .... and remember it?

b Work in pairs. Ask and answer the questions in 3a. Share your answers with the class.

Grammar

1 **a** Match 1–9 to a–i to make sentences.

1 The café had only just
2 I've always
3 I had never
4 I had just
5 They had
6 They were
7 We'd just
8 It's
9 I've

a associated the smell of coffee with clattering cups.
b been to visit the antique market in San Telmo.
c held once a week.
d opened when I moved in.
e planned a holiday in Spain.
f seen the sea before.
g started working for a family.
h seen the tango so many times.
i lulled to sleep by the waves.

b Look at the verbs in the completed sentences in 1a. Which verbs are in a) the present perfect? b) the past perfect? c) the passive? What do the three forms have in common?

2 Look at the GRAMMAR PANEL. Read the list of uses for the three verb forms. Which uses can you find in the sentences in 1a?

3 **a** Complete the sentences so that they are true for you. Use past participles at the beginning of each gap. Use the verbs in the box to help you.

award build choose fly forget give go locate love meet pass play sail study try visit want

1 I've never ....
2 I've always ....
3 I've .... three times this week.
4 If I'd .... I'd have been a very different person.
5 I'd never .... before this year.
6 My primary school was ....
7 One of my favourite TV shows was ....
8 I was really happy when my teachers told me that I had ....
9 I wasn't very happy when my friends told me that they had ....

b Work in pairs. Compare your answers. Were any of them the same?

4 Choose two of your answers in 3a and read out the words you wrote in the gap. Can the class guess which sentence you are reading from?

Review

Past participles

The past participle is used to form.

- perfect tenses (*have* + past participle)
- the passive voice (*be* + past participle)

Uses of the present perfect

- to talk about an action or situation that started in the past and continues in the present
- to talk about an action that happened at some time in the past, but we don't focus on when exactly it happened
- to talk about experiences in general

Uses of the past perfect

- to show that one action happened before another
- to report speech
- with *if* to describe an imaginary or hypothetical situation in the past

Uses of the passive voice

- to emphasise who is responsible for an action using *by*
- when we don't know who or what is responsible for an action
- when it's obvious who or what is responsible for an action
- to describe a process

See page 151 for grammar reference and more practice.

Speaking

1 **a** Work in pairs. Look at the photo. Where do you think it was taken? What time of day is it? What is the weather like?

b Imagine the rest of the scene. What do you think is happening around the fountain? Imagine the sounds, smells and sensations. If you were there, what would you be doing?

2 **a** Work in pairs or small groups. Imagine that there are some people in the scene in 1b. Two (or more) of the people are having a conversation. What do you think they are talking about? Act out their conversation.

b Repeat the conversation for the class. Can the class guess the relationship between the people?

- PRACTISE VOCABULARY
- TALK ABOUT DIFFERENT WAYS OF LEARNING

a

b

c

d

What's new?

The website that keeps you in touch

A Rote learning, it seems, is back in the news… and for a whole host of different reasons. From memory championships to learning a new language, from school exams to becoming a cab driver, everyone's talking about rote learning, the pros and the cons. Here's a quick digest of the basics. Click on the links to find out more.

1 *So, what exactly is rote learning?*

2 *Why are so many people against it?*

SPEAKING

1 Work in pairs. Look at the images. What do you think the people are trying to learn? Which do you think is the most difficult to learn by heart*? Why?

* **to learn something by heart** – to memorise something so that you can repeat it perfectly without having to read from a book or a piece of paper

2 Work in pairs. Look at the list. Discuss the questions.

multiplication tables	equations in Maths and Science
poems	periodic table
lines in a play	verb lists
the words to a song	notes for an exam
pieces of music	

- Did you learn any of these things by heart when you were at school? Which was the easiest? And the most difficult? Can you still remember them now?
- Have you ever had to memorise anything else? If yes, what? How long did it take you? Can you still remember it today?

READING

1 **a** Read the introduction to a web page about rote learning. What information do you think the texts in links 1–3 will give about rote learning?

b Read texts B–D and check your answers to 1a. Match texts B–D to links 1–3.

2 **a** Look at the symbols and their meaning. Read texts B–D again and write the symbols alongside the texts to show your reactions.

! = I didn't know that / that's really interesting
√ = yes, I agree or I knew that already
? = I'm not sure I agree / understand
X = I disagree

b Work in pairs. Compare your notes. Explain why you wrote the symbols where you did. Did you write any symbols in the same places and for the same reasons? Share your answers with the class.

3 **a** Look at texts A–D again. Which text tells us the following information?

1 a lot of people are talking about rote learning
2 a lot of different people use rote learning in their day-to-day lives
3 rote learning is good for you
4 rote learning is no longer a relevant skill
5 rote learning is a valid and important skill in some professions
6 rote learning does not encourage critical thinking

b Has your attitude to rote learning changed at all after reading the information web page? Why/Why not?

3 *Why do so many people swear by it?*

Memorisation, and rote learning in particular, is still a very important skill in a number of fields. Actors need to perfect memorisation techniques in order to learn their lines. London cab drivers need to memorise routes across the city in order to get their taxi driver's licence. Professional musicians memorise whole symphonies, professional dancers memorise whole choreographies. And recent research suggests that exercising our memories in this way can help keep our brains healthy and fit, and prevent the early onset of senility. For those of us who don't need to memorise things as part of our jobs, doctors advise taking up pastimes like chess or dance classes like square dancing or Bollywood, activities that involve memorising complex sequences in order to keep our brains young and flexible well into old age.

C Rote learning is a memorisation technique that basically involves repeating something over and over until we have committed it to memory. School children use it as a way to learn poems, actors use it as a way to learn their lines, politicians use it to help them remember their speeches. We also use it when we need to remember a phone number or key dates and names for a history exam or the directions that someone's just given us on the street. Facts, figures and texts that are committed to memory in this way can be stored for a minute or for the rest of your life. The key is in the number of repetitions.

D Rote learning has gone out of fashion in some circles. People criticise it for being 'mindless', that we don't concentrate on the content or the message when we're learning by rote, we are merely 'parroting', repeating the sounds with no sense. Educationalists are calling for deep understanding and critical thinking. They believe that knowledge is best stored when it has been processed and understood. They criticise the practice of rote learning in schools, saying that it is no longer a necessary skill. In the age of the internet it is much more important to know how to access information, and how to analyse it, evaluate it and use it.

VOCABULARY: review

1 Look at the words in the box. You have exactly two minutes to memorise them. When you have finished, close your books and write down as many of the words as you can remember.

ranch sign language placard speech browse crops graffiti disturbing earthquake exhibition gesture newspaper

2 Repeat the exercise with the words in the box. This time notice that the words are in alphabetical order.

barrier dump holiday join junk link mask myth parade stuff tale version

3 Repeat the exercise again with the words in the box. But before you do, work in pairs, decide if the words are nouns, verbs or adjectives and match them to the four unit topics. Some words can be more than one.

Topics

1 Permission and prohibition
2 Ideas and solutions
3 Identity
4 Memory

access benefit childhood clumsy compulsory confidence enable innovative remind short-term trespassing vague virtual

4 a Work in pairs. Which memory test did you find the easiest to do? Why?

b Read the short commentary on the memory tests. Do you agree?

> Most people find that it is easier to remember the list of 12 words when they have processed them in some way. Categorising or grouping usually works well, as does trying to create or remember a context for a word. Words which are presented in some kind of order, e.g. alphabetical, are usually easier to remember than ones which don't seem to have any order at all. Most language experts agree that one of the best ways to learn and remember vocabulary is to read as much and as widely as you can, encountering the new words again and again in a variety of contexts.

5 Choose five of the words from 2 and 3. Write a definition for each one. Close your books and read your definitions to the class. Can your classmates remember the words?

6 a 12.6 Listen to three people talking about how they learn vocabulary. Make notes on the main techniques they use.

b Work in pairs. Compare your notes. Which technique do you think is the most effective? Why? Do you know of any other techniques for learning vocabulary?

TUNE IN

1 Look at the images. What do you think each person is apologising for? What do you think they are saying, or are going to say? Whose apology do you think is most heartfelt?

2 a 12.7 Listen to four short conversations. Match conversations 1–4 to images a–c. Which conversation does not match an image?

b Work in pairs. Compare your answers. What image does the fourth conversation create in your mind?

FOCUS ON LANGUAGE

3 a Look at the extracts from 2a. Which conversations do they come from?

a I'm sorry, I'll do it for the next class.
b I really am very sorry. There was no excuse.
c I'm so sorry! That was so clumsy.
d I'm really sorry. I promise it won't happen again!

b Match extracts a–d in 3a to responses i–iv.

i It's OK. Just don't let it happen again!
ii Yeah... until the next time!
iii Well, I suppose that'll have to do!
iv Don't worry, I'll get a cloth.

4 Listen again and decide which apology sounds a) the most sincere, b) the least sincere.

Intonation

12.8 Listen to three people saying *sorry*. Who is
a) apologising?
b) asking someone to repeat what they said?
c) being sarcastic?
Listen again and repeat with the correct intonation.

5 a Work in pairs. Write short apologies for situations 1–4.

1 you bump into someone in a bar and spill their drink
2 you arrive late at a meeting
3 you forgot your best friend's birthday
4 you forgot to bring your wallet and can't pay for something in a shop

b Think of appropriate responses for each apology. Act out the situations with your partner.

6 a 12.9 Listen to three more apologies and answer the questions.

1 Where are they?
2 What are they apologising for?

b Work in pairs. Compare your answers.

7 a Put the words in the correct order to make formal apologies.

1 announce regret we to
2 inconvenience for apologise we any
3 phone we're answer afraid can't the we

b Match apologies 1–3 in 7a to their informal equivalents a–c.

a We're sorry if we've caused you any problems.
b We're really sorry, but we can't answer the phone.
c We're sorry to say...

OVER TO YOU

8 a Look at the situations. Decide
a) if you think a formal or informal apology would be better.
b) if it would be better to apologise in person, on the phone, by email or by text.

1 You are on your way to meet a friend, you're running late and will probably arrive about half an hour after the time you'd agreed.
2 You will not be able to attend a work meeting tomorrow because of an unexpected personal problem.
3 You borrowed your friend's bike and it got damaged in a crash.
4 You don't think you'll be able to attend a distant relative's wedding party because of work commitments.

b Work in pairs. Act out one of the face-to-face or phone apologies to the class.

9 Do you generally prefer to apologise face to face or in writing? Why?

TUNE IN

This particular story has grown into a kind of family legend, the myth of the monster mushroom. I was four when it happened. We were on a camping holiday in the North of Scotland. I can remember my bed in the camper van. I can remember wearing red boots and splashing in puddles in the rain. And I think I remember the story of the giant mushroom, but then again it's been told so many times that I'm not sure anymore what's a real memory and what isn't!

But back to the story. We had stopped for the night in a field near a river. In the morning I got up and put on my favourite boots. Dad was up and looking for mushrooms. I was just playing around, apparently, when I came across this enormous mushroom. According to the story I've heard so many times, I picked the mushroom up and it filled my little four-year-old arms. There was lots of cheering and clapping and the mushroom went into the frying pan. Now that's something I remember really clearly. I remember that the mushroom almost completely filled the pan. There are no photos of that. I think those really are my memories, but they may just be images I created to illustrate the story in my mind. Can a mushroom really be as big as a frying pan? And apparently the mushroom was one of the most delicious mushrooms ever, or so the story goes. Of course I can't remember that bit. Everybody knows four-year-olds hate mushrooms!

1 **a** Look at the two images, read the story and explain the connection.

b Read the story again. How much of the story does the writer actually remember and how much of it has he been told later in life?

2 Work in small groups. Discuss the questions. Share your answers with the class.

- What are your earliest childhood memories? How old were you?
- How do you know they are real memories and not images that have been created by other people's stories?
- Can we ever trust our early memories to be 100% accurate? Why/Why not?

NOTICE *FOUR-YEAR-OLD*

When we use *four-year-old* as an adjective or a noun, *year* is not in the plural.

... my four-year-old arms

... four-year-olds hate mushrooms

When we talk about how old someone is, we use *years*.

He was four years old.

PREPARE FOR TASK

3 **a** Look at the text in 1a. Underline the sections that explain what actually happened in the story. Identify

1. the main event.
2. an action that happened the day before.
3. an action in progress when the main event took place.

b Which verb form is used to describe each action, the past simple, past continuous or past perfect?

4 Write a short paragraph describing what you think happened after the mushroom was cooked. Use a variety of verb forms.

5 Find the words and phrases in the box in the text in 1a. What function are they performing? What do they tell us about the story?

according to the story   apparently
or so the story goes

TASK

6 **a** Think of a story from your childhood. Make notes about

- how old you were, where you were and what you were doing there.
- who was with you and their part in the story.
- the main events.
- how it ended.

b You are going to write the story as an entry to an online competition. Write the story as you remember it.

REPORT BACK

7 **a** Work in pairs. Swap stories from 6b. Read your partner's story and write two or three questions you would like to ask to find out more about the story.

b Ask and answer.

➜ Go to Review D, Unit 12, p. 138

VOCABULARY

Ideas & solutions

1 **a** Change the sentences using the word in brackets.

1 This invention really helps people who live a long way from each other. *(benefit)*
2 It means that they can communicate with each other cheaply. *(enable)*
3 And it really helps people who live on their own. *(a great help)*

b R21 Listen and check. What invention do you think the sentences are describing?

2 **a** Look at the image of the bicycle. Write a similar text to 1a about its benefits.

b Work in pairs. Talk about an invention that has really helped you.
My mobile phone allows me to do so many things ...

Phrasal verbs (1)

3 **a** Choose the correct phrasal verb to complete the questions.

1 Have you *taken up* / *burnt out* a new sport or free-time activity recently?
2 Have you ever had to *give up* / *keep up* something because you didn't have enough time to do it?
3 Do you sometimes find it difficult to *keep up* / *take up* with your workload?
4 Do you know anyone who has worked so hard they've *burnt out* / *carried on*?

b Work in pairs. Ask and answer the questions.

Metaphorical language

4 **a** R22 Listen to four people. What insight is each person talking about in each case?

b Listen again and complete the gaps. The first letter of each word is given.

1 Suddenly I s............ the l............ , I knew had to...
2 Then it just c............ , I r............ I had to ....
3 I was at the c............ , I could go one w............ or the other...
4 Then I had a f............ of i............ , the way forward was to open my own business...

GRAMMAR

Passives

1 **a** Complete the sentences using an appropriate form of the passive and the verbs in brackets.

1 I .... never .... to a wedding. *(invite)*
2 I .... once .... to represent my school in athletics. *(choose)*
3 Our house .... this week. *(redecorated)*
4 English .... in most of the shops and restaurants in the town centre. *(speak)*
5 My hometown .... by the Phoenicians over 3000 years ago. *(found)*

b Work in pairs. Are the sentences true for you or your town? If not, change them so that they are.

Who, which, that

2 **a** Join the sentences using a relative pronoun (*who/which/that*). In which cases is the pronoun NOT necessary?

1 That's the test. I failed it.
2 I love films. They make me scared.
3 I like people. They make me laugh.
4 I bought a watch. It cost 100 dollars.
5 I don't understand people. They are impolite.
6 Marlene's the woman. I was talking about her yesterday.

b Work in pairs. Change the sentences so that they are meaningful to you. Compare with your partner.

FUNCTIONAL LANGUAGE

Getting things done

1 **a** R23 Listen to two conversations. Where is each taking place? What does each person want to do?

b Listen again. Tick the expressions that you hear.

1 A I need to *have* / *get* my driving licence renewed.
B It will be *renewed* / *sent* within ten days.

2 A Can you get this suit *cleaned* / *washed* by the end of the day?
B We can get it *done* / *ready* for seven tonight.

2 Work in pairs. Think of a service that you need someone to do for you. Act out the conversations.

LOOKING BACK

- Think of five gadgets or machines that you have used today. Which do you think is the most useful and why?
- Think of five common turning points in people's lives.
- Think of five useful expressions that you have learnt in this unit. In which situations could you use them?

VOCABULARY

Roles

1 a Complete the gaps with a suitable role and a verb from the list.

Roles	Verbs
fan loner lover performer	care entertain escape support

1 She's a big .... of Chelsea, she .... them even when they lose.
2 She's a real animal .... , she really .... for them.
3 He's a natural .... , he likes an audience and he was born to ....
4 She's a bit of a .... , she likes to .... and get away from other people.

b R24 Work in pairs. Listen and check. Do you know someone who could match the roles?

Gaming

2 Work in pairs. Which two of these words can NOT be preceded by 'virtual' or 'online'?

community self identity shopping world age computer space

Personality adjectives

3 a Think of an adjective to match these descriptions.

1 He's always losing things and forgetting appointments.
2 She's always tripping over or spilling things, it's terrible.
3 He's really sociable and likes meeting new people.
4 He can never make his mind up.
5 She's a very private person, she keeps things to herself.

b Which of the descriptions in 3a could apply to somebody you know?

GRAMMAR

Imaginary situations

1 a Write consequences for these imaginary situations.

What would happen if...
... everyone drove a car?
... everyone spoke English?
... nobody needed to work?
... there were no borders between countries?
If everyone drove a car, the cities would be even more polluted.

b Work in pairs. Compare your ideas. Then think of an imaginary situation of your own.

If only / I wish

2 a Look at the picture. What does this person wish? Make sentences with *if only* and *I wish*.

b Work in pairs. Think of some things that you would like to change about yourself and your world.

FUNCTIONAL LANGUAGE

Giving advice

1 a R25 Listen to someone giving advice to a friend and complete the chart.

Problem	
Suggested solutions	

b Listen again and complete the advice.

If I were you, I'd...
You could always...
Have you thought about...

2 a Work in pairs. Look at the three situations. Choose one and write three pieces of advice using the structures in 1b.

- your friend wants to sign up for a language course abroad
- your mum wants to buy a new computer
- your teacher wants to do something different in class

b Compare your advice with the rest of the class. Who gives the best advice?

LOOKING BACK

- Think of five different ways of describing your identity.
- Think of five pieces of advice that you have given or been given recently. Was the advice followed?
- Which vocabulary would you most like to remember from this unit? How are you going to remember it?

VOCABULARY

Remembering (verbs)

1 Match 1–6 to a–f to make sentences. There may be more than one answer.

1 I'll never forget	a that smoking is not permitted.
2 Please remind me	b meeting the president.
3 I can't remember	c saying that, I'm really sorry!
4 If I remember rightly	d to set the alarm, ok?
5 I mustn't forget	e the keys this time!
6 I must remind you	f we're meeting on the 16th.

2 **a** Use prompts a–f in 1 to make your own sentences.

I'll never forget when Spain won the World Cup.

b Work in pairs. Compare and discuss your sentences in 2a with your partner.

Remembering (adjectives)

3 **a** Rewrite the underlined sections in the sentences using adjectives in the box and make any other changes necessary. Two do not apply.

early long-term photographic precious
selective short-term vivid

1 Like most people, I can remember things that I have heard recently.
2 I have a clear idea of my first few years, it's all very detailed.
3 One of the first things I remember is going to the fair with my parents and riding on a merry-go-round.
4 I don't forget a place easily, the image stays in my mind.
5 I think it's true that sometimes people remember just what they want to remember about a situation.

b R26 Listen and compare. Make the sentences true for you.

Phrasal verbs (2)

4 **a** Think about 1–5 and make notes.

1 A kind of taste or sound or smell that takes you back to childhood or brings back special memories.
2 A time when you looked after something or someone.
3 A place you went to that was so interesting you had to tear yourself away.
4 A time when you just sat back, watched the scene and took it all in without actually doing anything.
5 Your favourite place for soaking up the sun.

b Work in pairs. Compare your notes and discuss.

The smell of fresh cut grass reminds me of when my dad mowed the lawn.

GRAMMAR

Imaginary situations: past

1 **a** Look at the situations. Write sentences about them using *would have* + *if* + past perfect.

Regrets

1 I didn't study abroad when I had the chance.
2 I gave up music lessons when I was a child.
3 I didn't have any children.

Things I'm happy about

4 I went to university.
5 I got married.
6 I continued playing football.

b Work in pairs. Compare your ideas and then create your own situations.

Review

2 **a** Complete the sentences in any way you like to make true sentences about you and your life.

1 I've always .... to ....
2 Yesterday, X told me that he/she had ....
3 I had just .... when ....
4 I had never .... until recently
5 I have .... for ....
6 My favourite .... was ....
7 The .... is going to be ....

b R27 Listen to somebody doing the same exercise. Were their answers similar to yours?

FUNCTIONAL LANGUAGE

Apologising

1 **a** R28 Listen to three people apologising. What are they sorry about? Does the other person accept the apology?

b Listen again and complete the gaps.

A I'm (1) .... (2) .... I forgot your birthday...
B Don't (3) .... I don't celebrate it any more...

C I (4) .... (5) .... (6) .... that I haven't had time to do that work you asked me for... I've just...
D Well, that's (7) .... (8) .... (9) ....

E I'm (10) .... (11) .... I don't know how it (12) ....
F Well, I do actually... just don't (13) .... (14) .... (15) .... again, OK?

LOOKING BACK

- Think about what aspects you think you have improved most during the course.
- What has been the most useful thing about this final unit?

LISTENING

1 a Work in small groups. Look at the word cloud showing different language and skills that people might need more practice in. Which of these could be a priority for you?

slang/colloquial expression
pronunciation
grammatical accuracy
formal/polite register
listening practice
fluency practice

b R29 Listen to two people talking about the areas they need to work on. Tick the words they mention in 1a.

2 Listen again and answer the questions.

1

1 Why was the interview such a key moment for the speaker?
2 Which of the things in 1a does he consider to be a priority and which not?
3 What are his plans for the future?

2

4 Why is the speaker still not fluent?
5 What does she think would help her?
6 What are her aims? What is she looking forward to in particular?

3 Choose the correct options to complete the text.

Didac

Well, I had an interview the other day and after that I realised that I had to prioritise different things in my English studies. I want to be a doctor and study in the UK. Anyway, the interview didn't go very well. I (1)*am / was* asked lots of different questions and sometimes I didn't understand them the first time. So I think I (2)*will / would* benefit from more listening practice. I wish I (3)*have / had* done a bit of that before the interview, it was embarrassing to ask them to repeat. Also, the man (4)*who / which* interviewed me spoke very formally. That wouldn't (5)*be / have* been a problem if (6)*I had / I'd had* been familiar with that kind of language, but I wasn't. So, I think I (7)*will / would* find learning more formal expressions very useful as well. The good thing was that the interviewer understood me and the assessor (8)*who / which* I spoke to at the end said I sounded very English.

Juliana

The thing (9)*which / who* I find really difficult still is sounding fluent. I still speak in short sentences. I have to think about what I'm going to say next. I really need to work on that. If I (10)*had / have* more time, I (11)*could / can* do a language exchange. That's where I could get some more practice. I (12)*have been / will be* told that just chatting a little bit everyday should help. I think that (13)*will / would* be worth doing. I don't really need English for work. And I don't want to sound like a native speaker (14)*which / who* says everything perfectly. I just want to sound like myself, with the same confidence I have in my mother tongue. I wish teachers (15)*would tell / had told* me that when I was studying. Next week, I'm seeing an Australian friend (16)*who / which* is going to teach me all the slang and street language from Australia. That'll be great!

SPEAKING

4 Work in pairs. Who do you feel most similar to, Didac or Juliana? Why?

5 a Work in groups. Look back at the word cloud in 1a and discuss the questions.

- What are your general aims and priorities after finishing this course?
- What specific areas of English do you think you need to work on?
- How are you going to do this?

b Report back on your discussion to the rest of the class. Make a list of your priorities and plans.

QUICK CHECK

Complete the checklist below.

Can you...	Yes, I can.	Yes, more or less.	I need to look again.
1 describe a process and/or how something works?	☐	☐	☐
2 talk about solutions and innovations ?	☐	☐	☐
3 enquire about certain services you want done?	☐	☐	☐
4 talk about your identity?	☐	☐	☐
5 explain problems and give advice?	☐	☐	☐
6 give a good impression when introducing yourself?	☐	☐	☐
7 talk about changes and their consequences?	☐	☐	☐
8 recount a childhood memory?	☐	☐	☐

Compare your answers with a partner.

- What else do you know now after studying units 10–12?
- Do you need to look again at any of the sections?
- Do you need any extra help from your teacher?

Unit 1 Grammar Reference

1.1 Tense review

Present simple or present continuous?

Use the present simple to talk about
- habits and routines: *I talk to my brother once a week on the phone.*
- things which are generally true: *Animals often use body language to talk to each other.*

Use the present continuous to talk about things that are happening now or around now: *Can you be quiet, please. I'm talking to someone on the phone.*

Past simple or present perfect?

Use the past simple to talk about
- completed actions in the past: *I read a fascinating article about communication last week.*
- repeated, habitual actions in the past: *I read a lot of books when I was younger.*

Use the present perfect to talk about experiences with no specific time reference: *I've met a lot of interesting people through my work.*

Future: *will* or *going to*?

We can use both *will* and *going to* to make predictions: *It's going to be/It'll be a great party!*

We often use *going to*, but not *will*, to talk about intentions and plans: *I'm going to study media and communications.*

▶ 1.1

1.2 Question forms

Questions with *be*

verb + subject: *Were you at the concert?*

Yes/No questions

auxiliary verb + subject + main verb: *Did you see the match?*

Wh- questions

Wh- questions begin with a question word or expression, e.g. *which, what, who, why, how much, how old, how long, what kind, what type, which way, which one*, etc.

There are two types of *wh-* questions:

Object questions (the *wh-* question word is the object of the verb)
wh question word + auxiliary + subject + main verb: *What did you make?*
Use *do/does* and *did* in the present and past simple.

Subject questions (the *wh-* question word is the subject of the verb)
wh question word + verb: *Who made the sign?*
Do NOT use *do/does/did* in the present and past simple:
Who made the sign? NOT *Who ~~did make~~ the sign?*

▶ 1.2

1.3 State & dynamic verbs

State verbs (e.g. *love, know, understand*) describe emotions, beliefs and sensations. They are not usually used in the continuous: *I don't know this.* NOT *~~I'm not knowing~~ this.*

Dynamic verbs (e.g. *watch, do, run, read*) describe conscious actions. Use continuous verb forms for actions in progress: *I was watching the sun set.*

We often use verbs of the senses (*see, hear, smell, taste, feel*) to describe sensations with *can* or *could*: *I can't smell anything, I've got a cold.*

Some verbs can be both state and dynamic, e.g. *see, have, think.*

Their meanings often change:

I can't see without glasses. (*see* = sense) *I'm seeing Jane on Friday.* (*see* = meet)
I don't have any money. (*have* = possess) *We're having a party.* (*have a party* = action)
I think you are right. (*think* = believe) *I'm thinking of you* (*think* = mental process)

▶ 1.3

1.1

a Correct the verbs in **bold**.

1 **I'm always finding** it really difficult to speak to people when I meet them for the first time.
2 **I work** really hard on improving my pronunciation at the moment.
3 When I was younger **I've really wanted** to learn to speak Japanese.
4 **I didn't visit** any English-speaking countries.
5 Next year **I'll study** abroad for six months.
6 I think that really **helps** me improve my English.

b Rewrite the sentences so that they are true for you.

1.2

a Look at the sign. Write questions about it using the prompts.

1 When / you write it?
2 Why / you write it?
3 What / be it for?
4 What / happen when other people saw it?
5 it / have the effect you wanted?
6 How many people / come along?

b Imagine you wrote the sign. Answer the questions.

1.3

a Look at the verbs in *italics*. Which should not be in the present continuous? Rewrite them using *can*.

1 *I'm hearing* a strange noise.
2 *I'm listening to* music.
3 *I'm looking* out of the window.
4 *I'm seeing* some friends this evening.
5 *I'm smelling* something really nice, it's making me feel hungry!

b Are any of these sentences true for you at the moment? Write four more sentences describing what you are doing at the moment and your sensations.

2.1 Past simple & past continuous

Use the past simple to talk about single events, especially when we are telling a story. Use the past continuous to explain the background to the story and describe a situation or action that was in progress at the time: *We were watching the TV when we heard a knock at the door.*

We were watching TV. We heard a knock at the door.

▶ 2.1

2.2 Past perfect & past simple

Past perfect

Form the past perfect with *had* + past participle.

+	I'd (I had) been there before.
–	I hadn't been there before.
?	Had you been there before?
Y/N	Yes, I had. / No, I hadn't.

Use the past perfect to talk about an event that happened before a point in time in the past or to describe a situation that was in progress up to a point in time in the past:

He had died one week earlier.

Their two families had been at war for years.

Past perfect & past simple

Use the past simple to describe the main events in a story. Use the past perfect to explain that one event happened before another: *His father **had only been** dead for a few weeks when the Prince met his ghost.*

His father died. The Prince met his father's ghost.

▶ 2.2

2.3 *Used to* & *would*

Similarities

We can use both *used to* and *would* to talk about repeated actions and habits in the past:

I used to work in a bar at weekends. I'd work on Saturday evenings and Sunday lunchtimes.

Differences

Use *used to* to talk about feelings, states and actions:

We used to walk to school every morning. (action)

I used to hate getting up in the morning. (feeling)

Use *would* with actions only:

We would always stop at the shop to buy some sweets. (action)

I used to love that sweet shop. (feeling) NOT *I ~~would love~~ that sweet shop.*

In questions and negative forms there's no *d* at the end of *use*:

Did you use to play tennis in school?

No, I didn't use to like sport very much.

▶ 2.3

2.1

Complete the story using the past simple or past continuous form of the verbs in the box.

call carry come hear look like move see take walk

We [1] .... home one night when we [2] .... a noise. It [3] .... from a garden at the end of our street. There was a light flashing at one of the windows of the house. It [4] .... a torch. The light [5] .... from window to window. Suddenly we [6] .... two dark figures standing at the front door. They [7] .... a flatscreen TV set out of the house! I [8] .... out my mobile and [9] .... the police.

2.2

Complete the sentences with the verbs in brackets in the correct form. Use one in the past simple and one in the past perfect.

1 I .... (*just/finish*) work when my mobile .... (*ring*).
2 My boyfriend .... (*forget*) his keys and he .... (*need*) to get into his flat.
3 Luckily he .... (*give*) me a spare set of keys a few days before and I .... (*have*) them in my bag.
4 When I .... (*get*) to his flat, I had such a surprise. He .... (*organise*) a surprise birthday party for me!

2.3

a Complete the conversation with the correct form of *used to*.

A When you were a kid, [1] .... you [2] .... watch TV much?

B No, I [3] .... My parents [4] .... let us watch during the week – only two hours a day at the weekend.

A Really? That's pretty strict!

B I know. All my friends [5] .... talk about all these great programmes that I never saw!

b Look at the verbs in **bold**. Find three examples where *would* cannot be used. Replace *would* with the past simple.

When I was young, we [1]**'d** get up at six o'clock every morning to get ready for school. We [2]**'d** catch a bus from the top of our road at 7.15. Sometimes we [3]**'d have to** wait for ages when the weather **would be** bad. I remember one winter in particular when it [4] **would snow** a lot. Some days the bus just [5] **wouldn't come** at all and we could stay at home. The journey to school [6] **would always be** long and slow. Sometimes we [7] **wouldn't get** to the school gates until 8.30 – just in time for the first class.

UNIT 3 GRAMMAR REFERENCE

3.1 GRADABLE & ABSOLUTE ADJECTIVES

Gradable adjectives (e.g. *tired, good, special*)	can be made weaker or stronger: *it's quite nice, it's very nice*	to make weaker: *quite, fairly* to make stronger: *very, extremely*
Absolute adjectives (e.g. *exhausted, fantastic, unique*)	cannot be made weaker or stronger	to add emphasis: *totally, absolutely, completely, quite*

Quite

When *quite* is used with a gradable adjective, it makes the adjective weaker. When *quite* is used with an absolute adjective, it emphasises the strength of the adjective: *It was quite nice.* (*quite* = fairly) *It was quite unique.* (*quite* = totally)

▶ 3.1

3.2 *AS ... AS*, COMPARATIVES & SUPERLATIVES

	comparative	superlative
Long adjectives (two or more syllables)	*more* + adjective	*most* + adjective
Short adjectives (one syllable or two syllables ending in *-e* or *-y*)	adjective + *-er*	adjective + *-est*

When a one-syllable-adjective ends in consonant-vowel-consonant, double the final consonant: *big → bigger → biggest*.

As... as

Use *as* + adjective + *as* to show the similarity between two things. Use *not as* + adjective + *as* to show the difference: *The horse is as tall as the boy.* (= they are the same) *The horse is not as interesting as the boy.* (= they are different)

Modifying comparatives & superlatives

Comparative	Superlative	*As ... as*
big difference: *a lot, much, far* small difference: *a little, a bit, slightly*	*by far*	*just*

It's much bigger than I expected. It's by far the biggest. It's just as big as the others.

▶ 3.2

3.3 ADJECTIVES & ADVERBS

Adjectives & adverbs of manner

Adjectives (*big, happy, good*)	Adverbs of manner (*quickly, slowly, well*)
add information about people, things or places	add information about how we do something
position: before a noun: *She's got a pretty smile.* after a linking verb: *She looks happy.*	position: after the verb: *She sings wonderfully.* NOT after linking verbs: *Her voice sounds wonderful.* NOT *Her voice sounds ~~wonderfully~~.*

-ly adverbs

Many adverbs of manner are formed using an adjective + *-ly*: *careful – carefully*

But not all words which end in *-ly* are adverbs, e.g. *friendly, lovely, brotherly*. These are adjectives.

Some adjectives and adverbs have the same form: *fast, right, late, early*.

He has a fast car. (adjective) *He drives too fast.* (adverb)

The adverbial form of *good* is *well*.

▶ 3.3

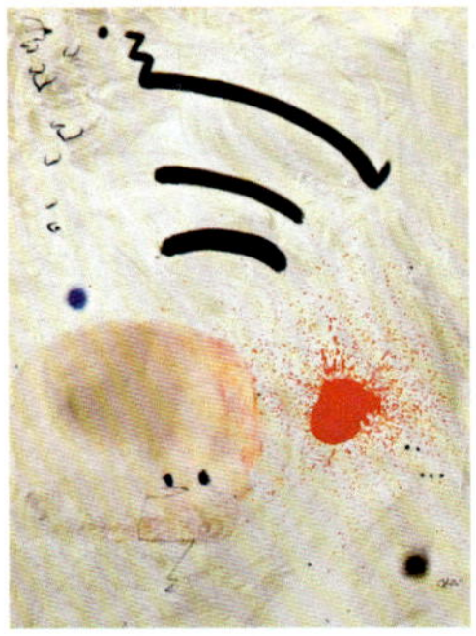

3.1

a Look at the image and choose the correct modifier to complete the sentences.

1 It's *very / absolutely* simple in one way.
2 But in another it's *quite / totally* complex.
3 The use of the colours and space are *very / completely* unique.
4 It's *very / totally* fascinating – I could look at it for hours.
5 It's *quite / completely* difficult to understand what it's showing.
6 I love its simplicity – I find Miro's paintings *really / absolutely* thought-provoking.

b Do you agree? Write two sentences giving your opinion. Use adjectives and modifiers.

3.2

a Complete the text with the words in the box.

by far just much not slightly

I work in a modern office block. It's got 12 floors and it's (1) .... the tallest office block in the neighbourhood. It's (2) .... taller than any other building in town, except for the Telecom tower, which is (3) .... taller. It's (4) .... as ugly as some of the other blocks, but it's (5) .... as faceless and boring as any other modern office block in our town.

b Write a short description of the building you live, work or study in. Compare it to the other buildings in your neighbourhood or town.

3.3

a Add *-ly* to eight words in the text.

Last Sunday I was sitting quiet in the park. It was a love afternoon and I was reading my book and watching the world go by. There was a couple who were sitting on the next bench. They were staring romantic into each other's eyes and then sudden they started arguing. It didn't sound like a friend argument! At first I tried not to listen, but they were arguing really loud. I didn't know what to do! I got up slow and moved towards them. They stopped shouting and looked embarrassed. 'Sorry!' they said and got up and walked away quick without looking back.

b Look again at the words you added *-ly* to. Are they adjectives or adverbs?

c Write a short text about something you did over the weekend. Use at least five words ending in *-ly*.

4.1 Present perfect simple

Use the present perfect simple to talk about a completed action or series of actions that happened during a period of time continuing up to the present:

We have seen three sharks here in the last month.

Always, ever, never

We often use the adverbs *always*, *ever* and *never* with the present perfect simple:

Have you ever seen a tornado? (= in your whole life up to today)

I've never travelled by boat. (= in my whole life up to today)

We've always been lucky with the weather on holiday. (= in my experience up to today)

Already & yet

Use the present perfect with *already* or *yet* to emphasise that an action has or hasn't happened before the present moment:

I've already told you. (the action has happened)

I'm sorry, I haven't spoken to him yet. (the action hasn't happened)

We usually use *already* in affirmative sentences. It comes between the auxiliary (*has/have*) and the past participle:

I've already been there three times.

We usually use *yet* in negative sentences. It comes at the end of the sentence:

I haven't been there yet.

We can use both *already* and *yet* in questions. There's a small difference in the meaning:

Has Jack already left?/Has Jack left already? = (I'm surprised, he left very early!)

Has Jack left yet? = (I expect he has, I'm just checking.)

▶ 4.1

4.2 Present perfect continuous

Form the present perfect continuous with *have/has* + *been* + verb + *-ing*.

Use the present perfect continuous to talk about actions that started in the past and continue in the present:

The people of Kullu Valley have been growing crops here for more than 3,000 years.

Present perfect continuous or simple?

We don't usually use the present perfect continuous with state verbs (verbs that describe feelings and thoughts):

I've always hated... NOT *I've always ~~been hating~~...*

I've never understood maths. NOT *~~I've never been understanding~~ maths.*

We can often use both the present perfect continuous and the present perfect simple with very little difference when we are talking about an action that has continued over a long period of time up to the present:

He's worked here for as long as I can remember.

He's been working here for as long as I can remember.

Time expressions with *for & since*

Use time expressions with *for* or *since* to talk about a period of time which started in the past and continues in the present. Use *since* + the point in time when the action started. Use *for* + the period of time:

I've been studying English since I was ten. I've been studying English for six years.

▶ 4.2

4.1

a Complete the sentences with the words in the box.

already always ever never yet

1 It's the most beautiful **thing** I've .... seen.
2 I've .... been **there**, but I'd love to go.
3 I've .... been **there**, but I'd love to go again.
4 I haven't tried **that** ...., but I hope to try it one day.
5 I've .... loved doing **that**. You should try it. You'll love it, too!

b Replace the words in **bold** in 4.1a with a place, object or activity so that the sentence is true for you.

4.2

a Complete the sentences using the present perfect simple or continuous of the verbs in brackets. Use the continuous where possible.

1 I .... (*study*) English since ....
2 I .... (*know*) my best friend since ....
3 I .... (*attend*) these English classes for ....
4 Our neighbours .... (*live*) next door to us for ....
5 I .... (*have*) my mobile phone for ....

b Complete the sentences in 4.2a with *for* and *since* to make the sentences true for you.

c Write questions using the prompts and the present perfect continuous. Then write answers using *for* or *since*.

1 How long / you / play [add an instrument or a sport you play]?
....
2 How long / you / sit at your desk?
....
3 How long / you / use [add a social network or computer application you use]?
....
4 How long / you / follow [add a sport team or musical artist or group you follow]?
....

5.1 FUTURE FORMS (1): PLANS, INTENTIONS, HOPES & FEARS

Present simple

We can use the present simple to talk about schedules in the future. We often use it to talk about timetables or the starting and end times of shows, the opening times of shops and restaurants; school terms:

... the new term starts in September.

The film starts at 7.30.

Present continuous

We can use the present continuous to talk about plans and arrangements in the future. We often use a future time expression, e.g. *tomorrow*, *next week*, *later today*:

I'm meeting Jaime this evening for a drink.

Going to

We can also use *going to* to talk about future plans and intentions. We usually use *going to* and not the present continuous when no definite arrangements have been made:

I'm not going to do any work this weekend. (this is an intention, but no arrangements have been made)

Will

We often use *will* to express our hopes and fears about the future:

I hope there'll be some tickets left for the concert tonight!

▶ 5.1

5.2 FUTURE FORMS (2): PREDICTIONS

We can use both *will* and *going to* to make predictions and talk about beliefs about the future. There is little difference in meaning between the two forms:

Weather patterns will/are going to change dramatically in the next few years.

We often use *will* with the passive voice (*will* + *be* + past participle) to talk about predictions:

I think Mandarin will be studied by lots more people in the future.

▶ 5.2

5.1

a Choose the correct forms to complete the conversation.

ANA	Jed and I (1) *are going / will go* to the cinema tonight. Do you fancy coming along?
BORG	What's on?
ANA	That new Bond film – you know, the remake, oh what's it called?
BORG	I know the one you mean. What time (2) *does / will* it start?
ANA	(3) *We're going / We'll go* to the last show. It (4) *starts / is starting* at 8.30.
BORG	8.30? Ah, sorry, I can't. (5) *I'm playing / I'm going to play* football till 9. I (6) *don't / won't* finish in time.
ANA	We're going for something to eat afterwards. Maybe you could catch up with us then? We're (7) *trying / going to try* that new Asian restaurant near the clock tower. You know the one?
BORG	Yeah, I think so. Have you booked a table?
ANA	No, we don't think (8) *we're needing / we'll need* to. It's quite big.
BORG	Great, well, (9) *I join / I'll join* you after the football then!

b Borg finds out that the football has been cancelled and that he can go to the cinema after all. He calls Ana and arranges a time and place to meet. Write the conversation between Ana and Borg.

5.2

a Complete the predictions using *will* + infinitive or *will* + *be* + past participle.

1 All university textbooks .... (*be*) digital.
2 Print books .... (*become*) a thing of the past.
3 Teachers .... (*replace*) by robots.
4 Most classes will .... (*hold*) online.
5 Electronic portfolios and digital assignment .... (*take*) the place of many traditional exams.
6 Keyboards and flat screens .... (*use*) instead of paper and pen.
7 No-one .... (*know*) how to write by hand.

b Look again at the predictions. Which (if any) do you think is the most likely to come true in the next 20 years in your country? Write one sentence explaining your answer.

Unit 6

6.1 Sentences with *if*: real situations

If + present simple + present simple
- to talk about things that are generally true
- you can replace *if* with *when*:

  If/When the sun shines, we go to the beach.

If + present simple + future tense
- to talk about situations that are likely in the future
- you can also use a modal verb or imperative in the main clause:

  If I have time, I'll go to the shops on the way home.
  You must go to see the town centre if you have time.
  If you're in town, don't miss the open air theatre.

Position of *if*
At the beginning of the sentence, add a comma at the end of the clause:

If I finish in time, I'll meet you in the café.

In the middle of the sentence, no comma needed:

I'll meet you in the café if I finish in time.

We often use sentences with *if* to offer advice or to make recommendations and suggestions.

▶ 6.1

6.2 Modal verbs: making deductions

We can use the modal verbs *can't*, *could*, *might* and *must* to give opinions and say whether or not we think something is true or possible:

He must be very proud. I guess she might be late. They can't be far behind.

must	I have no doubt that this is true.
could, might	I think this is possible.
can't	I don't think this is true.

Don't use *mustn't* to say that something is not possible. Use *can't*:

That can't be true! NOT *That ~~mustn't~~ be true!*

▶ 6.2

6.3 Future time clauses

When we use time expressions like *when*, *until*, *before*, *once*, *by the time* to talk about the future, we always use a verb in the present tense:

When we get to the airport, we'll call my dad to pick us up.
We'll wait in the airport snack bar until he gets there.

Do not use *will* or *going to* in these future time clauses:

When we get home, I'll show you my photos. NOT *When ~~we'll get~~ home...*

This is also true for clauses with *if* and *unless*.

▶ 6.3

6.1

Match the two parts of the sentences. In which sentence/s can you replace *if* with *when*?

1 If I go on a trip,
2 If you need any help,
3 If it rains,
4 If we cancel the trip,
5 If we arrange an alternative activity,
6 If you're running a business,

a it usually ends up costing more money.
b just call me on my mobile.
c something always seems to go wrong!
d we'll have to cancel the trip.
e you have to keep your customers happy!
f we'll need to offer some kind of alternative.

6.2

Complete the conversations using *might*, *must* or *can't*.

1 A He ...... live here. I always see his car parked in the street outside.
  B He ...... be visiting a friend or a member of his family.

2 A They ...... be sisters, they don't look anything like each other.
  B That's true, but they ...... be good friends, they're always together.

3 A She ...... be on the phone, I keep on trying to call her but it goes straight into her answer phone.
  B Or her phone ...... be out of order.

6.3

a Look at the verbs in **bold**. Find and correct five mistakes.

We're leaving Rio at 3 p.m., the flight takes about three and a half hours, so when **we'll land, it'll be** about 6.30, unless **there'll be** a delay – there often is! **It'll be** 7 by the time **we're going to get** through passport control and customs. There are buses to the town centre every 15 minutes. If **we'll catch** the 7.30 bus, **we'll be** in the centre at about 8.30. What time do you get home from work? Will you be there when **we're going to arrive**?

b Write a short email in reply, offering to meet your friends at the airport.

UNIT 7 GRAMMAR REFERENCE

7.1 QUANTIFIERS

	Uncountable	Countable	Both
Large quantity	much, how much, so much, too much	many, how many, so many, too many	a lot of, lots of, plenty of, enough
Small quantity	a little, very little	a few, very few	not enough

Much & many

We do not often use *much* or *many* on their own in affirmative sentences. We prefer to use *a lot of* or *lots of*: *I have lots of space.* NOT *I have ~~much space.~~*

Very few, very little, too much, too many, plenty of, (not) enough

Very few/very little means a quantity is not sufficient: *I have very little free time.*

Too much/too many means more than necessary. It is often used to criticise or complain: *There's too much noise! Turn that music down!*

Plenty of means a quantity is more than sufficient: *We've got plenty of food for everyone.*

Enough means sufficient quantity: *I think we have enough time to finish this last exercise.*

Not enough means quantity is not sufficient: *I don't have enough time for a coffee.*

▶ 7.1

7.2 USING *ONE* & *ONES*

Use *one* and *ones* to refer back to something that has already been mentioned:

Have you seen my shoes? Which ones? The red ones with the high heels.

We can use *one* or *ones* with:

• ***the***	*The ones you want are in the hall.*
• ***other***	*Don't sit in that chair, try the other one.*
• ***this/that/these/those***	*You're right, this one is much better.*
• **adjectives**	*The red one is the best.*
• ***which?***	*Which one do you prefer?*

▶ 7.2

7.3 ARTICLES

Basic uses

A/an	with singular countable nouns: *a label*	to talk in general about an object, person, thing or place
The	with uncountable and countable nouns: *the label, the labels*	to talk about specific objects, people or places
No article	with uncountable and plural countable nouns: *labels, labelling*	to talk about general and abstract concepts

Other uses

A/an	when someone or something is mentioned for the first time
The	• when someone or something has already been mentioned. • when an object or person is the only one in the context: *the internet* • to talk about one object as an example of a group: *the car* • with rivers, mountain ranges or names of countries that include a political label (e.g.*state, republic*): *the Nile, the Andes, the United Kingdom*
No article	with most proper names of people or countries: *Sonia* NOT *~~the Sonia~~*; *Spain*. NOT *~~the Spain~~*

▶ 7.3

7.1

a Look at the image. Write six sentences describing the contents of the fridge. Use as many words and expressions as you can with the words in the box.

> a few a lot of enough not enough not many not much plenty of too many too much very little

b In what ways is it similar to or different from the contents of your fridge? Write three sentences describing the contents of your fridge.

7.2

a Complete the text with *one* or *ones*.

> I love this collection of old TV sets. There are big (1) .... and small (2) ...., (3) .... that were kept in wooden cupboards and (4) .... that were round and sat on the dining room table. My favourite (5) .... of all is this old, black and white set. It's just like the (6) .... my parents had when I was a kid. Our family was (7) .... of the last families in the village to get a TV! Everyone else had a colour set, but we had to make do with black and white. I remember when dad finally bought a colour (8) .... I invited all my friends round to see it!

b Write sentences describing your first TV set, using *one* and *ones* in your description.

7.3

a Choose the correct article to complete the text.

> Yesterday (1) *a / the / -* friend gave me (2) *a / the / -* present. It was (3) *a / the / -* small box. In (4) *a / the / -* box was (5) *a / the / -* piece of (6) *a / the / -* paper. On (7) *a / the / -* paper someone had written (8) *a / the / -* message. (9) *A / The / -* message was written in Japanese. (10) *A / The / -* characters were beautiful, but I couldn't understand them. (11) *A / The / -* Japanese characters are so difficult to understand! I took it to (12) *a / the / -* Japanese neighbour and asked him if he could help me. He read (13) *a / the / -* message. It said, 'Those who ask for (14) *a / the / -* help, find (15) *a / the / -* friend'.

8.1 Reported speech

To report and summarise what someone said in the past, we use a past reporting verb e.g. *said*, *told*, *asked*, *explained*, *promised*. We often report the words in a past tense:

'People like Fide have nothing,' my mother said. → *My mother told me that people like Fide had nothing.*

Present simple *'I **don't know**.'*	Past simple *She said she **didn't know**.*
can, will, may *'I **can** read.'*	could, would, might *He said he **could** read.*
Present perfect *'I**'ve never visited** New York.'*	Past perfect *I explained that I **had never visited** New York.*
Present continuous *'I**'m studying** literature.'*	Past continuous *I told them I **was studying** literature.*

Reporting questions

Use the word order of an affirmative sentence. Do not use a question mark at the end of the sentence:

She asked me what I did. NOT *She asked me what ~~did I do~~?*

To report a *yes/no* question, use *if*:

'Do you have a brother?' → *She asked me if I had a brother.*

▶ 8.1

8.2 Reporting requests & instructions

Reporting requests

Use *ask* + person + (*not*) *to* + infinitive:

'Can you show us where you sleep?' → *We asked them to show us where they slept.*

'Please don't take photos.' → *They asked us not to take photos.*

Reporting instructions

Use *tell* + person + (*not*) *to* + infinitive:

'Bring a camera!' → *They told us to bring a camera.*

'Don't stand near the doors.' → *They told us not to stand near the doors.*

Reporting information or advice

Use *tell* + person + question word + *to* + infinitive:

*They told us **how** to get to the station.*

*They told us **where** to find the best beaches.*

▶ 8.2

8.1

a Report the words in the speech bubbles. Use past tenses.

1 I'm really tired. I'm going to bed.

2 Sorry I'm late. I missed my bus.

3 I'll do it tomorrow.

4 Sorry, I can't come, I'm working late.

1 She said ....

2 He told her he .... that he ...., but he ....

3 You promised you ....

4 I said I ...., but I .... because I ....

b Have you said any of these things recently? If yes, who to? What did they say back to you? Report their words to you.

8.2

a Complete the reported speech using no more than three words in each gap.

1 'Be here at nine.'
He told us .... there at nine.

2 'Please don't be late, as the train won't wait for you!'
He asked us .... late.

3 'Remember to bring an umbrella as it may rain.'
He told us .... an umbrella.

4 'If you're coming by car, the best place to park is next to the station.'
He told us .... to park.

5 'If you're coming by bus, take the number 21.'
He told us .... bus to take.

6 'If, for any reason, you have to cancel, please let me know as soon as possible.'
He asked us .... know as soon as possible if we have to cancel.

b What kind of trip do you think they are going on? Write down three more things the guide might ask or tell them.

9.1 Permission, prohibition & obligation (1): present

Modal verbs & phrases

Use the following modal verbs and phrases to talk about permission, prohibition and obligation in the present.

Permission	*can, is/are allowed to*
Prohibition	*mustn't, can't, isn't/aren't allowed to*
Obligation	*must, have to*
Lack of obligation	*don't have to*

We usually use *must* on signs or when giving direct orders. We tend to use *have to* when we talk about obligations in general.

Make & *let*

Use (*don't*) *make* + object + infinitive to talk about obligation and lack of obligation: *They make us do homework every night. They don't make us pay for internet access.*

Use (*don't*) *let* + object + infinitive to talk about permission and prohibition:

They let us bring our laptops to school. They don't let us use our mobile phones in class.

▶ 9.1

9.2 Permission, prohibition & obligation (2): past

Modal verbs & phrases

Use the following modal verbs and phrases to talk about permission, prohibition and obligation in the past.

Permission	*could, was/were allowed to*
Prohibition	*couldn't, wasn't/weren't allowed to*
Obligation	*had to*
Lack of obligation	*didn't have to*

Make & *let* in the past

Use *made/didn't make* + object + infinitive to talk about obligation and lack of obligation: *My parents always made us go to bed early on week days.*

Use *let/didn't let* + object + infinitive to talk about permission and prohibition:

They didn't let us stay up to watch TV.

▶ 9.2

9.3 Talking about ability (past & present)

General ability

Use *can* to express ability in the present and *could* in the past:

The machine can help me get to places... that I couldn't go to before.

Manage & *succeed*

Use *manage to* + infinitive and *succeed in* + verb + *-ing* to refer to the ability to do something in a specific situation. We use both verbs to talk about something which is difficult and requires skill or effort:

I finally managed to find a parking space. He succeeded in passing his driving test on the third attempt.

▶ 9.3

9.1

a Choose the correct modal verb.

Let me show you to your room. There are a few simple rules. You (1) *can / cannot* keep pets. And no animals are allowed in your room. You (2) *can / cannot* smoke in your room. In fact the whole building is non-smoking. You (3) *are / aren't* allowed to have visitors in your room, but they (4) *must / mustn't* leave before 10.30 p.m. They (5) *must / mustn't* tell the porter when they are leaving. You (6) *can / cannot* come in at any time of day or night and you (7) *must / mustn't* be careful not to disturb the other residents after midnight. A night porter is at reception all night.

b What kind of accommodation do you think this is? Have you ever stayed anywhere similar?

9.2

Complete the rules using the words in the box.

could | didn't have to | had to | let | made | wasn't allowed

When I was at high school I worked on the local milk round. I (1) .... get up at five o'clock every morning. I (2) .... wear a uniform, but it was important to dress warmly. The boss always (3) .... us wear reflective clothing so that cars could see us on the road. I (4) .... wear headphones and listen to music if I wanted, but I (5) .... to play computer games. At Christmas the customers gave us really generous tips. The milkman usually (6) .... us keep the money and we shared it out between us.

9.3

Rewrite the sentences in *italics* using the word in brackets.

1 It was really difficult finding a new flat. *But we found one in the end.* (managed)

....

2 He studied long and hard. *We were so pleased when he passed all this exams.* (succeed)

....

3 I was amazed when I saw Peter swim. *I had no idea he was such a good swimmer.* (could)

....

10.1 PASSIVES

In a sentence with a passive verb, the object of the action (the thing or person affected by the action) becomes the subject of the verb.

Active: *They have installed 10,000 new solar panels.* (object)

Passive: *10,000 new solar panels have been installed.* (subject)

To form the passive voice of a verb use an appropriate form of *be* + the past participle.

More and more money is being invested in alternative energy.
Wind farms were introduced in Denmark in the early 1900s.
Fossil fuels will be replaced by alternative energy sources.

When we want to include the person or thing responsible for the action we use *by* + noun.

Active: *Alternative energy sources will replace fossil fuels.*

Passive: *Fossil fuels will be replaced by alternative energy sources.*

We can also use *by* to describe the means by which an action is performed:

The books were written out by hand.
The information was sent by email.

We don't use *by* when:

it's obvious who/what is responsible for the action	*The food was brought to our table.* (a waiter or other member of the restaurant staff brought it, we don't need to know exactly who)
we don't know who/what is responsible for an action	*The cake had been eaten.* (we don't know who ate it)
to describe a process	*The coffee is harvested, processed and sent to the main plant.*

▶ 10.1

10.2 *WHO, WHICH, THAT*

Relative clauses

We use *who*, *which* and *that* to introduce a relative clause. Relative clauses add information about a person or thing.

Who	person	*He was the one who won the race.*
Which	thing	*This is the prize which he got for winning.*
That	person or thing	*There's the runner that won the race.* *There's the runner who won the race.*

Omitting *who, which, that*

Sometimes we omit the relative pronoun. We can omit *who*, *which* or *that* when it is not the subject of the verb that follows (when there is another subject or subject pronoun):

The photos (which) we took that day are hanging on the kitchen wall.
(*we* is the subject of the verb, so we can omit *which*)

We cannot omit *who*, *which*, *that* when it is the subject of the verb that follows:

It was a special moment which will stay with me forever.
(there is no subject after *which* so we cannot omit it)

▶ 10.2

10.1

a Rewrite the sentences using the passive voice.

1 You attach the cell charger to your bike.
The cell charger ....
2 As the wheels turn, they charge the dynamo..
As the wheels turn, the dynamo ....
3 The company sold thousands of chargers in the first few months.
Thousands of chargers .... in the first few months.
4 People in rural areas where there are no electricity supplies are buying the chargers.
The chargers .... by people ....
5 Environmentalists have praised the invention.
The invention .... by ....
6 They hope that more and more people will adopt them over the next few years.
They hope that they .... by .... over the next few years.

b Look at the photo of a traditional use of bicycles in many parts of the world. Write three sentences about it, using a passive verb in each.

10.2

a Replace *that* in the relative clauses with *who* or *which*.

1 an object *that* .... is very important to me
2 a film or TV programme *that* .... I have seen recently
3 a friend *that* .... I have spoken to today
4 a person *that* .... taught me how to do something
5 a thing *that* .... I have to do today
6 a member of my family *that* .... lives far away

b Look again at the relative clauses in 10.2a. When can you omit *that*, *who* or *which*?

c Write a sentence about 1–6 in 10.2a using *who*, *which* or *that*.

My cell phone is the object which is most important to me.

UNIT 11 GRAMMAR REFERENCE

11.1 Imaginary situations: present or future

Imaginary situation in the present or future	Imaginary action/ response in the present or future	Real situation in the present or future
if + simple past	*would/wouldn't* + infinitive	
If I had a car,	*I'd drive/I wouldn't drive to work.*	I don't have a car and I don't have any plans to buy one.

Notice that although we use a past verb form we are NOT talking about a past situation:

*If I **had** the chance to study abroad,...* (at the moment I don't have that opportunity and it is unlikely that I will have a chance in the foreseeable future)

We can use either *was* or *were* with *if* + *I*, *he*, *she* and *it*:

If I was/were super rich... (but I'm not)

If she was/were just a little bit more sure of herself... (but she isn't)

▶ 11.1

11.2 *If only / I wish*

Use *if only / I wish* + past simple to say how you would like reality to be different. Notice that although we use a past verb form we are NOT talking about a past situation:

I wish I had more time to study English. (reality: I don't have enough time.)

If only I didn't have to work so hard. (reality: I have to work really hard.)

We can say *I wish I/he/she/it was* or *I wish I/he/she/it were. I wish I/he/she/it was* is more informal.

▶ 11.2

11.1

a Answer the questions with *would* or *wouldn't*.

1 What would you do if you saw someone stealing from a shop? Would you try and stop them?

....

....

2 Where would you go if you won two free airline tickets to the destination of your choice? Who would you take with you?

....

....

3 Who would you go to if you needed advice about a personal problem? Why?

....

....

b Complete the sentences with the verbs in brackets and *would* or the past simple.

A Can I ask you a question?

B Yes, sure, go ahead.

A What (1) .... (*you/do*) if they (2) .... (*offer*) you a free place on a Spanish language course for a month?

B I'd take it, of course!

A Yes, but what if you (3) .... (*have*) plans to go on holiday at the same time?

B Well, I (4) .... (*try*) and combine the two things, I guess.

A Yes, that's what I (5) .... (*like*) to do.

B So, have you been offered a free place?

A Yes. I can choose to do it in Madrid, Buenos Aires or Santiago.

B Santiago in Chile? That's definitely where I (6) .... (*go*)!

11.2

a Complete the sentences with an appropriate form of the verbs in brackets.

1 I wish I .... (*can*) speak Japanese.
2 If only I .... (*know*) how to play the guitar.
3 I wish I .... (*be*) taller.
4 If only I .... (*have*) a car.
5 I wish it .... (*be*) warm and sunny.

b Look again at the sentences in 11.2a. What is the real situation in each case? Why do you think the speaker wants to change the situation? Write two sentences explaining your answers for each situation.

1 *The speaker can't speak Japanese. Maybe he or she would like to travel to Japan.*

12.1 Imaginary situations: past

We use sentences with *if* + past perfect (*had* + past participle) + *would/ wouldn't have* + past participle to talk about imagined situations in the past, and their imagined results.

Imaginary situation in the past	Imaginary action/response in the past	Real situation in the past
if + *had* + past participle	*would/wouldn't have* + past participle	
If I had known about the accident,	*I'd have said something/I wouldn't have said anything.*	I didn't know about the accident.

▶ 12.1

12.2 Review

Past participles

We can use the past participle to form perfect tenses (with *have*) and the passive voice (with *be*).

Perfect tenses	Passive voice
have + past participle	*be* + past participle
present perfect: *I've never been to New York.* past perfect: *I'd just finished work for the day.*	present simple passive: *It's made by hand.* past simple passive: *It was built in 1996.* present perfect passive: *The house has been sold.* modal + passive voice: *It can be used several times.*

Present perfect: basic uses

We can use the present perfect to talk about

- an action or situation that started in the past and continues in the present: *I've known him most of my life.*
- an action that happened at some time in the past, but we don't focus on when exactly it happened: *He's left the office, he'll be home soon.* (we don't know when, we just know that he left)
- experiences in general: *He's starred in a number of films. I've been to Mexico a few times.*

Past perfect: basic uses

We can use the past perfect to show

- that one action happened before another: *I had just finished work when I heard a knock at my door.*
- to report speech: *She told me she had passed her exam.*
- with *if* to describe an imaginary situation in the past: *If I'd arrived on time, I'd have seen him.*

The passive voice: basic uses

We use the passive voice

- to emphasise/clarify who is responsible for an action using *by*: *Laws are passed by the parliament.*
- when we don't know who or what is responsible for an action: *The window had been broken.* (we don't know who broke it)
- when it's obvious who or what is responsible for an action: *The law was finally passed.* (it's obvious that parliament passed the law)
- to describe a process: *The books are printed in China and then they are shipped to the USA.*

▶ 12.2

12.1

a Choose the correct forms to complete the text.

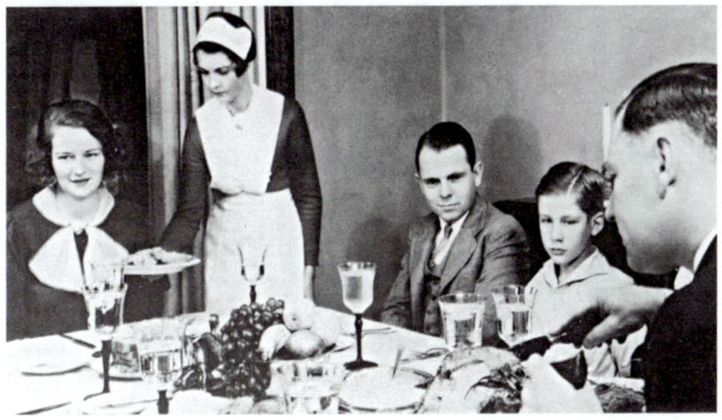

If I (1) *had / would have* been born 100 years ago, my life (2) *had / would have* been very different. I probably (3) *hadn't / wouldn't have* gone to university. I (4) *had / would have* stayed at home and looked after my children. If I (5) *had / would have* had the luck to be born into a rich family, I (6) *had / would have* had maids and other people to look after me. If I (7) *had / would have* come from a poor background, I (8) *had / would have* been a maid myself.

b Complete the sentence so that it is true for you and where you live. Use *would have* and the past perfect.

If I had been born 50 years earlier...

12.2

a Complete the conversations using the past participle form of the verbs in the box.

build buy decide invite leave pay take

1
A We'd just (1) .... the restaurant when the waiter ran out after us.
B Really? Why?
A He said we hadn't (2) .... the bill... he was really angry.

2
A Have you been (3) .... to Paula's birthday party?
B Yes, I have, but I haven't (4) .... if I'm going yet. I've (5) .... tickets for a concert on the same day and I'm trying to sell them.

3
A The bridge was (6) .... in 1855. It was the first bridge to span the Mississippi.
B How did people cross the river before that?
A Passengers, animals and heavy loads were (7) .... across by boat.

b Look again at the past participles you added in exercise 12.2a. Which form part of a) a perfect tense? b) a passive form?

Writing Bank

1 A promotional poster

1 Work in pairs. Look at the images which show two different kinds of clubs.

1 Do either of them appeal to you? Why?
2 What do you think people do when they meet in these clubs?
3 What could be the benefits of being a member?

2 Read the poster written to persuade people to join the club. Match it to one of the images. Would you or anyone you know be interested in joining? Why/Why not?

3 Read the poster again. Match paragraphs a–e to functions 1–5.

1 Provides practical information.
2 Attracts the reader's attention.
3 Explains more about the paragraph above.
4 Provides final words of persuasion.
5 Gives information about the club and activity for different types of people.

4 a Find examples of the following types of language in the poster to complete the chart.

Questions	*Don't get enough exercise?*
Exclamations	....
Positive & superlative adjectives	....
Use of *will*	....
Imperatives	....

b What style do these features help create?

5 Choose three phrases that you like or that are catchy. Why do you think they are effective?

6 Change the sentences to make them more catchy. Use the suggestions in brackets.

1 If you care about the environment, you might be interested in joining our club. (questions)
2 You love food, but hate cooking it. You can do a cookery course with us. (exclamations)
3 Yoga is a good way to relax. If you're tense, learn to relax at the Yoga Club in the right atmosphere. (positive/superlative adjectives)
4 Video games are your hobby, but you don't like online forums? You can make new friends at our weekly meetings. (*will*/imperatives)

a Don't get enough exercise? Need to get out of the office and breathe fresh air? Want to make new friends of all ages? Come and join us at the **New England Hiking Club**!

b At the **New England Hiking Club**, we organise hiking tours throughout the region. In spring and summer, we organise trips along the Appalachian Trail, from Maine to Connecticut. In the fall, we take you to the forests of New England to see the spectaular colors as the trees shed their leaves.

c Whatever your level of fitness, our team of experts will help you choose the tour that best suits you. And if you are already a committed trekker, we'll introduce you to new challenges.

d There are one-day to ten-day packages available with accommodation in lodges throughout the region. A year's membership is only $150, and packages start from as little as $400. There are special packages for families, and discounts for students. We're sure you'll find a vacation to suit you!

e Get in touch! Get into shape! And enjoy the beauty of your region as you've never seen it before. At the **New England Hiking Club**, we're waiting to hear from you.

***Special deal:* Already a New England Hiker? Introduce a new member and get a discount on your annual fee for you and your guest!**

7 a Work in pairs. Decide on a suitable club that promotes an activity that you could do where you live.

b Write a poster promoting the club. Use the poster in 2 as a model. Consider

- the questions you are going to ask potential club members to attract their attention
- the basic information that people will need
- any particular promises or invitations you would like to make
- a catchy slogan to get people interested

8 Read another group's poster. Did the club sound attractive? Would you join it? Why/Why not?

Tip

Remember to make joining the club as attractive as possible. Don't forget to attract the reader's attention with questions and invitations.

2 SUMMARISING THE FINDINGS OF A SURVEY

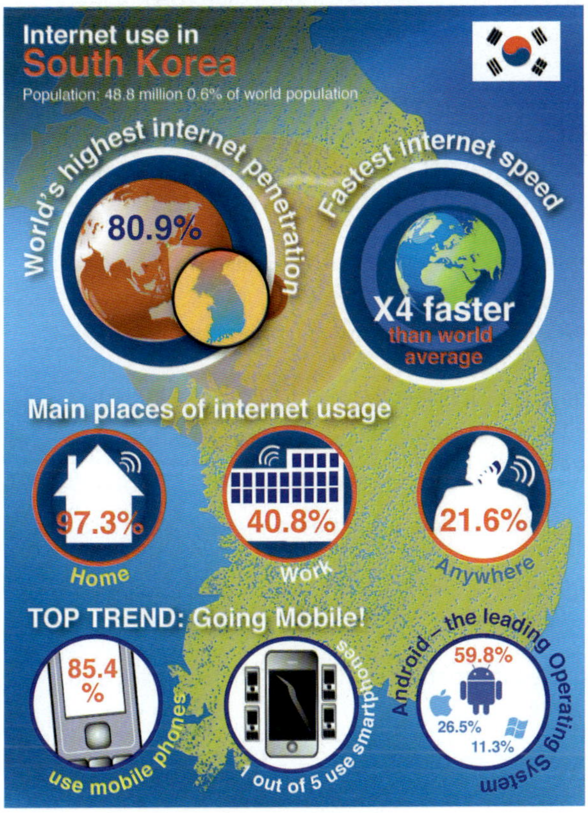

1 **a** Look at the infographic. What does it show? What differences do you think there would be in the information for your country?

b Compare your answers with a partner and complete the summary.

Recent statistics show that South Korea has the world's (1)........... level of internet penetration. More than (2)........... % of the population have access to the internet. And South Korea also has the (3)........... internet speed in the world. **Almost all** internet users have access to the internet at (4)............ **Just under half** have access to the internet at (5)........... and **more than a fifth** of the internet users can access the internet (6)........... via their mobile phones and devices. The use of mobile phones is growing, and around (7)........... % of mobile users have smartphones. It is expected that this figure will rise dramatically over the next few years. South Koreans spend an average of 11 hours a week online. **Most people** use the internet for news and information, with games and entertainment coming a close second.

2 **a** Look at the phrases in **bold** in the summary in 1b. Match them to the percentages.

1 around 40–45%
2 more than 90%
3 20% or higher
4 more than 50%

b Look at the information. Write four sentences using the same phrases to explain the statistics.

Regular internet use by age	
6–29	95%
30–40	86%
41–49	44%
50 +	27%

Almost all 6-29-year-olds use the internet regularly.

3 Look at the questionnaire. Which questions are not covered in the summary in 1b? What do you think the answers might be? Discuss your ideas with a partner.

Q1 Can you access the internet
a) at home? **b)** at work? **c)** on your phone?

Q2 What do you use the internet for most? *(tick two answers)*
- shopping
- news and information
- social networking and instant messaging
- entertainment (music, video clips, games, etc.)
- studies
- work

Q3 How many hours (approx.) a week do you spend on the internet?

Q4 What time of day do you usually access the internet?
- all times
- mainly during the day
- mainly during the evening/night
- varies

Q5 Do you think you will use the internet more or less in the future? Why?

4 **a** Work in small groups. Answer the questions in the questionnaire. Note down all the answers in your group.

b Work in new groups. Share your previous group's answers from 4a. Bring all the information together and work out the statistics for the whole class.

5 **a** Write a summary of the results of the questionnaire.

Most of the class can access the internet at home, and more than a third of the class can access the internet on their phone.

b Compare your summary with the rest of the class. Are your answers all the same? Are there any surprises in the results?

TIP

It's a good idea to summarise numerical statistics using these and other similar, phrases, as it makes the information more accessible and easier to understand for most people.

3 AN OPINION

a

b

1 Work in pairs. Look at the two images and answer the questions.

1 What are the differences and similarities?
2 Which adjectives would you use to describe each place?
3 In which place would you prefer to be now? Why?
4 Which place is most similar to where you live?

2 Petar and Rachael have posted texts on a discussion board for their English class. Read the texts and answer the questions.

1 What do the two texts have in common?
2 How old do you think the two people are? Why?

Town or country? Which are you?

Petar
I thought I'd always live in the country, but then my dad got offered a new job and we moved to the city. I'd say it's much better living here. I can study whatever I want and also it will be easier for me to get a good job in the future.
There are lots more things to do and so many different kinds of people here, and I love that variety. There are almost too many distractions! Also, in the country, everybody knows you, but here you feel freer. So, yes, on balance, I'm happy with the move!

Rachael
I've always been a city person, but recently I decided to make a change. I sold my apartment and, for the same money, I could afford a large house in the country with a garden. The nearest village is two miles away!
It's a better quality of life and I have more space and time. Besides, as you get older, you don't need all that a city provides. Now, I can enjoy reading a book, cooking, gardening, and I finally have time to walk my dog. He's much happier! So, all in all, I think I made the right move.

3 How would you feel if you were Petar or Rachael? Would it be easy for you to make the change? Why/Why not?

4 **a** Read the posts again. What advantages do Petar and Rachael mention? Complete the chart.

Petar – city life	Rachael – country life

b Compare your answers with a partner. Do you agree with Petar and Rachael? Think of three disadvantages for life in both the country and the city.

5 Complete the sentences with the disadvantages you wrote in 4b.

1 Life in the country is very quiet and peaceful. *However*, it can also be ....
2 Life in the city is really exciting, *whereas* life in the country is ....
3 Country life may be better for older people, *but* it ....
4 *Despite* the job opportunities in the city, it can also be ....
5 *Although* country life is simpler, it could also be ....

6 Read the information about linkers of contrast and complete 1–5.

Linkers of contrast
Linkers are used to show the connection between two ideas.
In this case the ideas are (1)*similar/different*.
- *Although*, *however*, *but* and *whereas* are all followed by (2)*a noun/a verb*.
- *Despite* is followed by (3)*a noun/a verb*.
- *However* often begins a new sentence and (4)*is followed/isn't followed* by a comma.
- *But* is often used in the middle of a sentence and (5)*is followed/isn't followed* by a comma.

7 **a** Read the posts in 2 again. How does each open and finish? Which expressions are used to conclude an argument?

b Write your own comment to add to the discussion board explaining which you prefer: life in the city or life in the country. Before you write, decide which advantages and disadvantages you are going to mention and in which order.

c Work in pairs. Read your partner's comment in 7b and write another short comment stating whether you agree or disagree with them.

TIP
Remember to try and give a balanced opinion. You can state the advantages of one thing, but remember to also mention some disadvantages to show that you have considered various options.

4 SAYING THANK YOU

a

b

c

1 Work in pairs. Look at the images which were attached to three separate thank-you messages.

1 Who do you think the person is writing to?
2 What do you think they are saying thank you for?
3 When was the last time you thanked someone for something? Did you write to them or tell them in person?

2 Read the messages and match them to the images.

1

To: Elizabeth Janik
From: Gemma

Dear Mrs Janik,

I am writing to thank you very much for my graduation gift. It was very kind of you. I would like to move to the city soon, so the money will certainly come in handy.

I've attached a photo of the ceremony – I thought you might like it as a souvenir.

I hope you're enjoying your retirement. Take care of yourself.

Best wishes,

Gemma

2

Edgar Carrillo messages

Hi there

Just want to say thanks a million for that great day at the beach. Had a fantastic time! Here's a photo of Ana's flip-flops, just as a reminder ;-) Shame to be back in the office tomorrow morning :-(

Speak later

3

Harry & Jean

Our stay in your lodge was just fantastic – one of our most memorable vacations. Thanks so much for the great hospitality.

See the photo of us all out on the deck after a long walk (We've put it on the notice board). Don't you worry, we'll be back!

Keep in touch!

Connie & Gerardo (Wisconsin, Milwaukee)

3 Read the messages again and check your answers to question 1. Summarise what each person is saying thank you for and why.

1 Gemma says thanks for Mrs Janik's gift of money. She'll use it ...

4 Underline the different phrases for saying thank you and complete the gaps in the chart.

Formal	....
Informal	....
Very informal	....

5 Put the expressions from the messages into the chart in 4. What is the function of each?

Keep in touch!
Speak later
Take care of yourself
Best wishes

6 In informal texts, we often miss out words. Can you find some examples in messages 2 and 3? What other aspects of formal and informal style can you find in the texts?

Addressing the person at the start of the message ....
Referring to a photo ....

7 Work in groups. Think of situations in which you would write a thank-you message. Write the messages in a formal and informal style. Consider the following:

- What other information are you going to mention? Why?
- How are you going to sign off?
- What photo are you going to attach?

TIP

Remember to say what you are thanking the person for, and include some extra information, news or a reference to meeting up so that your message finishes with a personal touch.

5 FILING A COMPLAINT

1 **a** Work in pairs. Look at the image and the title of the task. What do you think the problem might be?

b Read about what happened. Did you guess the problem in 1a?

> What a nightmare! You won't believe what happened to us on the way home. We got to the airport for our flight to London and they'd changed the time of the flight! The plane had already left. We couldn't believe it. They said they'd sent out text messages to all the passengers 24 hours before. I showed them my phone. I hadn't received any messages. The girl at the check-in desk said she couldn't help, and that we'd have to buy new tickets. We were furious!

2 Work in pairs. Discuss what options the passengers have now, and what you think is the best thing to do. Share your answers with the class.

3 **a** The passengers were asked to fill in an official form of complaint in order to ask for their money back.

Look at the useful phrases in the box. Use a dictionary to help you and decide which phrases you can use to

1) describe what happened.
2) demand some action.

> We were shocked and disappointed to find that...
> We were forced to...
> We couldn't believe that...
> We were informed that...
> The least you can do is...
> We hope you will be able to...
> We expect a full and prompt repayment of all expenses incurred.

b Work in pairs. Complete the form with the information you have so far and the useful phrases in 3a.

To register an official complaint, please complete the form below. We will endeavour to reply within seven working days.

Airport	London Gatwick
Flight number	AX 278
Date	15 July
Who attended to you?	
What exactly was the problem?	
Were you given any assistance?	
Any other comments	

4 **a** Compare your answers with another pair. Check that you have

1) used full sentences to describe what happened and what you would like the company to do now.
2) expressed your anger and disappointment.
3) included information about any money you had to spend because of the delay.
4) made it very clear what you expect the company to do about the situation.

b Make changes to your form if necessary.

5 **a** Work in small groups. Think of situations you have been in where you were not happy about the service or the facilities. Use the ideas in the box to help you.

> a shop   a restaurant   a concert   a party
> an online service   a hairdresser's

Discuss what happened and what exactly you were unhappy with.

In a shop: the sales staff were rude and impatient and refused to exchange a shirt I had bought for a friend that was too small.

b Fill in a complaint form explaining exactly what happened.

6 **a** Check your complaint against the checklist in 4a.

b Read your complaint to the class. Ask them to decide what the best response would be.

TIP

When writing a letter/email of complaint, or filling in a complaints form, remember to use polite language, no matter how angry you are. Your complaint will be taken more seriously if you remain polite at all times.

6 AN ONLINE PROFILE

An online profile is a short introduction to you. It gives people a quick first impression of who you are and what you do. It also helps them decide if they are interested in finding out more. Profiles are used in a number of different ways and in a number of different places.

a

b

c

1 a Read the three profiles and match them to images a–c.

1

Life is good! I've just left home and am studying Information Systems at uni. Studying hard but, above all, enjoying the bright lights and the nightlife. Don't tell my mum! Follow me to share photos, stories and experiences of life away from home.

2

My family and I run a small organic farm with a couple of acres of wild woodland. We love experimenting with new techniques on the farm. At the moment we're investing in wind turbines. The kids help us track and protect the wildlife in the woods. They're great amateur photographers, so as well as sharing the technical side of organic farming and sustainable energy, we'll be posting all kinds of images from our day-to-day, back-to-basics lifestyle.

3

Melissa Okonedo studied writing and film at the MET film school. She works as both a screenwriter and internet marketer, and has great passion for both disciplines. Her screenplays have received numerous awards and glowing reviews from the top agencies. Her recent script, *A beginning and an end*, has received considerable attention.

b Work in pairs. Look again at the three profiles and answer the questions.

1 Which do you think was posted on
   a) a company website? b) a blog? c) a social network?
2 What differences can you see in
   a) the content? b) the style?
3 Which person would you like to know more about? Why?

2 a You are going to write two 'about me' pages: one for professional use and one for social use. Follow the steps below.

1 Decide what information you want to include in each profile.
2 Decide what kind of style you want to use.
3 Check the advice in the tip at the bottom of the page.

b Write your profiles in a maximum of 120 words each.

3 a Show your profiles to a partner. Suggest two more pieces of information you partner could include in their profiles.

b Change the profiles to include the suggestions.

4 Read all the profiles in the class. Which do you think is the most interesting/funny/useful?

TIP

When you're writing a personal profile, remember to think about who is going to read it. Think about the impression you want to make. Keep the profile concise.

COMMUNICATION BANK

1.1 Pronunciation, page 7, Exercise 2b

When we form the third person present simple of a verb that ends in *-s*, *-sh*, *-ch*, *-tch* or *–x*, we add *-es*. It is pronounced as an extra syllable. When we add *-ed* to a verb that ends in *-d* or *-t*, the *-ed* ending is pronounced as an extra syllable.

1.5 Speaking task, page 13, Exercise 6b

Strategy 1

Organise large events with authors present giving lectures.

Strategy 2

Launch the book online through social networking sites, invite guests to publisher's head office for big launch party with drinks and music.

Strategy 3

Visit schools/colleges explaining to teachers the book's approach.

Strategy 4

Send out free copies of the book to important clients.

3.3 Speaking & Vocabulary, page 31, Exercise 2b

1 **go about your business** – be busy doing the things you need to do in day-to-day life
2 **listen in on conversations** – listen to the conversations of other people when you are not actually part of them
3 **tune in to** – focus your attention on something
4 **pass the time of day** – not do anything in particular, just fill time
5 **watch the world go by** – sit still and look at the people around you and what they are doing
6 **stare into space** – not look at anything in particular or think about anything in particular

5.5 Speaking task, page 57, Exercise 6

Group A

You are going to conduct a class debate. The statement under debate is:

We believe that increased surveillance is the most efficient way to fight crime.

In a formal debate, it doesn't matter what your personal opinion is, the important thing is to be able to argue a position. Your group will argue against the statement. Take five minutes to prepare as many arguments as possible to attack the statement.

3.1 Speaking, page 27, Exercise 1a

1

2

3

4 page 38, Exercise 3a

4.2 Speaking, page 43, Exercise 2a

Student A

Read the text about The Cooper Point House in Big Sur, near San Francisco. Prepare to tell your partner about it.

Californian architect Micky Muennig has designed this beautiful grass-roofed house in Big Sur that saves energy by blending into its environment. The windows face south in order to make the most of the heat and light from the sun in the winter months. Natural ventilation keeps the inside of the house cool during the summer.

The layout of the house and large floor-to-ceiling windows means that it has beautiful views of the Pacific Ocean. The roof is covered with local plants that are watered with recycled rain. It is an off-grid house which means it doesn't depend on the national power grid, but it uses solar panels.

5.5 Speaking task, page 57, Exercise 6

Group B

You are going to conduct a class debate. The statement under debate is:

We believe that increased surveillance is the most efficient way to fight crime.

In a formal debate, it doesn't matter what your personal opinion is, the important thing is to be able to argue a position. Your group will argue that the statement is true. Take five minutes to prepare as many arguments as possible to defend the statement.

7.2 Vocabulary, page 76, Exercise 1a

7.3 Speaking, page 78, Exercise 1

All of these objects are exhibits in the British Museum in London. They were all featured on a BBC radio programme called *A History of the World in 100 Objects*. The programme looks at interesting man-made objects throughout history, and talks about what they can tell us about life at the time when they were made.

8.4 Over to you, page 90, Exercise 7a

Conversation 1: Student A, you are going to phone Student B and leave a message for Student C. Before you start, Student A needs to think of a reason for calling Student C. Do NOT tell your partners what you have chosen. Student A, call Student B. You must conduct your conversation in whispers so that Student C cannot hear you.

Conversation 2: Student B, you are going to pass on the message to Student C. Decide if you're going to do it on the phone or face-to-face. You must conduct your conversation in whispers so that Student A cannot hear you.

Conversation 3: Student C, you are going to call Student A in response to his/her message. You must conduct your conversation in whispers so that Student B cannot hear you.

10.2 Speaking & Vocabulary, page 111, Exercise 1a

Label the footwear with the words in the box. Use a dictionary where necessary.

boots flip-flops high heels sandals slippers
trainers walking boots work shoes

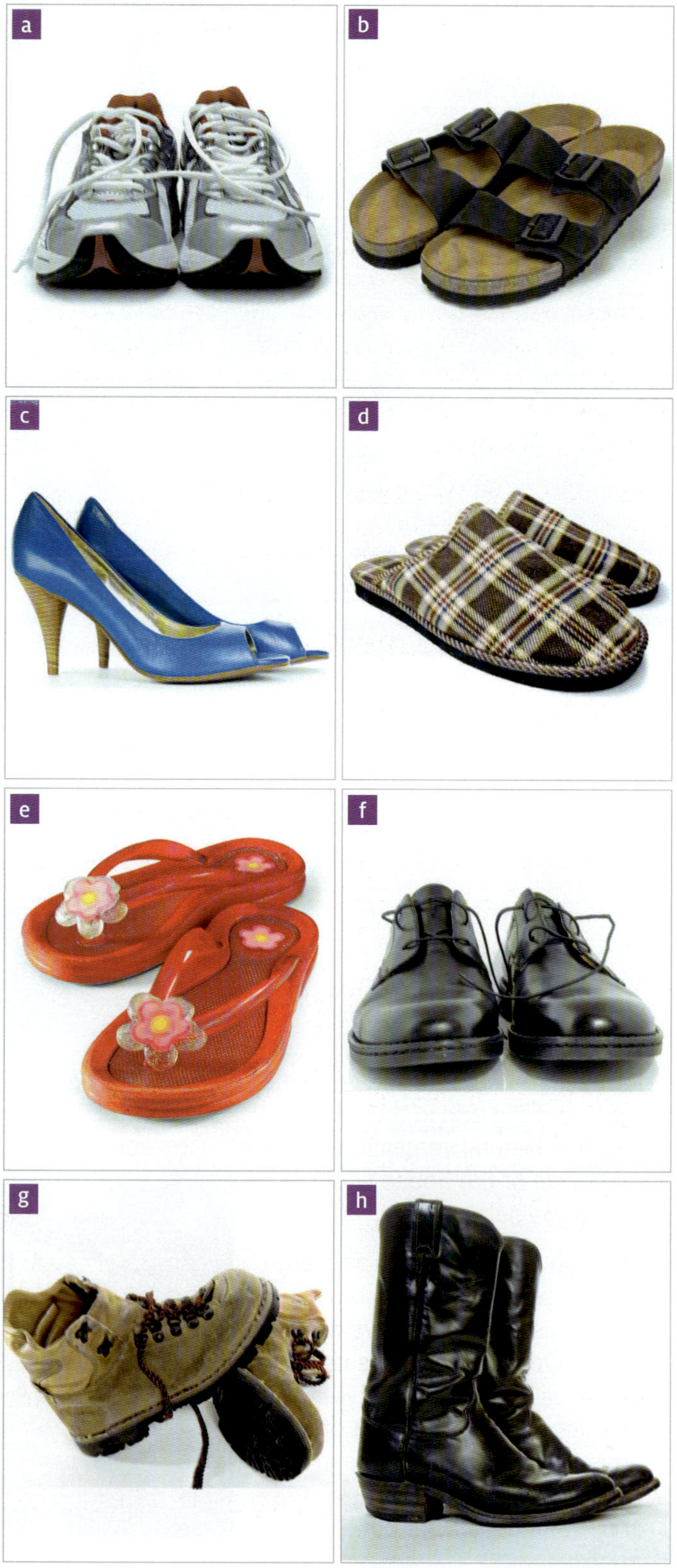

3.4 Tune in, page 32, Exercise1b

The Experience Music Project and Science Fiction Museum, Seattle

You either love it or hate it. That's the verdict on the Experience Music Project and Science Fiction Museum in Seattle, finished in 1999 and designed by architect Frank Gehry. The building itself is a work of art and the city's most well-known icon, but nobody can agree about this strange building and its controversial design.

11.4 Tune in, page 124, Exercise 1b

PROBLEM 1: I'm so distracted at home. I just can't concentrate on anything and I don't get my work done. My attention span is just terrible. Noise doesn't help, either.

PROBLEM 2: Sometimes, I lose my work. I forget to save it on the computer, or my computer crashes, or I erase a file, or something like that, and I have to do my work all again. What a waste of time! It normally happens when I have a tight schedule as well.

PROBLEM 3: I didn't read that part of the contract. I think I'll have problems now. You should read things more carefully, or you just end up getting into trouble with the law.

5.2 Speaking & Reading, page 52, Exercise 1a

The **Oresund Bridge** is a combined twin-track road and railway bridge and tunnel that crosses the Oresund Strait. It connects Sweden and Denmark and it is the longest road and rail bridge in Europe, nearly eight kilometres long. The bridge company itself insists on calling it the Oresundsbron, a compromise between the two languages. This symbolises a common cultural identity for the region, and the nature of the project as a friendship bridge.

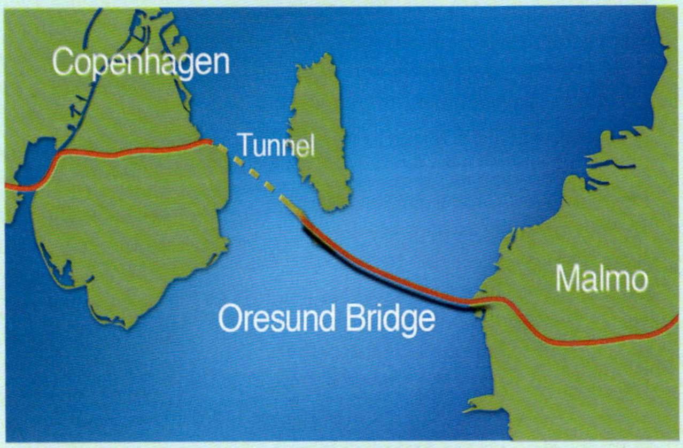

4.2 Speaking, page 43, Exercise 2a

Student B

Read the text about an Earthship home in New Mexico. Prepare to tell your partner about it.

The idea came from Michael Reynolds, an American architect who has been developing these environmentally friendly homes for decades. Earthships are made from local and waste materials. No bricks and only the minimum of concrete and wood are used. It mixes the advantages of an adobe house with the modern technology of greenhouses. The external walls are made from tyres and decorated with recycled cans and bottles. They hold the heat in winter and help cool the building in summer, like a cave. The roof of an Earthship is insulated – often with earth or adobe for solar energy efficiency.

10.5 Prepare for task, page 115, Exercise 5a

Making coffee

1.1, p. 4, Ex 2

1 Ah yes, this is a Kabuki dancer, isn't it? And umm, each dance tells a story, with the costume and the make-up and the movements all, er, all communicating something different – the only problem is ... you have to know the language of Kabuki dance to understand what he's saying!

2 She's obviously angry about something and umm... she's decided to protest about it, she's using a placard to communicate her message – and the strength of the crowd as well – that umm, that makes the message much louder and err, and more powerful.

3 This gesture speaks a thousand words, doesn't it? So gentle, so tender... it's communicating love and protection – it's amazing how a hand gesture can say so much!

4 I love this photo, the way the two people are looking at each other, the way they, umm, the way they seem to be so deep in conversation... They're not just talking with words, the expressions on their faces, the, uhh, gestures they're making with their hands, it's all part of the conversation.

5 Mmm ... There are two things going on in this photo – I mean first of all there's the keyboard, and that's so much part of modern communication, isn't it? You know, people staying in touch by email, or on social networks, or umm, instant messaging services – but it's also the hands. Look, the, err, the henna on her hands, that tells a story, too. It communicates a lot about the person who's typing, don't you think?

6 OK, this one is obviously showing sign language. I wonder where they are. I wonder if they're both deaf, or perhaps they're communicating with someone else.

1.3, p. 7, Ex 3a

Today I've texted friends, tweeted with colleagues at work, I've emailed work contacts, I've skyped with my partner, I've talked on the phone to a few people, I've chatted to people in the street. In fact I've discussed all kinds of things and I've watched lots of people speak on their phones, and I'm sure I've used my body to say things – but I'm not sure if any of us have communicated very much with each other!

2.2, p. 16, Ex 2

Beloved by Toni Morrison. This looks like a romantic novel, I mean the title suggests that, but actually it's about the slave trade in the United States. It follows the life of a mother and daughter as they try to rebuild their lives after escaping from slavery. It's set in the United States at the end of the nineteenth century. So, I think historical novel is the best description for it.

Norwegian Wood by Haruki Marukami. This is like a love story and a drama and a humorous novel all in one. The narrator looks back on his life in the 1960s as a student in Tokyo, so it's very nostalgic. It talks about the love affairs he had when he was younger. It's funny at times, but it has its tragic side as well. But if I had to choose, I think love story is the best description.

The Road by Cormac McCarthy. This is a story about the end of the world. We follow the story of a father and son as they walk across America which has been virtually destroyed, and there are few people who have survived. Some people might think this is like science fiction or fantasy, but I think it's very real, which makes it so frightening. It's hard to classify but I suppose it's an action/adventure story, but a very tragic one.

The No.1 Ladies Detective Agency by Alexander McCall Smith. This story is set in Botswana, Africa. As the name suggests, it's a detective novel but with a difference. It tells the story of Precious Ramotswe and her decision to become the first female private detective in Botswana. The crimes are ordinary crimes and the problems are the everyday problems of the people of Botswana. There are touches of comedy, but also of tragedy, and above all there's the taste of Africa, in all its colours, sights and sounds.

3.1, p. 24, Ex 2b

1

A: I love this mural. It's amazing how he uses these derelict old buildings and turns them into a work of art. I was amazed when I first saw it, really amazed!
B: Yes, I know what you mean. But the images are pretty disturbing sometimes. I mean, all those rats!
A: Yeah, I guess his murals of rabbits are less shocking.

2

A: Hey, this is a great photo. What is it?
B: It's an installation in an open air sculpture park not far from where we live. It was a really hot day, and we were really surprised – and so pleased – when we came across this last installation. We had no idea it was there. There was just a, er, a tunnel into the hillside, and then we came out into this, like, underground room and there was this pool, and in the middle a strange tower. It was so cool and fresh. Just what we needed!

3

A: So, did you get to see the Mona Lisa then?
B: Yes, eventually, but we had to queue up for hours, and then when we finally did get to see the painting, it was so disappointing. It's so small! And the, um, the room was so full of people, you couldn't see a thing! It was so annoying – all these people taking photos on their phones!

4

A: Is that Rodin? The thinker? Where is it?
B: There was, er, there was an exhibition in the centre of town. Six or seven Rodin sculptures. And this one of course. The kids look really bored, don't they? But actually they're just imitating the statue's pose.

5

A: Have you ever seen any of these 3D street drawings? You know, people make them with chalk. They draw them on the floor, but they're in 3D, and it looks like there's a hole or something. Look, I've got a photo of one on my phone. I tell you, this one was so lifelike that the first time you saw it, it was terrifying.

3.7, p. 31, Ex 1a

This is one of my favourite places in town. I love sitting here with a coffee and watching the world go by. It's a large town and a huge variety of people walk along this street, young and old, tourists and locals, all kinds of cultures and backgrounds, all going about their business.
I love watching them and imagining where they're going, what they're like, what they're thinking. It's so much more interesting than just staring into space.
Sometimes I watch the people at the next table and tune in to their conversations. Is that bad? I know I shouldn't really listen in on other people's conversations, and if they're too personal, then I turn away, but on the whole they're simply passing the time of day, or talking about work. It's surprising how many people come here to have business meetings over a cup of coffee!

4.2, p. 40, Ex 1b

A = Anchor **S** = Sarah **J** = Jarun
B = Bob **G** = Gai

A: Good evening everybody and welcome to another City Watch! Every city has its dangers, some more serious than others, some man-made, some caused by nature. This week, we travel the globe to hear people talking about how these dangers can be prevented. We asked local people across the globe to comment on the dangers around the corner in their part of the world. We start our journey in Melbourne, Australia... So, I take it that the main problem here are fires, is that right?
S: Yes, there are more and more forest fires every year, it's not good at all... – and they're getting bigger and more destructive. We've already had three major fires this year – and it's only February! People have lost their homes, their businesses, but luckily no one's lost their life – yet! And the tragic thing is they're so easy to start! It only takes a cigarette thrown out of a car window to start a catastrophe here. The land is so

dry and the heat is so intense and one of the biggest problems can be a sudden change in the wind direction – if the wind is blowing in the wrong direction, it can be fatal. Most local people are aware of all this, but it only takes one person to start a fire – but sometimes visitors, or people from the city aren't so aware. Maybe they haven't travelled in the bush before, and maybe they don't know the dangers – so we have to keep campaigning.

A: Thanks. And now, to an area where a terrible natural disaster took place not so long ago... Phuket in Thailand... What's being done to take precautions in the future?

J: The terrible tsunami that came in 2004 caught us all by surprise. Luckily, we haven't seen anything like it since then, but we all know it could happen again. Locals and tourists need to know what to do in case there is another tsunami. We've built new evacuation sites, and we've put up signs like this to mark the sites very clearly. Look, here's one. As you can see the sign shows that you need to get up on high ground, above the waves. We've built more shelters on higher ground as well.

A: That sounds good. Sometimes, more minor accidents involving water can occur. Our next visit is closer to home... to the English countryside. What's the problem here?

B: Well, Norfolk is very prone to flooding. The land is very flat and very low. When it rains, roads and bridges can get flooded very quickly. And these flash floods have become more and more common recently. Warnings of flash floods in the area are always broadcast on the TV and the radio, but too many people ignore the alerts. They go out in their cars without thinking and then get stuck when the water level rises. Here the weather can change very fast, we get torrential rain and on flatlands like this, that's dangerous. The water can move at quite a speed and the strong currents can carry away cars and other vehicles. This sign is quite new. We've put up a lot of them in the area. We want to make sure people don't just ignore the sign, so we've given it a humorous message – hopefully that way they won't forget!

A: Right. And finally, the kind of disaster that doesn't happen very often and a sign that certainly is alarming. We finish our tour in Recife, on the north-east coast of Brazil. We interviewed a resident of Boa Viagem beach where the main danger lurks... and what a danger!

G: As you can see, the sign really hasn't made any difference. People haven't stopped coming to the beach. There hasn't been a fatal attack on this beach yet this year, thankfully, and I suppose maybe until there is one, they'll just keep swimming in the sea.

A: Have you ever seen a shark attack?

G: No, I haven't. I've seen sharks in the waters, and they come up really close to the shore. But we've always been able to warn people in time. I've never actually seen one attack a person, but we all know they can – and they do.

A: So why do people continue to swim here?

G: They think if they aren't swimming in deep water it's OK, if they stay close to the shore – but you know, when there are sharks around an attack can happen anytime, anywhere. We've put up more signs and we've visited the local schools and told the kids of the danger, they're the ones who take the most risks. Kids and tourists ... that's why the signs are also in English – for the tourists, of course.

4.3, *p. 45, Ex 2b*

In the fight to cut back on plastic, more and more governments are trying to phase out plastic bags, or at least make customers pay for them at the checkout. In Ireland recently the government introduced a tax on plastic bags, and in the first year bag use fell by 95%. It's a high-profile campaign in many countries, but is it really worth it? Well, probably it is, when you look at how many bags we use each year. More than 10 billion in the UK alone. And especially when you look at what usually happens to most of them.

Let's look at the typical lifecycle of a plastic bag. A plastic bag starts out its life on a production line. It'll be distributed to shops and retailers and may have a logo stamped on it. In the shop we, the customer, pick it up and use it to take our shopping home. Once at home, it may get used again, to carry more shopping, or possibly to clean up after our dog. We may take it out with us on a picnic. We may even put it in a litter bin, or better, a recycling container. But only a very small proportion of bags actually ever get recycled. A much larger proportion are disposed of along with other household waste and end up on open rubbish dumps, where they may get caught by the wind and carried far and wide. A lot of plastic bags end up in the sea. The sea is full of plastic - and not only plastic bags; there are plastic bottles and plastic wrappers and plastic boxes, even children's plastic toys. And all this rubbish gets carried by the currents and trapped in huge floating rubbish dumps. One of the largest of these is the Great Pacific Rubbish Patch. It's bigger than the state of Texas, and it is continually growing. Governments say it's too expensive to clean it up. Meanwhile, environmentalists are studying the effects of plastic on marine life, and the results are truly scary.

5.1, *p. 49, Ex 1b*

A: Well, the computer screen is an easy one to analyse, isn't it?

B: Yes, social networking sites like Facebook allow you to contact anybody in the world.

A: Yeah, for example, you can find someone you've lost touch with... it provides that link, so I guess that Facebook could be building bridges.

B: And... and we could also say, the internet reaches across borders, too.

A: But then that can be a problem, can't it? Some people see Facebook and Twitter as an invasion of privacy, you know...

B: OK, so, then you can put up barriers, even block particular people completely... so they can never get in touch with you.

A: Right, I see what you mean.

B: You have to do something, to prevent everyone from seeing everything about your private life, otherwise it can be dangerous. Too much information!

A: Yeah, you're right about that. OK. What's next?

B: Now I really like this photo... it's beautiful really, I mean...

A: I think it symbolises reaching out... breaking down barriers between ages, bridging the generation gap? Sometimes there's this big gap between two people because of age.

B: I guess that's why it's there, it's like a contrast with the Facebook image, the woman sitting on her own looking at the screen, and here the two people are together, shaking hands, about to enjoy each other's company however different they may be.

A: Yeah... and joining hands refers to establishing new links with people and how we can do that. And now finally this sad image.

B: No entry... yeah, that's sad, I guess.

A: You know I was told that this photo was taken on the border between the USA and Mexico, in the state of Arizona.

B: Wow, OK, that's symbolic. So, it's saying you can't cross this land for two reasons: one because it could be private land or two because it might be a different country. So that's a barrier, as well, of course, something that divides nations and people, that stops them connecting... it's the opposite of the image of the two people shaking hands, connecting. Here a border or a wall can only separate.

5.4, *p. 53, Ex 2a*

With today's technology it doesn't matter that a mountain range or a sea divides two countries. There are ways round these obstacles. One of the most important projects in the world in this respect has just reached a milestone.

Yes, Switzerland's Gotthard Base Tunnel is about to become the world's longest rail tunnel. The engineering team are just completing the drilling work in the Swiss Alps. The tunnel covers a distance of 57 kilometres. It actually consists of two single-track tunnels, which together with the shafts and passages that link the two tunnels cover a total of 115 kilometres.

But you'll have to wait some time before you can actually travel through it. The Swiss Federal Railway intend to open the tunnel to the general public in 2017. The tunnel is expected to shorten travel times dramatically for locals, business travellers and tourists between Switzerland and Milan. The train journey from Zurich to Milan will be cut by two hours to 90 minutes and is bound to increase traffic and trade between the two cities.

However, the project has been controversial – eight people have been killed in the building work and green campaigners complained of environmental damage to these beautiful mountains.

On the other side of the world, a different kind of milestone is being celebrated, the very beginning of a project. The Chinese authorities have just given the go-ahead for what is certain to be the longest road bridge in the world – joining the city of Macau to Hong Kong. In fact, there will be a series of road bridges and tunnels that will connect Hong Kong on the east side of the Pearl River Delta with Macau and the mainland Chinese city of Zhuhai on the west. At present it takes four and a half hours to complete the journey by road. The new bridge hopes to cut the driving time to 40 minutes. Local politicians and economists claim that it is bound to have a positive effect on the economy of the developing regions west of the delta.

"The new transport network aims to improve finance, logistics, and professional services in the Pearl River Delta," said a statement posted on the Hong Kong government website.

The bridge will eventually be a six-lane expressway and is expected to cost at least 107 billion dollars. It will include the building of two artificial islands. It is due to be completed in 2016. The project also plans to boost the construction industry and when completed the link will be a vital route for both trade and tourism. Environmental groups complain, though, of damage to the natural habitat of the Chinese white dolphin among other species.

6.2, *p. 58, Ex 3b*

So, that's a good example of a festival that now takes place in a country that never used to celebrate it. Globalisation and shifting populations are responsible for that. Nowadays, many countries also celebrate well-known festivals such as Christmas, Easter, Halloween or Carnival even though they have no direct link with their culture. This might also be because consumerism is taking over these celebrations.

Two not so well-known events that have a Japanese connection are interesting in this respect because they show that globalisation does not just mean Americanisation. Americans adopt customs from other countries as well. The first is the Cherry Blossom Festival, known as Hanami, which is celebrated every spring in Japan and people have outdoor parties and admire the trees. And it is also well-known in the USA now. There the celebration commemorates the date March 27, 1912, when the Mayor of Tokyo gave a present to the city of Washington. Mayor Ozaki donated cherry trees in an effort to enhance the friendship between the United States and Japan and also celebrate the continued close links between the two nations. Now the festival takes in a parade, a ten-mile run and an alternative music festival called Cherry Blast, all very American phenomena. A Japanese festival has evolved into an American festival.

Another celebration, Cosplay, is also of Japanese origin. Cosplay means costume play. The idea is that you can dress up as characters from comics, video games and fantasy movies. In fact, you take on the role of any person from the real or virtual world. This Japanese festival has now taken off in many countries all over the world. The photo in front of me shows young Cosplay fans dressed as characters from Japanese manga, outside the Frankfurt Book Fair in Germany. Another example of how an international event adapts to the changing tastes of a globalised world. But when local cultures are transformed, are these changes for the better or for the worse? Are they permanent or temporary? Do countries lose something of their cultural identity if they modify their behaviour in this way?

6.5, *p. 62, Ex 1*

I = Interviewer E = Eshan

I: Hi, in our podcast this week, Eshan Brice tells us about a new group of superheroes who are hoping to take over the world. Hi Eshan. So, tell us something about these new superheroes? Who are they?

E: Well, the 99 are a group of young people from all over the world. Each one comes from a different country, each one has a special, unique superpower that they have been given by one of 99 mystical Noor stones.

6.5, *p. 62, Ex 1*

I = Interviewer E = Eshan

E: Each one comes from a different country, each one has a special, unique superpower that they have been given by one of 99 mystical Noor stones.

I: Noor stones?

E: Yes, these stones represent the 99 virtues – the 99 positive qualities of Allah – that are described in the Qur'an. The 99 – this is the name given to this group of young superheroes – are the world's first Islamic superheroes. Their creator, Naif al-Mutawa, wanted to take the universally popular figure of the superhero – an American invention – and make it more relevant to young Muslims. He wanted to give young Muslims everywhere role models they could be proud of and offer the world a positive image of the teachings of Islam.

I: So what's the story behind it all?

E: Well, the story starts in the thirteenth century. The great library in Baghdad known as the House of Wisdom has been destroyed, but the knowledge contained in its thousands of books has been saved. It has been stored in 99 mystical stones, the Noor stones, or the stones of light.

I: The stones you talked about earlier?

E: Exactly. Those stones are said to contain all the knowledge and power of all human wisdom. To save the stones from the invaders they are sent to the furthest corners of the world – each stone to a different destination where they remain hidden for hundreds of years.

I: Until now I suppose?

E: Yes, that's it. Now, in the twenty-first century, a psychiatrist, a descendant of the guardians of the House of Wisdom, Dr Ramzi Razem, is looking for the stones. He believes he can use their power to fight evil and save the planet.

I: Of course – the classic mission of all superheroes! So, who are the 99?

E: They are 99 young people from around the world and each one finds one of the stones. And the stone gives them a superpower. Each power is different, each power is unique. Some have classical superpowers like super strength or super speed; others have more unusual powers, like the ability to create light or to become invisible. Dr Razem's mission is to bring these young people together, to teach them how to use their powers to fight darkness and evil.

I: But who exactly are they fighting against?

E: The main bad guy in the story is Rughal. He too knows about the stones and their powers, but, of course, he wants to use the powers for his own personal gains. He wants to create an army of superheroes who will follow his commands and take over the whole world. He has no superpowers himself, but he's a strong character. None of the 99 is strong enough to fight him alone. If they want to win, they have to work as a team and learn about the three key values of tolerance, acceptance and cooperation.

I: So, has the series been a success so far?

E: The series has become incredibly popular. The comics have sold millions of copies, both in the Arab world and beyond. In 2009, the TV series was launched. In 2010, the 99 teamed up with Superman, Batman and the other superheroes of the Justice League to fight together against evil. So yes, I guess they're a success.

I: Thank you, Eshan. So, are the 99 just another set of comic book heroes, or can they really be a new force for good in real life? Write and let us know what you think! Send us an email or leave a comment.

7.1, *p. 72, Ex 2a*

1

These treasured possessions – a few chairs, a carpet, a photograph and some old records – are looking for their owners. They are in a way lost property. But nobody threw these things away. These are household contents which have been left by a natural disaster, Hurricane Ivan. Ivan was one of the most intense hurricanes ever recorded and caused heavy damage in Jamaica and Cuba in 2004 before affecting Florida and the Gulf of Mexico. This photo was taken in Pensacola, Florida. Homes were destroyed and private property scattered everywhere. Did anyone ever claim these articles, I wonder?

2

These family belongings – toys, chairs, laundry baskets – are not in the street because these people are moving house or are homeless. They are there because the police have just removed them from an apartment in Lafayette, Colorado. The people who rented the place could not make their monthly payment, and the owner evicted them with the help of the police. As the economic crisis continues, many Americans are finding it hard to pay their rent or mortgage. If this continues, more and more stuff like this will start appearing on our streets.

3

This photo shows six objects that the family and friends of miner Edison Peña sent to him while he was trapped underground. Edison was one of the 33 Chilean miners trapped underground for 69 days at the San José mine after it collapsed on the 5th August 2010. He received these objects through a narrow tube that acted as a lifeline, allowing food, water and regular contact between families and their trapped loved ones. The six objects include a picture of his idol Elvis Presley, some socks and earplugs. Not long before his rescue, Edison sent these personal items back up to the surface.

7.4, *p. 76, Ex 1a*

Today we're in the National Toy Hall of Fame, a museum which houses a collection of some of the most popular games and toys of all time, new ones and old ones, digital and traditional, all much loved by adults and children alike. To join the collection a toy must be recognised and loved across the world. It must have been used by children for several generations and it must encourage creativity and learning.

The inside of the museum looks more like a giant playroom than a museum. There are toys and games from – and for – all ages. You can touch and explore and play. There are giant building blocks, and an enormous train set. There are board games and puzzles. Choose your favourite one and sit right down and play.

8.1, *p. 83, Ex 4a*

1

Well, I'm not sure. I don't think women like football much. Football stadiums are usually full of men, aren't they? But, yes it does bring people together. People are always exchanging stories and opinions about it. My problem with football is that it's always in the media. Every time you turn on the news or open a newspaper, it's always the same old story – football, football, football. What if you're not interested in football?

2

Yes, absolutely right. Hip hop is a great way to express yourself. It's like poetry that you recite, that you read aloud. People can find a voice when they rap, and women do it, too, of course! Just because of one or two well-known cases years ago, now all we get is negative stereotypes about it. People prefer to marginalise it and make up these lies. It's time to tell the other side of the story.

8.5, *p. 89, Ex 1a*

A: Did you read that article I sent you?
B: Yeah, interesting... I was thinking about that the other day...
A: What, citizen journalism?
B: Yeah, you know, and all the stuff about Twitter and people finding out about the news from the people who are there, you know, like in the fire the other day.
A: The fire? Oh, you mean the one in the hotel?
B: Yeah... I mean, you know, the first thing I heard was from my flatmate – he came home, he'd been cycling near there and he said he'd seen this huge cloud of smoke... but he didn't know where it came from...
A: I saw that cloud too – it was massive!
B: Yeah, well, we looked it up on the internet ... you know, on the local newspaper's website...
A: And there was nothing there?
B: N... no... There was a story there, with a photo and some eye witness reports – you know, guests who were staying at the hotel, passers-by, that sort of thing...
A: ... yeah...
B: ... and the story said there were 40 people stuck on the roof... but that's all... no more information, so we went on Twitter and it was amazing!
A: Really?
B: Yeah – there were two people actually tweeting from the rooftop! With photos and comments and quotes from the other people on the roof... it was fascinating... so much detail... and a minute-by-minute commentary... we got really sucked in!
A: I bet!
B: Yeah... I mean, the news story was interesting, but normally I'd have given it about two minutes of my time, but the Twitter side of the story was like following a film or something!

8.6, *p. 90, Ex 1a*

S = Secretary **N** = Natalie **M** = Marc **D** = Damian

1

N: Hello. Can I speak to Peter Moorcroft please?
S: Hold the line, please.
N: OK, no problem.
S: Hello, I'm afraid Peter isn't picking up the call. Do you want me to take a message?
N: I just wanted to check that he'd received a file from me.
S: Who's speaking?
N: It's Natalie Martin. I sent him a file this morning and I just wanted to know if he received it. It's important. Could you ask him to call me, please?
S: Of course, he has your number I take it, Natalie?
N: Yes.
S: OK, I'm just making a note of this.
N: Thanks.
S: Fine, I'll let him know.

2

You've reached the voicemail service of Sabine Meyer, please leave a message after the tone.

M: Sabine, listen. It's Marc here. You won't believe this, I'm still at the airport. Uhhh ... there are terrible delays, same old story ... Umm... I won't be able to travel tonight. So ... do you think you could call Petra? Tell her not to wait for me at the airport or, er, or text me her number, I don't have it for some reason. Erm ... thanks for that! Bye!

3

The cell phone you've called is currently unavailable. Leave a message after the tone.

D: Sarah, hi this is Damian. I'm in the square. Where are you? You asked me to be here at 4.15, didn't you? I texted you before ... Umm, call me, I'm here, OK, in front of the town hall? Right, bye!

9.2, *p. 94, Ex 1a*

I = Interviewer **R1** = Respondent 1 **R2** = Respondent 2

I: So, what's the situation in your school? Are you allowed to access the internet on the school computers?

R1: In the library we have laptops that we can use to access the internet, but there's a very strong firewall. We can't access YouTube or Facebook for example and a lot of music sites and chatrooms are blocked.
In class we use laptops as well – and sometimes our general studies teacher lets us use our mobile phones to access sites that are blocked on the computers. Most of the teachers hate mobile phones! They make us switch them off as soon as we enter the class. One teacher makes us leave them on the desk at the front of the classroom and we aren't allowed to have them back until the end of the day!
I think that's a bit extreme, but I guess I kind of understand as well, I think they can be really distracting sometimes.

I: So, what's the situation in your school?

R2: Our school computers are fairly carefully controlled, a lot of social networking and music sites are blocked. Students aren't allowed to access music sites or chatrooms on the school computers. I think it makes sense from a security point of view. And anyway they can do all that on their mobile phones.

I: What about phones? Are those banned?

R2: No, not at all. Students are allowed to bring their mobile phones to class. It can be really good because then we don't have to rely on the school WiFi, which isn't always very efficient! And they're great for making recordings, taking photos, preparing presentations and so on. Of course students must be taught to be responsible – we don't share phone numbers in case of cyber-bullying and we have to monitor their use very closely. They mustn't misuse the internet whether it's on their phones or on a computer. We're very strict with offenders, they have to learn about good and bad internet use and I think that's something we really must help them with, it's such an important skill for their futures. We talk about it a lot in class too ... responsibilities and duties and safety, above all safety. They really need to know about the dangers of the internet. I think that's a really important part of my job.

9.5, *p. 96, Ex 3*

P = Presenter **F** = Fiona

P: Today we have a story of a modern day Quixote fighting against the windmills of the new Spanish smoking law. Fiona Allen reports from Marbella, where bars, restaurants and cafés are coming to terms with the new smoking ban while others are breaking the law! Fiona.

F: I'm here in Marbella, on a street lined with bars and restaurants, all showing the obligatory no-smoking signs. Under the old law, smaller establishments could choose whether to be smoking or non-smoking while larger establishments had to designate a special, sealed-off area for smokers. This could not be more than one third of the total area available to the public. A lot of smaller establishments went for the smoking option. They lost some customers, families with small children for example, but their smoking clients were more than happy. They didn't have to stand outside to enjoy a cigarette, they could continue to smoke as they ate or drank. But then the law changed.

P: And what did that change mean?

F: Well, all public bars and restaurants, along with all public buildings, children's parks and entrances to schools and hospitals became no smoking areas. Restaurants and bars were no longer allowed to choose. It was a blanket ban and it came accompanied by heavy fines and the risk of closure. Most people accepted the change. Some grumbled and complained, but on the whole it was seen as being inevitable. But one bar and restaurant owner here in Marbella simply refused to accept the new law. He refused to accept that he wasn't allowed to choose what to do in his own establishment and he decided to make a stand against the new law.

P: So what did he do?

F: He posted signs in his bar and restaurant stating that smoking was allowed. He claimed that banning smoking would ruin his business. He let his customers continue to smoke over their food and didn't make them stand out in the street. His regular customers were happy, but the neighbouring bars and restaurants weren't. They reported him to the authorities and he was threatened with a fine of 145,000 euros and immediate closure of his business. The rebel bar and restaurant-owner stuck to his guns – when the authorities came to inform him of the closure, he invited a group of friends to join him in a protest at his bar and restaurant, where they spent the whole night smoking cigarettes and cigars. There was a party atmosphere, but the party soon came to an end. After long talks with his lawyer and the local authorities, and almost a week of forced closure, the bar and restaurant owner finally agreed to take down all the smoking signs and posters attacking the anti-smoking law and replace them with the regulation no-smoking signs.

P: And did he?

F: Yes, he did and now his bar and restaurant is just like all the others, and all his customers have to step out onto the street if they want to smoke. Will this ruin his business? Only time will tell!

10.1, *p. 106, Ex 2a*

Of the world's total population of 6.5 billion, 5.8 billion people, or 90%, don't have regular electricity, clean water, or shelter – a simple roof over their heads. The exhibition Design for the Other 90% explores low-cost, innovative solutions to support this majority, Here are three unique ideas that we hope will enable people to live their lives more happily.

Firstly, The FLAP (Flexible Light and Power) Bag is a portable solar bag designed for those people who have no electricity. It includes a solar panel, a reading light, and a mini-USB port for recharging the batteries on small devices. Portable Light Bags are created by local workers in Mexico's Sierra Madre. The bags are made from a material that absorbs the heat from the sun during the day, and give light at night. A light, personalised bag, they can be carried to provide temporary or permanent access to light and power depending on the situation and are of great benefit to local industries. It has become an essential tool for leading a happier, more prosperous life in communities without a reliable power supply.

Then, we have the The Life Straw™ - this has become an absolutely essential object in parts of the developing world. It's a personal mobile water tool that is designed to turn any water into drinking water. The straws are effective against diseases such as cholera and typhoid, and remove particles as small as 15 microns, enabling people to drink from puddles in the road! The Life Straw™ will be highly beneficial to rural communities, allowing people to access drinking water without having to walk miles to find it.

Finally, this bike cell charger works using an innovative dynamo to convert your cycling into power. The phone is held to the bars of the bike with a big rubber band. The charger will first be available in Kenya at an affordable price and will go on sale worldwide by the end of this year. If you pedal at 6 mph for just 10 minutes, you'll get almost half an hour of talk time or 37 hours of standby. The minimum speed required to charge a phone is 4 mph, or walking speed, so even a short trip should be enough to keep your cell phone going for a whole day. This affordable invention will prove a great help to communities without a reliable electricity supply and where people exploit cell phones for far more than just chatting.

10.3, *p. 110, Ex 3a*

N = Natalie **B** = Bogdan

N: How's the running going, Bogdan? Still out every morning before breakfast?

B: Yes, absolutely. But things have changed recently.

N: What? You're training for a marathon or something?

B: No, no... not that. I've started running in a different way.

N: In a different way? I thought there was only one way of running.
B: You won't believe this but I've taken up barefoot running... it's the latest thing!
N: Barefoot running? Are you mad? That must be so bad for your feet!
B: No, listen, before you start, just let me tell you how I heard about it. I read this book called *Born to Run*. It's by this guy called Chris McDougall and his whole argument is that it is healthier to run barefoot.
N: Because?
B: Well, he first read about this runner that won a 100-mile race through the mountains wearing only a pair of sandals, at the age of 55! And McDougall thought how can he run like that without getting an injury?
N: I bet this runner he met was a freak or something like that.
B: No, apparently he was a member of this tribe, the Tarahumara, who all run like that – barefoot or with sandals. It's a way of life for them. They do it in a very natural way.
N: And so?
B: Well, that was his inspiration, and the book talks about a whole new way of thinking about running. For example, there are people who say that conventional running shoes give you more support and protect your feet from the impact when you're running on hard ground. But when you read *Born to Run*, you realise it's the opposite. In fact, sport shoes cause injuries. They put pressure on your feet and...
N: I'm not sure I believe that. It seems more comfortable to me to run in trainers, there's no comparison. Going running barefoot? I can't imagine the pain!
B: No, it's not like that. Well, at first, it's not easy but you get used to it after a while.
N: I'm not sure I could, you know.
B: Well, if you don't like that idea, you can try out these sports shoes which make you feel like you're barefoot. They're called Five Fingers and they're incredible. They have thin, flexible soles which are really comfortable and they look amazing, like having gloves on your feet.
N: Now I've heard everything – hi-tech shoes that make you feel like you're running barefoot. That just doesn't make sense.
B: There are lots of runners who have got rid of their shoes, and they've got rid of their stress and injuries, as well. They've changed their habits and they're having a lot more fun running.
N: What's that got to do with stress?
B: Well, the book says that the way we run is all wrong. First, there are races which require special preparation and equipment and there are companies that make a lot of money from running products. It's big business. Then, there are people who run marathons and are obsessed with beating their time and keeping up with others and then, when they don't reach their goal, they just burn out or give up. There are people who say you have to suffer, that running has to hurt. I think that's all wrong. For the Tarahumara, running isn't work, it's an art and I believe that, too.
N: Well, good for you, but I think your barefoot running's crazy, honestly I do.

11.5, *p. 123, Ex 1*

Rashid

How will I be using English in the future? Well, I hope to have a successful career in which English plays a part, sure. Maybe in some big global organisation where I have to give presentations or something like that. But I don't see my relationship with English stopping there. I like the idea of meeting new people through work, people from other cultures, that's very attractive for me – socialising and getting to know other cultures. I can see myself having trouble at first because I'm not a very confident speaker. I get very nervous sometimes, but I guess people will help me out. What else? Well, travelling for work really appeals to me, sure, and English can allow me to do that. I can imagine myself in airports, talking in English, that kind of thing ... chatting with new friends in bars and restaurants, having fun.

Louise

How will I be using English in the future? Well, to start with, I'd like to live in an English-speaking country, to feel part of a community, to talk to the neighbours, you know... to get to know another way of life through the language, that would be important to me. Some things will be easy to achieve, I suppose, the day-to-day stuff, asking for directions, going shopping, but I like to think that I could talk about deeper stuff as well. I mean, it'd be great to have a conversation about politics sometime. I just don't know how achievable that is, really. It might never happen, but I can still imagine it! Well, anyway, English is essentially a very useful language. I can see it helping me out in lots of tricky situations in the world, because it's the world's common language.

11.9, *p. 125, Ex 4*

1

Well, thank you everybody for coming. I'd like to thank Logic Systems for inviting me to speak to you all today. My name's Ralph Sharma and today I'm going to speak about the field of industrial design. I'd like to start by explaining the outline of my talk.

2

A: Good morning, pleased to meet you Jonathan, come in.
B: Pleased to meet you, too. Many thanks for giving me this opportunity.
A: Now, tell me why are you interested in this post?
B: Well, I feel I'm well-qualified for the post because of my previous work experience ... as you can probably see from my CV.
A: Yes, I was going to ask you about that. Are you experienced in organising a team?

3

C: Goodbye. It was nice to meet you. We'll be in touch by email.
D: Yes, likewise. I look forward to hearing from you when it's convenient.
C: That's great. You should hear from us within a week.
D: Excellent, thanks very much. Please don't hesitate to contact me if you need any further information.

12.4, *p. 130, Ex 2*

1

I love the smell of fresh coffee. It really takes me back. It reminds me of the time when I lived in a flat over a café. I always woke up to the smell of coffee. It used to fill the flat in the morning. The café had only just opened when I moved in and it was really popular. I only lived there for six months, and ever since I've always associated the smell of coffee with the clatter of cups and the chatter of voices.

2

I grew up in the Czech Republic. I'll never forget the first time I saw the sea. I was 19. I had never seen the sea before. I had just started working for a family, looking after their three kids. They had planned a holiday in Spain and they took me with them. Seeing the sea for the first time was incredible! It was such an amazing sight. So big, so open. I just stood there and looked at the sea, trying to take it all in. And once I actually got in the water, they just couldn't tear me away! I loved the waves, the sound they made on the sand. We could hear them from our hotel room. The kids slept so well, they were so tired. It made my job really easy as they were lulled to sleep by the waves.

3

I love this photo. We took it on holiday last year in Buenos Aires. It brings back great memories of our trip. This was one of the highlights, we'd just been to visit the antique market in San Telmo – it's great. It's held once a week on Sunday, it's a great place to just to soak up the atmosphere – anyway, we were just sitting down for a coffee, when this couple started dancing in the square in front of us. It was amazing, they were so good. I've seen the tango so many times in dance halls and theatres, but nothing beats seeing it live in the streets of downtown BA. Whenever I look at this photo, the scene just comes flooding back and I can hear the music playing in my mind.

Irregular verbs

Infinitive	Past simple	Past participle
be	was, were	been
beat	beat	beaten
become	became	become
begin	began	begun
bite	bit	bitten
blow	blew	blown
break	broke	broken
bring	brought	brought
build	built	built
buy	bought	bought
catch	caught	caught
choose	chose	chosen
come	came	come
cost	cost	cost
cut	cut	cut
do	did	done
dream	dreamt/dreamed	dreamt/dreamed
drink	drank	drunk
drive	drove	driven
eat	ate	eaten
fall	fell	fallen
feel	felt	felt
fight	fought	fought
find	found	found
fly	flew	flown
forbid	forbade	forbidden
forget	forgot	forgotten
forgive	forgave	forgiven
get	got	got
give	gave	given
go	went	gone, been
grow	grew	grown
have	had	had
hear	heard	heard
hide	hid	hidden
hold	held	held
keep	kept	kept
know	knew	known
learn	learnt/learned	learnt/learned
leave	left	left
lend	lent	lent

Infinitive	Past simple	Past participle
let	let	let
lie	lay	lain
lose	lost	lost
make	made	made
meet	met	met
pay	paid	paid
put	put	put
read /ri:d/	read /red/	read /red/
ride	rode	ridden
ring	rang	rung
rise	rose	risen
run	ran	run
say	said	said
see	saw	seen
sell	sold	sold
send	sent	sent
set	set	set
shake	shook	shaken
shine	shone	shone
shoot	shot	shot
show	showed	shown
shut	shut	shut
sing	sang	sung
sit	sat	sat
sleep	slept	slept
speak	spoke	spoken
spend	spent	spent
split	split	split
stand	stood	stood
steal	stole	stolen
stick	stuck	stuck
swim	swam	swum
take	took	taken
teach	taught	taught
tell	told	told
think	thought	thought
throw	threw	thrown
understand	understood	understood
wake	woke	woken
wear	wore	worn
win	won	won
write	wrote	written